THE DACHSHUND

E. FITCH DAGLISH

Revised by Amyas Biss and J. V. Crawford

POPULAR DOGS

London

Popular Dogs Publishing Co Ltd
3 Fitzroy Square, London WIP 6JD

An imprint of the Hutchinson Publishing Group

London Melbourne Sydney Auckland
Wellington Johannesburg and agencies
throughout the world

First published (as *The Popular Dachshund*) 1952
Second edition 1956
Third edition, revised 1958
Fourth edition, revised 1960
Fifth edition 1963
Sixth edition, revised (as *The Dachshund*) 1967
Seventh edition, revised 1968
Eighth edition, revised 1973
Ninth edition, revised 1975
Tenth edition, revised 1980

Printed in Great Britain by The Anchor Press Ltd
and bound by Wm Brendon & Son Ltd
both of Tiptree, Essex

ISBN 0 09 139950 5

CONTENTS

ILLUSTRATIONS

Between pages 128 and 129

IN THE TEXT

PUBLISHERS' NOTE

This sixth edition—now republished as *The Dachshund*—includes fresh information about all six varieties as Addenda, cross-referenced with the original text. The list of breed clubs and their secretaries has been brought up to date and overseas clubs are now included.

New Appendices giving Kennel Club registration totals from 1946 onwards and a list of Champions from 1955 to 1966 inclusive have also been added. A few of the plates have been replaced with new photographs.

Following the death of Dr. Eric Fitch Daglish in April 1966, the publishers are much indebted to Colonel Amyas Biss for his help with these revisions and additions.

1967

The Addenda and Appendices were again revised and brought up-to-date by Colonel Biss for the seventh, eighth and ninth editions.

1968, 1973, 1975

Following the death of Colonel Biss in 1975, the Addenda and Appendices have been brought up to date by Mr. J. V. Crawford, and the breed standards have also been updated. Seven photographs have been replaced and three added.

1979

CHAPTER I

ORIGIN AND EARLY BRITISH HISTORY OF THE DACHSHUND

IN setting out to write a monograph on so distinctive and well-established a breed as the Dachshund it seems logical to begin by trying to trace its history back to those far-off days when the long-bodied, short-legged little hunter first took shape from the less specialized ancestral stock from which it sprang. Many such attempts have been made by previous writers, but none of the results have been convincing and all have been peculiarly lacking in finality. In the past some breed devotees have been at pains to show that the Dachshund is the oldest of known breeds of dogs, the Simon Pure of all the varieties into which the modern representatives of *Canis familiaris* are sub-divided. Some have subscribed enthusiastically to the theory, first strongly advocated by the great German authority Major Emil Ilgner over half a century ago, which claims to trace our breed's history through thirty-five centuries. That theory is based on evidence adduced from replicas of small dogs of Dachshund type that appear on the monuments of two of the kings of Ancient Egypt. On one of them the word Teckal is included in the inscription and is supposed to be the name of the dog depicted. This has been seized on as additional support for the belief; Teckel, the breed name by which the Dachshund is commonly known in Germany today, being held to be derived from that Egyptian name. Others have cited the stone or clay models of short-legged dogs discovered in Greece, Peru, Mexico and China as attesting the existence of the Dachshund type in times extending far back into the mists of antiquity. But such so-called evidence proves extremely flimsy and unreliable when closely examined.

The fact that dogs whose most striking physical characteristics were length of body and shortness of limb existed in various parts of the world thousands of years ago, cannot be taken as proving the antiquity of the Dachshund. Our breed is by no means the only one in which these peculiarities occur, and there is no justification for assuming that all dogs showing them are either related to one another or descended from common ancestors. Short-legged individuals in which the body is proportionately long, crop up from time to time as mutations, or "sports", in many animal types, as in sheep, pigs, cattle and horses, as well as in most breeds of dogs. Sports of this kind doubtless occurred in the past in widely separated localities and, should their shape have rendered them especially suitable for some particular purpose, like going to ground after fossorial quarry, such individuals may well have been kept and bred from, resulting in the stabilization of a number of local races which, though resembling one another in certain features, were unrelated. As regards the origin of the word Teckel, there is no vestige of evidence to show that it has any sort of connection with the Egyptian Teckal. The Germans are much given to the use of diminutives as terms of affection or endearment. Just as Mädel becomes Mädchen, Dachshund becomes Dachschen, Dachsel and Dachel. Today in many parts of Germany the word Dachshund is rarely used. The breed is almost universally referred to as the Dachel, of which Teckel is merely a variant, depending on the substitution of T for D and a slight change in the vowel sound: phonetic modifications often noticed in dialectic and colloquial German.

The truth is that, however fascinating speculation on the subject may be, we have no idea how, when or where the Dachshund had its origin. But though the Teckel may not have been a contemporary of the Pharaoh, there is good reason for thinking the breed has been in existence, in a form closely resembling that in which we know it today, for at least four centuries. Sixteenth-century wood-cuts show dogs of unmistakable Dachshund shape, long of body, short of leg, with deep chests, level backs and pendant ears, being used for badger digging: the form of venery still recognized as the Dachshund's true avocation.

The Bassethound is the only breed known in Britain that can be said to exhibit any close affinity with the Dachshund. A visitor to one of our shows where both are represented can hardly fail to be struck by their similarity. In both we see the same long body, short legs, strong quarters and large, pendant ears. There are, of course, many differences, particularly in colour, size and head properties, but the general resemblance cannot be ignored. These differences are accentuated by the fact that the Bassethounds seen at our shows are larger, heavier and more Bloodhound-like in head than were the hounds originally imported from France; which were closer to the type still to be found in that country. Years ago, too,

Dachshunds were larger and much more hound-like than at present, and not a few showed white markings, so that the similarity between them and the smaller type of Bassethound was very marked. In support of this view I quote a passage from the first edition of *British Dogs* written by a breeder of Bassethounds who adopted the pen-name of Wildfowler:

> ". . . a black and tan or red *Basset a jambes torses* cannot by any possible use of one's eyes be distinguished from a Dachshund of the same colour, although some German writers assert that the breeds are quite distinct. To the naked eye there is no difference, but in the matter of names (wherein German scientists particularly shine) then, indeed, confusion gets worse confounded. They have, say, a dozen black and tan *Bassets a jambes torses* before them. Well, if one of them is a thoroughly good-looking hound they call him Dachs Brachen; if he is short-eared and with a pointed muzzle they cap him with the appellation Dachshund. Between you and me, kind reader, it is a distinction without a difference and there is no doubt that both belong to the same breed."

This may be an extreme view, but when we read the description of the Dachshund given in the same volume, there seems to have been considerable justification for Wildfowler's opinion. The description is as follows:

> "The head, when of proper type, resembles that of a Bloodhound. The ears are also long and pendulous . . . the muzzle should finish square and the flews should be fairly developed. We have a brood bitch from one of the best kennels in Germany in which the dewlap is very strongly pronounced. . . . The forelegs are one of the great peculiarities of the breed; these are very large in bone for the size of the dog and very crooked, being turned out at the elbows and in at the knees. . . . The feet should be very large and should be well splayed outwards."

Here, surely, is a description much more appropriate to the modern Bassethound than to the Dachshund as we know it. From this and other similar references that might be quoted from dog books dating back to the early days of British Dachshund history, it seems probable that the Bassethound, perhaps the most ancient of all the French breeds that still survive, and the Dachshund owe their origin to a common ancestral type. The differences that now separate them are due to the divergent purposes for which the two have been bred over a long period of years.

From time to time much ink has been wasted in attempts to settle the question whether the Dachshund is a terrier or a hound. Some writers have taken the view that, since the Dachshund is essentially an underground worker and specially modified physically to fit it for the purpose, it is clearly a terrier. Others have stressed its fine scenting powers, its love of tracking and its penchant for hunting as one of a pack, to support their opinion that it is a hound. The truth seems to me to lie midway between these opposing dicta. The breed certainly possesses many of the qualities usually associated with terriers but it also shows several hound traits. When, before the last war, I had a kennel of Bassethounds and Beagles as well as Dachshunds, I had constantly brought to my notice the several aspects of character and behaviour typical of hounds which the Dachshunds exhibited. As individuals they are more independent than hounds but have a natural dignity and sense of self-importance not found in a terrier.

Having glanced at the vexed problem of the Dachshund's origin, we may turn to the history of the breed in Britain. This takes us back a little more than a century; for it was in the 1840s that the first Teckels reached this country. About that time the Prince Consort received several from Prince Edward of Saxe-Weimar, whose kennels were then among the best known in Germany. These early importations were kept at Windsor and, according to Stonehenge, were used in pheasant shooting. The publicity given to the canine aliens that had been accorded royal patronage, naturally aroused keen interest among British dog-lovers, with the result that a number of other specimens were imported and in the next decade the breed made considerable headway. The show history of the Dachshund appears to have begun in the late 1860s, when a few exhibits were entered, as German Badger Hounds, in the classes for Foreign Dogs put on at some of the larger shows. In 1873 the breed was offered separate classes for the first time, at the Crystal Palace show. The following year the first issue of the Kennel Club Stud Book was published and included several registrations under the breed name of Dachshunds, though the title of German Badger Hounds was printed in parenthesis, presumably in case the uninitiated reader might be left wondering to what breed the strange name might belong! From then the Dachshund's popularity increased rapidly. The demand for stock far exceeded the supply available in British kennels, many importations were made and high prices were paid for anything good enough to show. One of the most active in trying to satisfy the demand was a Mr. Schuller, who is said to have brought over more than two hundred Dachshunds from Germany in 1876–77.

The first of our breed to win the title of Champion was the dog Dessauer, imported from the kennels of Count Picked by Mrs. P. Merrick Hoare in 1874. This dog was described by a contemporary critic as being black with a bull-terrier head and whip tail but with good body, legs and feet. Press criticism was then a lot more outspoken than it is today. Mrs. Merrick Hoare deserves special mention as one of the leading pioneers of the show Dachshund. She owned and bred many outstanding specimens and her efforts on behalf of the breed to which she was devoted continued over a period of forty years. Dessauer sired three champions in Faust, Hoffman and Rapunzel, the first two in one litter. Of these Champion Faust was the sire of the two Champions Kossuth and Zither. Another prominent figure of that time was Mr. A. W. Arkwright, who in 1876 purchased a dog from the Royal Kennels in Stuttgart. This dog was registered here as Xaverl and soon won his title. He was very successful at stud, siring among many other good winners the two Champions Senta and Zigzag, Hans, who in turn sired two champion bitches, and Otter, the sire of that old-time celebrity Champion Olympian. Champion Zigzag numbered at least seven champions among his progeny, one of which, Champion Ozone, became famous as the sire of the litter brothers Champions Maximus and Superbus, regarded as the best specimens of the breed yet seen in this country. A long line of winners emanated from this distinguished pair, of which the most important was Champion Charkow, a son of Champion Maximus, which, when mated to the bitch Wagtail owned by Major Harry Jones, produced Jackdaw, born in 1886, which soon became a champion and was unbeaten throughout his long show career.

In his day Champion Jackdaw was regarded as typifying all the qualities most desired in a Dachshund. Between 1887 and 1894 he won the Fifty Guinea Challenge Cup of the Dachshund Club eleven times. Judging from his engraved portrait he was big, heavy and lacking in quality, with a pronounced dewlap and elbows which would be condemned by present-day judges; but he looks a handsome dog, well boned, strongly built, with well-dropped keel, good top- and underline and sound quarters. His head appears to have been rather coarse and his ears distinctly houndy. Of the many winners that owned him as sire perhaps the most notable was Wodin, the sire of Champion Snakes Prince, born in 1897 and bred by Mr. A. C. de Boinville; a dog acclaimed by both English and German authorities as the nearest approach to the ideal that had been seen.

Wodin's dam Jessamine was a daughter of Champion Pterodactyl, a red dog bred in 1888 by Mr. C. A. Wallroth and bought in 1891 by Major Harry Jones, in whose possession he had a brilliant career. His sire Don Quixote combined in his breeding the best of the old blood-lines, his grandparents being Champion Maximus, Champion Olympia (a granddaughter of Champion Zigzag), Champion Faust and Isis, a daughter of Champion Superbus. His dam Tekkel was unregistered and nothing can be discovered about her breeding. She may have been imported, but that, too, is uncertain. Champion Pterodactyl became as famous as the great Champion Jackdaw and proved as successful as a sire. Among the best of his progeny were Champion Blond Belle and Champion Primula, two of the best bitches of their era, and the dogs Champion Hotspur and Champion Wiseacre. Hotspur, bred by Major P. C. G. Hayward, was the sire of a great breed celebrity in Champion Sloane, and Wiseacre sired the three champions Beretta, Sly Boots and Walwyn. Pterodactyl was a clear, rather light red. Up to that time nearly all the most successful Dachshunds had been black and tan but red now became the fashionable colour and remained so for some twenty years.

The only known picture of Pterodactyl is a photograph, taken in the early days of photography, which is so poor that it is difficult to obtain any reliable impression of his good and bad points. In it the dog is badly posed and his outline appears to have been touched up by an unskilled hand. He seems to have been freer from loose skin about the throat and feet than Jackdaw, his ears look shorter and less houndy and his general build more compact. He shows plenty of bone and good quarters. Jackdaw and Pterodactyl have been given more detailed treatment than the other old-timers mentioned in this chapter because they each played a dominant part in building up the show Dachshund through the 1890s to the early years of the present century. In their day they were invincible in the show ring and were very widely used at stud. Almost all the outstanding winners that succeeded them up to the outbreak of the First World War carried the blood of these famous dogs.

To return to Champion Snakes Prince, his most important offspring was the bitch Champion Lenchen, bred by Mrs. Dewar from Fashoda, a grand-daughter of Champion Jackdaw. Lenchen was born in 1901. She was certainly the best bitch of her period, showing in a striking degree the many superlative qualities of her sire and was free from the loose skin, exaggerated crook and faulty back line that marred many of her contemporaries. The dog Brandesburton Magister, a brother of Fashoda, became famous as the sire of the bitch Carmen Silva, which, mated to a son of Champion Hotspur, produced the litter brother Champions Wirral Hollybranch and Hollyberry, two of the most consistent winners of their day, and whose descendants were winning right up to 1914.

Turning now to the dogs imported after the Jackdaw–Pterodactyl period, one of the most interesting was a small black and tan named Boch Bier, brought over by Captain Barry in 1893. He was a neat, clean-cut, sound little dog which should have done much to correct the faults most prevalent in the home-bred stock. He became a champion but was used comparatively little at stud on account of his colour, for this was the time when the craze for reds was at its height and the majority of breeders were unwilling to breed from a dog of any other colour. Florian was imported by Mrs. Nugent and Rother Beelzebub, a big dark red, by Mrs. Blackwell. Beelzebub has been described by one who knew him as the best Dachshund imported up to that time, and came over with a very impressive list of wins at Continental shows. Mr. Lever imported Hirschrot, which became an English champion and is of special importance as the sire of the bitch Hygeia, the dam of Champion Hyphen and Champion Honeystone, both bred by Major P. C. G. Hayward about 1912.

Champion Honeystone must be considered to have been one of the best Dachshunds of all time. He had a remarkable show career, extending over a period of eight years, in the course of which he won nineteen challenge certificates and set up an all-breeds record by being awarded the Challenge Trophy offered for the Best Sporting Dog or

Bitch at the Ladies' Kennel Association's Championship Show at the Crystal Palace four consecutive times. Champion Honeystone won that Trophy in 1914, 1915 and 1916. Thereafter it was not offered till 1920, owing to the Kennel Club's ban on war-time shows, when this remarkable dog, then a veteran, eight years old, was again placed over the best exhibits the other sporting breeds could produce. It is unlikely that this feat will ever be equalled by a dog of any breed.

The last of the pre-1914 importations that need be mentioned is the dog Racker von der Ecker, a small, very sound black and tan brought from Germany by Mr. John F. Sayer in 1903. He was not a particularly attractive dog, being rather short and somewhat cobby, but he excelled in feet, quarters and general soundness: those qualities which his importer considered stood in need of improvement in British stock at that time. Racker's show career was not very impressive but he was popular at stud. His most noteworthy son was the dapple Champion Spotted Dog, the first of his colour to become an English Champion.

The year 1881 is an important date in Dachshund history, for it was on the 7th January of that year that the Dachshund Club came into being. It was founded at a meeting held at Cox's Hotel, in Jermyn Street, London, attended by Mr. A. M. Arkwright, Major Harry Jones, Mr. Montague Wootten, the Rev. G. F. Lovell and one or two others. These gentlemen were among the most prominent and successful of the early exhibitors. Mr. Arkwright had been breeding on a fairly extensive scale since the late 1870s and many future champions first saw the light of day in his kennels. Among them were such notabilities as Champion Maximus, Champion Superbus, Champion Olympian, Champion Ozone, and Champion Senta. Major Harry Jones bred, or owned at some period of their lives, most of the great dogs of the late nineteenth century. Champion Jackdaw, Champion Pterodactyl, Champion Joan of Arc, Champion Wiseacre, Champion Jabin and Champion Jude are but a few of those which achieved fame in his possession. Mr. Montague Wootten bred the champions Zigzag, Hagar, Jezebel, Zedkiel, Zeyn and Zulemus. He became the first Hon. Secretary of the newly formed club; the first concern of whose members was to draw up a Standard of Points.

The German Dachshund Club did not come into existence till some years later, so that the British pioneers had no guide but their own conception of the ideal to which the breed should conform, which was, no doubt, based on the characteristics shown by the dogs they knew. Here is the result of their efforts:

	Points
Head and Skull. Long, level and narrow; peak well developed, no stop; eyes intelligent and somewhat small, following the body in colour.	12
Ears. Long, broad and soft; set on low and well back; carried close to the head.	6½
Jaws. Strong, level and square to the muzzle; canines recurrent.	5
Chest. Deep and narrow; breast bone prominent.	7
Legs and Feet. Forelegs very short and strong in bone, well crooked, not standing over; elbows well clothed with muscle, neither in nor out; feet large, round and strong, with thick pads and strong nails. Hind legs smaller in bone and higher, hind feet smaller. The dog must stand true, i.e. equally on all parts of its foot.	20
Skin and Coat. Skin thick, loose, supple and in great quantity; coat dense, short and strong.	13
Loin. Well arched, long and muscular.	8
Stern. Long and strong, flat at root, tapering to the tip; hair on underside coarse; carried low except when excited. Quarters very muscular.	5
Body. Length from back of head to root of stern two and half times the height at shoulder. Fore-ribs well sprung; back ribs very short.	13½
Colour. Any colour; nose to follow body colour; much white objectionable.	
Symmetry and Quality. The Dachshund should be long, low and graceful—not cloddy.	
Weight. Dogs about 21 lb.; bitches about 18 lb.	

To modern eyes this first Standard of Points appears strange indeed! It seems to include as desirable points nearly all the gravest faults a Dachshund can possess. Most of the provisions that now seem so odd owed their inclusion to the then generally accepted view that the Dachshund was a hound. The breed was still known as the Badger Hunting Hound and the dog depicted by this Standard is clearly a small hound, differing very little from a lightly built, whole-coloured Bassethound. There is the narrow, peaked skull, the loose skin, the long, flagged stern and the well-developed crook: all typical of the Bassethound both then and now. Looking through the advertisements of the stud dogs of the period we are left in no doubt as to the pride taken in the possession of specimens which possessed the points demanded by this Standard. Thus, Champion Clifton Wonder, born in 1897, a grandson of Champion Pterodactyl, is described by his proud owner as "of the correct hound type", while another dog, Taffy, born in 1895, a son of Woden, is advertised as "a big houndy dog, over 48 inches in length". How much of that was tail is not revealed!

When the German Dachshund Club was formed in 1888 it published a Standard which differed in many important respects from that put forward by the English club. It described a dog, which though long and low, was more compact, cleaner in outline, sounder and free from exaggeration, with well-ribbed body, only slightly arched loin and very little crook. For sixteen years the original English version remained unchanged. Today it seems surprising that no effort was made to bring the two divergent Standards into line, particularly as British breeders continued to go to Germany for blood with which to improve their own stock. But although the German Standard was not officially adopted, it certainly had a profound influence on the ideas of our breeders and judges. Many of the dogs imported had won high honours in the Fatherland before crossing the North Sea and continued their winning careers under British judges, the majority of whom were themselves successful breeders. Conversely, several of our best home-bred dogs were sent to compete at Continental shows and were placed high in the awards lists by German judges. From this it is clear that, despite the differences in the two Standards, the Dachshunds produced in Britain and Germany were of similar types, and long before the original English Standard was scrapped it had ceased to be taken seriously by the Dachshund fraternity in this country. By 1907 the position had become so absurd that the Dachshund Club was compelled to act. In that year a Special Committee was appointed to consider what should be done, and recommended that the English Standard be revised to make it conform to the German. This revised edition of the Standard is still in force, unchanged except for a few minor additions to the text which clarify, without altering, certain of its provisions.

CHAPTER II

THE SMOOTH DACHSHUND IN THE INTER-WARS PERIOD AND UP TO THE FIFTIES

IN the previous chapter we passed in brief review the rise of the Dachshund in what may be termed the first period of its history in this country. That period holds a peculiar fascination for students of breed history and one is strongly tempted to linger over its many interesting events. Space, however, is limited and no useful purpose would be served by dealing in greater detail with the exhibits which dominated the Dachshund stage prior to the coming of the First World War. With very few exceptions, to be mentioned later, those old dogs must be regarded as being of only historical interest to present-day breeders, for their blood became virtually extinct over thirty years ago.

The 1914–18 war inflicted a severe blow on all aspects of dog breeding in Britain and elsewhere. All breeds were affected, but none, perhaps, so tragically as the Dachshund. Ever since its first appearance among us the little Teckel had been recognized as the national dog of the Teutonic Empire, and with the outbreak of hostilities he came in for a share of the obloquy heaped on everything "made in Germany". Up to 1916 a few of the older breeders stuck staunchly by their favourite and continued to support the classes put on for the breed at the larger shows. But in that year the Kennel Club put a ban on both showing and breeding, and during the next four years interest in the Dachshund fell to zero.

The resumption of shows in 1920 found our breed in a most unhappy position. Almost all the pre-war exhibitors had dispersed their kennels, most of the old-time winners were either dead or too old to be of use, and young stock was all but unobtainable. Of the pre-war breeders Major P. C. G. Hayward alone possessed a number of first-class dogs and bitches, impeccably bred from his Honey strain which he had founded some quarter of a century previously and kept uncontaminated through the war years. Major Hayward had purchased his first Dachshund from that great enthusiast Major Harry Jones in 1893. This was a chocolate bitch which her new owner registered as Honey. Her breeding was of the best, for she was by Jimp, a son of Champion Jackdaw, out of a daughter of Champion Pterodactyl. She was mated to Duckmanton Winkle, a grandson of old Champion Charkow (the sire of Champion Jackdaw) and Champion Joan of Arc (a daughter of Champion Maximus). This mating produced the bitch Honeysuckle, which, when put back to Champion Pterodactyl, bred that great dog Champion Hotspur, born in 1896 and almost invincible in his day. The Honey strain was, therefore, founded on the most successful original British blood lines judiciously intermingled with the best of the German strains introduced by subsequent importations. During the first two years of the inter-wars show era, exhibits from the HoneyKennels accounted for most of the principal awards, the most prominent winners being Champion Honeystone, Champion Honeygirl, Champion Honeydrop, and Champion Honeymint.

Other breeders who had retained a few good specimens through the years of conflict were Miss F. E. Dixon, whose Champion Karkof, a daughter of Champion Honeystone, was a great winner in the early 1920s, Mr. E. W. Ricks of the Kensal prefix, whose most notable dog was Champion Kensal Call Boy, sold to the U.S.A., where he was never defeated by a dog of his own breed and was the first Dachshund ever to win Best in Show over all breeds in America, Mrs. R. Saunders, the great Dapple devotee, and Lord Wrottesley. This small band of enthusiasts under the leadership of Major Hayward, ably assisted by Mr. John F. Sayer, who had had his first Dachshund way back in 1894 and never lost touch with the breed till his death half a century later, set to work to raise the Teckel from the obscurity into which it had fallen to something approaching its former status. Their efforts were speedily crowned with success. Interest grew rapidly, many new disciples were attracted to the cause and the Dachshund once more took a place among Britain's most popular dogs.

As the demand for young stock increased, the need for new blood became urgent, and in 1923 Mr. A. C. Dunlop, who had first appeared as an exhibitor two years earlier, imported two dogs which were destined to lay the foundations of what may be called the modern type. These dogs were Theo von Neumarkt and his son Remagan Max. Theo, a black and tan, was a war-baby, born in 1917, and, therefore, ineligible by Kennel Club rules to compete in ring competition, but before coming to England he had won well in Germany. He proved very successful at stud, siring among many other winners the four champions Silva von Luitpoldsheim, Wanda von Luitpoldsheim, Honeymote and Honeystake, and the dog Fels von Luitpoldsheim, the sire of Champion Seraphina the dam of Champion Ludwig. He was, however, somewhat eclipsed by his son Remagan Max, born in Germany in 1920, whose name is still revered by all lovers of Dachshunds. Max's show debut was sensational. On his first public appearance he won five firsts, the challenge certificate and the Best of Breed award. Thereafter his show career was a procession of victories. In all he won eighteen challenge certificates and was generally acknowledged to be the best Smooth Dachshund ever seen in this country. Max was widely used at stud and sired an astonishing succession of superlative descendants, including such outstanding champions as Shrewd Saint, Saintly Sister, Spring Song, Ernemann, Ludwig, Red Rust, Master Michael, Ratho Tessa, Juno, Fernwood Marion, Firs Cruix Jewel and the bitch Honeymine, the dam of Champion Honeytime. Modern breeders owe much to this remarkable dog. He, more than any other, was responsible for stabilizing type and soundness in the first decade of the Dachshund's revival in England after World War number one. His name is to be found in the back areas of the pedigrees of most of our prominent winners and is still of significance to those to whom these family trees are something more than mere lists of names.

Mr. Dunlop put Dachshund lovers yet further in his debt by importing another great stud force in Faust von Forstenberg, by Asbecks Lehman ex Rauteldene von Forstenberg. Faust took his first challenge certificate at the Kennel Club show in 1924, where he made his debut, and quickly became a champion. He proved particularly well suited to bitches bred from Champion Remagan Max, and sired, among many other high-class winners, Champion Honeytime, Champion Honeyfire, Champion Honeygirl, Bronze of Greatwood and Kensal Nox, the sire of American Champion Kensal Call Boy. His greatest son was, perhaps, Champion Honeytime, the sire of the five champions Honeywag, Daw of Dilworth, Eve of Querns, Jade of Greatwood and Juduska.

The name of Mme P. P. Rikovsky and her Von der Howitt suffix is familiar wherever Dachshunds are known. She bought the bitch Isolde von Forstenberg from Mr. A. C. Dunlop about 1926. Isolde was a daughter of Champion Faust von Forstenberg and Roschen von Harlyburg. Her first litter to Champion

Remagan Max included a bitch registered as Brunhilda von der Howitt. This bitch was sold and her name changed to Wohlgeboren Brunhilda, but she was later bought back by her breeder and mated to the dog Wolf vom Birkenschloss, which Mme Rikovsky imported in 1930. Wolf was born in 1927, by Rotfink Schneid out of Mirzel vom Birkenschloss, and, besides becoming an International Champion, proved one of the most dominant stud forces of all time. He was a small, compact, strongly built dog, excelling in shoulder placement, front and feet, and impressed all who saw him by his absolute soundness and perfect movement. Mated to home-bred bitches carrying the blood of the old Honey strains, plus that introduced by Theo von Neumarkt, Remagan Max and Faust von Forstenberg, he got an innumerable progeny almost all of which showed many of their sire's outstanding qualities. Of these it is difficult to decide which to select for special mention, but perhaps Champion Zwiebach von der Howitt, Champion Firs Romany King, Champion Firs Sweet Briar, Champion Summer Shower, Fernwood Phantast and Wolfram of Loxwood are those through which his blood was most widely distributed and by which he is most represented in present-day pedigrees. The mating of Wolf to Wohlgeboren Brunhilda may be said to have founded the Von der Howitt strain, which has achieved world-wide fame during the last quarter of a century. From it came, besides Champion Zwiebach von der Howitt and Fernwood Phantast already mentioned, Champion Forelle, exported to America, Champion Rothart and Champion Petro von der Howitt, both sold to Canada, Champion Atilla and Hitlerin von der Howitt, the last a very beautiful bitch whose show career was cut short by the outbreak of war in 1939.

In the 1930s Mme Rikovsky also imported the elegant red Champion Cito von Alderschroffen, the red Champion Kunz Schneid, a great stud dog whose name ornaments the pedigrees of a host of contemporary winners, and the small black and tan Gernot von Lindenbuhl, a working champion in Germany and winner of two challenge certificates in England. Her two later imports, Champion Zeus vom Schwarenberg and the Austrian Champion Sepperl vom Hessenhorst, are well known, by name, at least, to all modern breeders, for they have contributed richly to the breed in the post-war period. Zeus has been especially successful as a sire, his offspring including Champion Silvae Zebo, Champion Grund von der Howitt, Champion Hollyhill Rigolo von der Howitt, Champion

Limberin Lounge Lizard and Tzigan von der Howitt, the sire of much winning stock including Champion Son of Tzigana.

Other importations were made in the inter-wars years, the most important being the red dog Champion Emmo von Rautenschild and the bitch Champion Fiffi von Alderschroffen, both owned by the great Scottish breed devotee the late Mr. C. F. Copland, Mrs. P. S. Allen's Darling von Falthor, the sire of Champion Max of Buckhurst, and Miss F. E. Dixon's Rothardt von Falthor, a grandson of Rotfink Schneid.

When Major Hayward retired from showing in 1923 most of his best dogs were purchased by Colonel G. S. Spurrier, D.S.O., to strengthen the Querns Kennels, which had been founded by his daughter, Miss Dorothy Spurrier, in 1920 with the bitch Hunker Monker, a daughter of Champion Honeystone. On the dispersal of the Honey Kennels Miss Spurrier became the owner of Champion Honeyfire, Champion Honeytime, Champion Honeyshine and Champion Honeywag. At the death of Mr. Dunlop the Querns Kennels also acquired Faust von Forstenberg and Theo von Neumarkt. Honeywag became a champion in five weeks at the age of nine months, thereby setting up a record that remains unbeaten. He was a neat, very sound black and tan weighing about seventeen pounds and was the sire of Flush of Querns, a most successful stud dog whose offspring included the three champion chocolate bitches Vickie, Kate and Velma of Querns. Champion Honeyshine sired Champion Crystal of Querns, an outstanding bitch which won eleven challenge certificates; then believed a record for her sex in the breed. Other notable inmates of these famous kennels included Champion Shrewd Saint, Champion Ernemann, Champion Junker Jan, Champion Jade of Greatwood, Champion Dicker von Kornerpark (imported), Champion Eve of Querns, the only Dapple bitch ever to become a champion, Storm of Querns and Juan of Querns. The last two would almost certainly have won their titles but for the intervention of the Second World War.

Mrs. Rhona Huggins was attracted to our breed in 1922 when she went to the Crystal Palace to visit her first dog show. Shortly afterwards she bought an imported dog, Friedel von Taubergrund, primarily for his soundness and beautiful action, and mated him to two English-bred bitches. This laid the foundation of the Firs strain which from the later 1920s to 1939 was the most successful in the country. Champion Firtinkergirl was one of several champions produced by in-breeding strongly to Friedel. Her sire, Firbeech, was by him, as was her dam, Firchime, and both went back on the maternal side to the Honey strain. The dog Champion Firochre was by Champion Red Rust, a son of Champion Remagan Max and Champion Honeymouse. From Champion Firtinkergirl came Champion Firs Chenille, by Champion Wolf vom Birkenschloss, which, mated to Champion Zwiebach von der Howitt, also by Champion Wolf, bred Champion Firs Black Velvet; in my opinion the best dog of the inter-wars period. He, in turn, sired Champion Firs Cruiser, another wonderfully good Dachshund, whose dam Firs Dreamship of Fullands was a daughter of Champion Firs Romany King, by Champion Wolf. Other superlative specimens bred by Mrs. Huggins were Firlustre, the sire of Champion Honeyshine, Champion Firs Red Line, bought by Mrs. V. Collins to strengthen her Kelvindale Kennels in Scotland and sire of Champion Red Letter of Kelvindale, Champion Firs Dimity, Champion Firs Cruix Jewel, Champion Firsgem and Champion Firs Black Sheen.

Champion Firs Cruiser sired many winners, one of the most notable being the English and American Champion Dimas Earthstopper, exported to the U.S.A. by Mr. John Mason, who had another worthy champion in Glycerine Honey. Earthstopper's dam, Red Glory, was by the imported Champion Emmo von Rautenschild, so that he was strongly line-bred to Rotfink Schneid. The Firs Kennel was disbanded in 1939, but its influence is still strong in the breed. Almost every winning Smooth of today carries the names of some of its representatives in its pedigree, and Firs type is still accepted as an ideal to which to breed.

Another important kennel of the 1930s was that bearing the Fernwood prefix, owned by Mrs. P. S. Allen. Champion Fernwood Marion and her daughter Champion Fernwood Tessa were outstanding in their sex and the dogs Champion Fernwood Brigand, Champion Fernwood Radio and Champion Fernwood Cassius were excellent examples of the smaller, all-quality type which has, alas, virtually ceased to exist. Anyone possessing stock going back to the Fernwood dogs might be well advised to try to collect up the blood by a carefully planned programme of line-breeding.

Mrs. P. E. Goodman owned the red dog Max of Buckhurst, born in 1934 by Darling von Fallthor ex the bitch Appelzinne, a daughter of Champion Wolf vom Birkenschloss. He became a champion and was very popular at stud, so that his name appears in the pedigrees of many contemporary winners. The most distinguished of his offspring was Champion Willow of Roding, a clear red of great elegance and perfect balance. Among other prominent breeders and exhibitors of the 1930s whose names call for special mention were Mr. E. W. Ricks of the Kensal Kennels and his brother Mr. George Ricks of the Grixfords, Mrs. D. W. Elliott, whose Burd Kennels included a great dog in Champion Burdrobert, Mrs. K. Fraser Ellis of the Dalling prefix, Mrs. L. Midwood whose Champion Daw of Dilworth was most successful both in ring competition and at stud, Mrs. Channer, owner of the Fullands dogs, Mr. C. A. Ealand of the Loxwoods, Mrs. Gilligan and Captain R. S. De Quincey.

The impact of the Second World War on the breed was much less severe than had been that of the earlier conflict. In the first excitement and alarm many kennels were shut down, much exhibition and breeding stock was destroyed, or given to pet homes, and all breeding operations were suspended. But as people became accustomed to war-time conditions, some found it possible to keep at least a few of their favourites, and the holding of local shows helped to keep breed interest alive. Although many pre-war breeders were employed on war-work or on military service, a few managed to keep their kennels going in a small way and a number of newcomers interested themselves in our breed and managed to rear a litter or two. Feeding was, of course, a great problem and no large-scale breeding was attempted, but enough was done to give a flying start to show activities immediately the Kennel Club lifted its ban on Open and Championship events. When the post-war position of the breed came to be assessed it was found that all the blood-lines built up in the twenty years prior to 1939 were represented in the surviving stock, and the intermixing of these has produced our present exhibits. Since the end of the war no Smooth Dachshund has been imported that has had a significant influence on the breed.* Every one of our post-war winners has been bred from stock descended from dogs that have already been mentioned.

Any review of the kennels that have played leading parts in the show history of the Smooth Dachshund since 1946 must give first place to that of Mrs. Grosvenor Workman, whose Silvae prefix has achieved unique fame. Mrs. Grosvenor Workman started exhibiting in 1935 and registered her prefix the following year. Much of her kennels' success is based on the

*Until the importation from Belgium of the red Heracles von Liebestraum in the late fifties. J. V. C.

bitch Silvae Radium, bred by Mrs. M. Gibson, by Champion Fernwood Radio ex Fernwood Bridget, a daughter of Champion Fernwood Brigand. Mated to Firs Tally, a son of Champion Firs Black Velvet and Champion Firs Olivia of Fullands, Radium bred the bitch Silvae Error, the dam of Champion Silvae Polish and Champion Silvae Lustre (both by Champion Silvae Zebo, a son of Champion Zeus vom Schwarenberg) and of Champion Silvae Post Horn, as well as several other well-known winners. It is impossible to give here a full list of the numerous champions and certificate winners which have borne the Silvae prefix or have been bred from stock emanating from this kennel, for it would include a large proportion of the most consistently successful exhibits of the post-war period. Among the most outstanding are Champion Silvae Lustre, Champion Silvae Banjo, Champion Silvae Zebo, Champion Silvae Post Horn, Champion Silvae Polish, Champion Silvae Woodnote, Champion Silvae Sailor's Quest, the litter brother and sister Champion Silvae Jolly Farmer, Champion Silvae Land Girl, Champion Silvae Bandolier, and his sons Champion Silvae Keeper and Champion Silvae Review.

In his day Champion Silvae Lustre held the record number of challenge certificates won. Champion Silvae Sailor's Quest has been the dominant stud force of the last decade. His progeny include such celebrities as Champion Ashdown Skipper, Champion Ashdown Coral, Champion Grunwald Glade, Champion Zilla von Weyher, Champion Tugboat of Thistleavon, Champion Urbatz von der Howitt, Champion Selwood Sailorette, Champion Selwood Sailaway and Champion Selwood Sailorman. He was by Champion Silvae Banjo (by Champion Silvae Zebo) out of Champion Silvae Polish and was born in 1946. His tragic death in 1951 while in his prime was a great loss, but his influence for good should be impressed on the breed through his descendants for many years to come.

Mr. R. W. Pilkington's and Mrs. Gath's Champion Ashdown Skipper emulated the feat of Champion Silvae Lustre as a collector of challenge certificates and has proved the successor at stud of his sire Champion Silvae Sailor's Quest. He had a great show career and has proved a prepotent sire. His offspring include such outstanding winners as Champion Hawkstone Matelot, Champion Ashdown Eminent, Champion Potsdown Cruiser, and Champion Dargarvel Corvette. Among numerous other champions bred in this kennel are Champion Ashdown Gracious, Champion Ashdown Grandee, Champion

Ashdown Starshine, Champion Ashdown Coral and Champion Ashdown Glamorous, the last named one of the great Dachshunds of all time. Miss G. Barker, owner of the Potsdown kennels has had many show successes with her home-bred stock. Her most notable exhibits include Champion Potsdown Persimon, Champion Potsdown Poetess, Champion Potsdown Cruiser and Champion Potsdown President.

The Von Weyher Kennels of Mr. J. E. Langdale, who started showing Smooth Dachshunds in 1934, have produced five champions since 1946. His present strain is founded on the bitch Erna von Weyher, a grand-daughter of Champion Wolf vom Birkenschloss. She was mated to Champion Firs Black Velvet and the resulting litter included Brunhilda von Weyher and the dog Theo von Weyher. The latter was sold to Miss Spurrier and renamed Querns Theo. He sired Querns Golden Sovereign, one of the greatest stud dogs of recent years. At the dispersal of the Firs Kennels Mr. Langdale bought the black and tan dog Firs Ingo, son of Champion First Cruiser and Champion Firs Dimity, which, mated to Brunhilda, sired Charlotte von Weyher, the dam of Champion Zilla von Weyher (by Champion Silvae Sailor's Quest). A later mating of Brunhilda to Imber Hero, a son of Champion Dimas Earthstopper, produced Elsa von Weyher, the dam of the litter brother champions Ingo and Rufus von Weyher, whose sire is Querns Golden Sovereign. Charlotte's mating to Theodore von Weyher, a son of Elsa and Querns Golden Sovereign, gave the New Zealand Champion Erica von Weyher and Dieda von Weyher, which, when mated to Champion Rufus, bred Champion Olivia von Weyher. Mr. Langdale's fifth champion Elissa von Weyher is by Champion Ingo ex Sandra von Weyher, a daughter of Charlotte.

Mr. and Mrs. G. A. Lloyd owe much of the success of their well-known Grunwald Kennels to the Irish Champion Zick of Grunpark, bred by Mrs. M. Macnaughton, Co. Dublin, in 1938, brought to England by Mme P. P. Rikovsky in 1941 and purchased by Mr. Lloyd within a few days of his arrival. He was a son of Zick von der Howitt and Suzane of Grunpark and carried a strong infusion of Champion Kunz Schneid blood. This clear-red, medium-sized dog sired many high-class exhibits, including Grunwald Avril, winner of thirty-six Best in Show awards, and never beaten by a Dachshund other than her dam, Grunwald Oda, Grunwald Victor and the Australian champions Grunwald Ochre and Barkescale Merry Boy. The bitch Grunwald Avril was out of Sally of Summerflowers, daughter of Champion Kunz Schneid and, when mated to Champion Silvae Sailor's Quest, bred Champion Grunwald Glade, a very consistent winner and popular stud dog. His progeny include Champion Grunwald Garland, Champion Grunwald Glenda, Champion Cinnamon of Roding and Champion Black Shelagh of Roding. Another well-known product of this kennel is Champion Grunwald Gleam, a son of Champion Silvae Sailor's Quest. By concentrating on the Champion Kunz Schneid blood, through I.K.C. Champion Zick of Grunpark and Sally of Summerflowers, Mr. and Mrs. Lloyd have built up a strain of pure-breeding reds of rich, clear colour.

Mrs. P. Hood-Wright's Selwood prefix has come rapidly to the front in recent years and is now borne by several Champions including Selwood Starturn, Selwood Sailorette, Selwood Sailaway, Seasprite, Salute, Sinderella, Selebrity, Seastar, and Selwood Sailorman. Starturn is by Dahabeah of Dachswald and out of Selwood Dimpseylight of Dachswald, the former a son of Champion Firs Cruiser, the latter a grand-daughter of I.K.C. Champion Zick of Grunpark. Among the latest of the Selwood champions is October Lad, a son of Sailorman.

Miss P. A. Clayton has been closely associated with the breed since 1934 and her Dachswald Kennels have produced many notabilities that have contributed significantly to the make-up of our post-war stock. Among her best have been Champion Democrat of Dachswald, Director of Dachswald, Damascene of Dachswald, the dam of Champion Silvae Zebo, Dahabeah and Selwood Dimpseylight of Dachswald, the sire and dam of the litter mates champions Selwood Sailorette, Sailaway and Sailorman mentioned above, the New Zealand Champions Dobbie and Dellah of Dachswald and the Indian Champion Daily Mail of Dachswald.

Miss N. Hill's Hawkstone prefix is among the best known in the breed. Her Champion Hawkstone Matelot is winner of 22 challenge certificates and has twice been Best In Show at all breeds championship shows. He is by Champion Ashdown Skipper and has, himself, an excellent record. Other notables are Champion Hawkstone Superb, a son of Champion Ashdown Eminent, Champion Hawkstone Eclipse, and Champion Hawkstone Treasure.

Of the breeders prominent in the inter-wars period who have continued strongly to influence the breed since 1946, special mention must be made of Mme P. P. Rikovsky. Among the best of her post-war winners are Champion Grund von der Howitt, Champion Hollyhill Rigolo von der Howitt, both by Champion Zeus vom Schwarenberg, Champion Dallas Victoria von der Howitt, Champion Red Ruby of Broadbeck, a grand-daughter of Champion Zeus, Champion Urbatz von der Howitt, by Champion Silvae Sailor's Quest ex Champion Grund von der Howitt, Champion Czardas and Champion Petuchok von der Howitt, the Italian Champion Kukuraza, the Indian Champion Cerno and the American Champion Peteo von der Howitt.

Miss Dorothy Spurrier, the President of the Dachshund Club, also continues to serve the breed with her Querns Kennels which have now won over two hundred challenge certificates. The most famous of her recent possessions have been Champion Victoria of Querns, a grand-daughter of Champion Crystal of Querns, Golden Sovereign of Querns, sire of the four champions Ingo and Rufus von Weyher, Victoria of Querns and Craigmere Cora (Mr. F. McSalley's), and of Rytona Diamond of Querns, winner of three certificates. Mrs. P. S. Goodman is also still active both as breeder and exhibitor with her Rodings Kennels, and has added to her list of champions with Delimit of Roding, a daughter of Champion Silvae Zebo, Selene of Roding, a grand-daughter of Champion Max of Buckhurst, Champion Cinnamon and Champion Black Shelagh of Roding.

Many champions besides those specifically mentioned in this necessarily short review have, of course, been made up in the period covered. My aim has been not to furnish a complete list of title-holders and their owners, but to indicate the main blood-lines represented in the principal winners of the past thirty years. The individuals named include those that can be said chiefly to have contributed to the building up of the Smooth Dachshund as it exists in Britain today.

Among other exhibitors whose stock has been very prominent in the awards lists of championship shows, special mention must be made of Mr. R. W. B. Pinches, whose Turlshill prefix is carried by several notable champions, Mr. and Mrs. E. G. Crowley, whose Aysdorn kennels have turned out a succession of celebrities, Mrs. B. Covell and Mrs. M. E. Thomson (Eastmead), Miss D. Walsh (Oysterville), Miss M. K. Stewart (Dargarvel), Mrs. J. Peach Lewis (Peachcroft), Mr. and Mrs. J. Gallop (Rhinefields) and Mr. M. J. Birley (Adyar).

For later information see Addendum 1, page 173.

CHAPTER III

A CRITICAL ANALYSIS OF THE SMOOTH STANDARD AND ITS IMPLICATIONS

THE Standard of the Smooth Haired Dachshund as issued by the Kennel Club is as follows:

Characteristics. First and foremost a sporting dog, the Smooth Dachshund is remarkably versatile, being equally adaptable as a house pet; his smooth, close coat is impervious to rain and mud. His temperament and acute intelligence make him the ideal companion for town or country. In the field of sport he is unequalled, combining the scenting powers of a Foxhound with unflinching courage, and will go to ground to fox, otter or badger.

General Appearance. Long and low, but with compact and well-muscled body, not crippled, cloddy, or clumsy, with bold defiant carriage of head and intelligent expression.

Head and Skull. Long and appearing conical when seen from above, and from a side view tapering to the point of the muzzle. Stop not pronounced, skull should be slightly arched in profile, appearing neither too broad nor too narrow. Jaw neither too square nor snipy but strong, the lips lightly stretched fairly covering the lower jaw.

Eyes. Medium in size, oval, and set obliquely. Dark in colour, except in the case of Chocolates, in which they may be lighter; in Dapples one or both wall eyes are permissible.

Ears. Broad, of moderate length, and well rounded (not narrow, pointed, or folded), relatively well back, high and well set on, lying close to the cheek, very mobile as in all intelligent dogs; when at attention the back of the ear directed forward and outward.

Mouth. Teeth must be strongly developed. The powerful canine teeth must fit closely. The correct bite is a scissors bite, any deviation being a fault.

Neck. Sufficiently long, muscular, clean, no dewlap, slightly arched in the nape, running in graceful lines into the shoulders, carried well up and forward.

Forequarters. Shoulder blades long, broad and set on sloping, lying firmly on fully-developed ribs, muscles hard

(*Sally Anne Thompson*)

Ch. Womack Wrightstarturn
(*Smooth*)

(*C. M. Cooke*)

Ch. Rebecca Celeste of Albaney
(*Long Haired*)

(*Anne Roslin-Williams*)

Ch. Gisbourne Inca
(*Wire Haired*)

Ch. Delphik Debbret
(*Miniature Long*)

(*Thomas Fall*)

Ch. Dandy Dan of Wendlitt
(*Miniature Smooth*)

(*H. J. Fountain*)

Ch. Drakesleat Klunk Klick of Andyc
(*Miniature Wire*)

Ch. Jackdaw
(*Smooth – born 1886*)

Ch. Remagan Max
(*Smooth – born 1920*)

(*Almond*)

Ch. Wolf vom Birkenschloss
(*Smooth – born 1927*)

Ch. Honeyshine
(*Smooth*)

(*Sport & General*)

Ch. Honeydrop and Ch. Honeymint
(*Smooth*)

(*Ralph Robinson*)

Ch. Firs Black Velvet
(*Smooth*)

and plastic. Chest very oval, with ample room for the heart and lungs, deep and with ribs well sprung out towards the loins, breast-bone very prominent. The front legs should, when viewed from one side, cover the lowest point of the breastline. Forelegs very short and in proportion to size strong in bone. Upper arm of equal length with, and at right angles to, the shoulder blade; elbows lying close to ribs, but moving freely up to shoulder blades. Lower arm short as compared with other animals, slightly inclined inwards (crook), seen in profile moderately straight; not bending forward or knuckling over (which indicates unsoundness).

Body. Long and muscular, the line of back slightly depressed at shoulders and slightly arched over the loin, which should be short and strong; outline of belly moderately tucked up. What is required is a general levelness of the back, the hindquarters (the rump) not being higher than the shoulders.

Hindquarters. Rump round, full, broad; muscles hard and plastic; hip bone or pelvic bone not too short, broad and strongly developed, set moderately sloping, thigh bones strong, of good length, and joined to pelvis at right-angles; lower thighs short in comparison with other animals; hocks well developed and seen from behind the legs should be straight (not cow-hocked). The dog should not appear higher at the quarters than at shoulders.

Feet. The front feet should be full, broad and close-knit, and straight or very slightly turned outwards, the hind feet smaller and narrower. The toes must be close together with a decided arch to each toe, with strong regularly placed nails and firm pads. The dog must stand true, i.e., equally on all parts of the foot.

Tail. Set on fairly high, strong and tapering, but not too long and not too curved or carried too high.

Coat. Short, dense and smooth, but strong. The hair on the underside of the tail coarse in texture; skin loose and supple, but fitting the dog closely all over, without much wrinkle.

Colour. Any colour other than white (except a white spot on breast). Nose and nails should be black. In red dogs a red nose is permissible, but not desirable. In Chocolates and Dapples the nose may be brown or flesh-coloured. In Dapples large spots of colour are undesirable, and the dog should be evenly dappled all over.

Weight and Size. Dogs should not exceed 11·3 kg. (25 lbs.). Bitches should not exceed 10·4 kg. (23 lbs.).

Faults. In general appearance weak or deformed, too high or too low to the ground; ears set on too high or too low, eyes too prominent; muzzle too short or pinched, either undershot or overshot; forelegs too crooked; hare or terrier feet, or flat spread toes (flat-footed); out at elbows; body too much dip behind the shoulders; loins weak or too arched; chest too flat or too short; hindquarters weak or cow-hocked, quarters higher than the shoulders.

Note. Male animals should have two apparently normal testicles fully descended into the scrotum.

Everyone hoping for distinction in the breed must study this Standard. Each paragraph deals with some aspect of anatomical structure required to fit the dog to perform the task of going and staying to ground in pursuit of its natural quarry. A Dachshund that is unable or unwilling to carry out that job successfully is unworthy of the name. The fact that our breed has been and is used for other purposes, or that the great majority of show dogs never have the chance of showing their prowess in the field, is irrelevant. The breed was evolved for a specific purpose, as its name, which is merely the German way of saying Badger Dog, clearly reveals, and all the provisions of the Standard are based on recognition of the need to keep it up to that job.

A breed Standard must of necessity be concise. It can only indicate essentials, and because of the need for brevity its wording may verge on the terse. Full appreciation of its nuances and inner implications often elude those who have been active as exhibitors and breeders, perhaps even as judges, for some years, so that it seems desirable to examine the official description in detail to assist the novice to get at the less obvious inferences of the phrasing.

First, then, we see under General Appearance it is stated that a Dachshund must be long and low. Here at once we come on a feature that is much misunderstood. When first looked at a Dachshund should convey the impression of a dog whose most striking characteristic is its length and lowness to ground. But this appearance of length should not depend wholly on great length of back—using the word here as applying to the region between the withers and the pelvis. The correct placement of the shoulders, the forward thrust of the breast and the conformation of the hips all help to add to the apparent length of the body. It is the trunk as a whole that should be long, not the back itself. An overlong back makes for weakness, but length derived from a back of medium length, obliquely set shoulder blades, a well-developed fore-chest with prominent

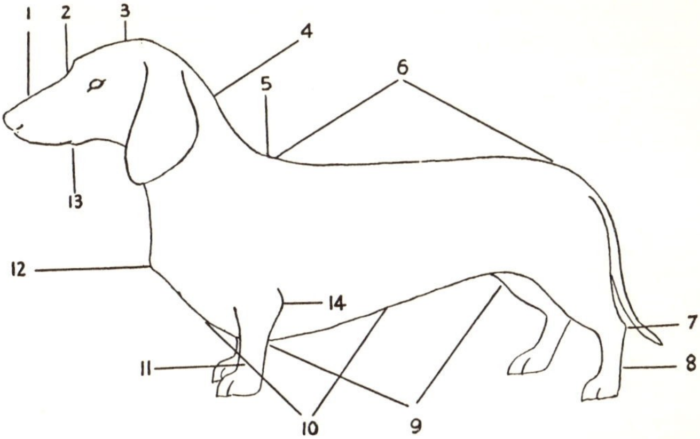

FIG. 1

DACHSHUND TERMINOLOGY

1. Muzzle
2. Stop
3. Skull
4. Nape
5. Withers
6. Top-line
7. Hock
8. Tarsus
9. Underline
10. Keel
11. Wrist
12. Projection of Breast bone
13. Corner of mouth
14. Elbow

breast bone and properly proportioned pelvis, makes for suppleness with strength: qualities essential in an animal required to work for long periods in the confined space of a twisting underground tunnel. The statement that the Dachshund must be low refers to the height at the withers. Lowness is needed to enable the dog to follow its quarry to earth; which usually means squeezing into a comparatively small hole. Many exhibitors still appear to think that the term "lowness to ground" refers to the depth of the keel, or lowest point of the chest, but the two are in no way connected. At our shows we see many exhibits with chests so deep as to all but touch the ground but which are much too high at the withers to have any hope of following a fox or badger to its earth. A dog possessing great length of body will always appear lower than a shorter dog, but this proportionate lowness should not be mistaken for the absolute lowness required by the Standard.

The description of the head is so clear that it calls for little comment. It has been said—indeed I have often said it myself—that this is the part of the Dachshund that a knowledgeable judge looks at last. But that dictum should not be understood to suggest that the head is unimportant. It merely indicates the overriding importance of such qualities as general soundness, body length, correct chest formation, good feet and movement. The ideal Dachshund head is unique: a combination of refinement and strength. Its length should be in proportion to that of the trunk, with almost flat skull, cleanly modelled foreface and fine muzzle; the top line showing no abrupt step between skull and foreface. On the whole, heads are fairly good today. One rarely sees the thick, bulgy-skulled dogs that were once all too common, and the heavy, houndy muzzle is happily a thing of the past.

A well-shaped head may be marred by faulty eyes, which may be too large, too round, too light or badly set. A small, oval, dark eye, neither so deeply sunk as to make the dog look sulky, nor so shallow as to impart a soft, languishing expression, gives a most attractive finish to a long, clean, well-modelled head. In reds the eyes should be at least two shades darker than the coat and in black and tans very dark hazel. Chocolates, it should be noted, are not to be faulted for light eyes. In this colour the eyes vary from pale gold to reddish-brown. Most of us prefer the darker shade but either is correct. The ears play an important part in giving the desired expression. They should be set on rather high and be large and broad enough to become a conspicuous feature, but when pulled to the front the leather should not extend to the tip of the muzzle. If hung too low and too thin in texture they become immobile and may tend to fold, like the ears of a Bloodhound or Bassethound. When a Dachshund is called to attention its ears should be turned so that the broad flaps face directly to the front. This ear movement is a breed characteristic and a judge is fully justified in handicapping an exhibit that fails to use its ears when put on the alert. Immobile ears are often, though not invariably, set on low or are too narrow at their bases. Small or short ears are ugly and very untypical.

The teeth should be large in proportion to the dog's size, white, strong and even. The so-called scissor bite is considered correct. Here the inner side of the upper incisors is in contact with the outer side of the under ones. This is supposed to afford a more secure grip. The late John F. Sayer was a great advocate of this dental arrangement. He was, I believe, largely responsible for getting the phrase referring to it incorporated in the Standard. Any suggestion of an overshot or undershot jaw is a grave fault, but I fancy there are very few judges who would penalize a Dachshund for teeth which meet exactly in what is termed the pincer bite, despite the wording of the Standard. I have yet to be convinced that the one has any advantage over the other in a hunting dog. When judging I have from time to time noticed exhibits in which one of the incisors in one or both jaws is not developed. There should be six incisor teeth in each jaw and any deficiency should be penalized. From recent correspondence I suspect the fault to be commoner than is generally realized. It should be watched for, as the condition appears to be inherited. The accidental loss of a tooth is, of course, a very different matter. This should not be counted a fault, neither should staining caused by distemper. I consider it irrational to put an exhibit down for either of these minor, acquired blemishes.

The proportions and outline of the neck contribute much to the air of pride and elegance needed in the perfect Dachshund. This part must be of good length, wholly free from loose skin about the throat, slightly arched at the nape from its junction with the base of the head to the point where it runs gracefully into the line of the back; strong and muscular without being thick or heavy. A short neck is a grave fault. Not only does it destroy the grace and symmetry of the whole outline, it also spoils the head carriage and gives the dog the appearance of being overloaded or "stuffy" in front. The fault usually goes with a short head and insufficient body length, and one sometimes sees exhibits which, though showing ample length from withers to rump, are disproportionately short in neck, so that the forequarters look too heavy for the part of the trunk behind the shoulders. Loose skin about the throat detracts from the apparent length of the neck and is very ugly. It is often associated with wrinkled forelegs, another very definite fault which, though less general than formerly, is still with us.

The skin of a Dachshund should cover all parts of the body like a well-fitting glove, giving the dog a clean-cut outline completely free from folds or puckers. In the paragraph dealing with Coat the Standard states the skin should fit "closely all over, without much wrinkle". When that phrase was introduced, in 1907, it probably seemed sufficiently revolutionary, for the original Standard had asked for the skin to be loose and "in great abundance". Since then our ideas concerning the ideal Dachshund have progressed far and I suggest it is high time the word "much" was deleted. When, some twenty years ago, I wrote strongly on the desirability of eliminating wrinkle some breeders and judges of the old school protested, insisting that the "loose stockings" effect had always been a characteristic peculiar to the Dachshund and that it should be retained. Soon, however, practically all the breed authorities adopted my view and today loose skin on any part of the body is generally regarded as most undesirable.

A few years ago a well-known breeder sought to excuse the wrinkle shown by some of her dogs on the ground that it is difficult to get heavy bone without some wrinkle. That, however, is not the case. The truth is, loose wrinkled skin round the forefeet gives a spurious impression of substance by causing the forelegs to look thick, but this apparent thickness is not indicative of heavy bone, as may easily be proved by handling. No competent judge should mistake thick, wrinkled skin for bone.

The longest paragraph in the Standard is devoted to the Forequarters, which indicates the importance attached to that region. The key to the whole structure lies in the shoulder girdle, in which the shoulder blade is the dominant component. This bone must be long, broad and sloping. If it is too short and upright it will give rise to many faults. A short shoulder blade is almost always attended by a short upper arm and, because of the angle at which these bones will articulate, the upper arm will be too straight. The weight of the body bearing too steeply on the upper part of the forelimb pushes out the elbow, which in turn causes the lower arm to slope inwards and, in an effort to establish some sort of equilibrium, the feet turn out. Loose or protruding elbows and out-turned feet are among the most prevalent of all faults in our breed, and are, in the great majority of cases, caused by badly placed, or wrongly proportioned, shoulder blades. A dog with upright shoulders cannot move correctly. Its gait is cramped and stilted. The long, easy, swinging stride desired in a Dachshund is only possible if the shoulder blades are long, obliquely placed and lie firmly against the thorax.

The whole shoulder girdle should be set well back. If it

is too far forward the dog will appear "loaded in shoulders" and the strong, forward thrust of the breast so much desired will be lacking, so that the dog will look flat-chested.[1] With this kind of front the shoulders tend to be too loosely placed against the rib cage and all the joints of the forelimbs to be loose. The elbows protrude, particularly when the dog moves, the wrists bend inwards and the feet turn outwards. When the condition

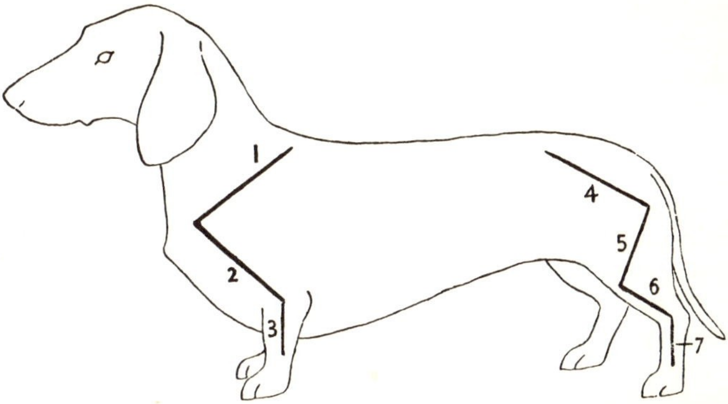

FIG. 2

POSITION AND ANGLES OF ARTICULATION OF THE BONES OF THE SHOULDER AND PELVIC GIRDLES

1. Shoulder blade
2. Upper arm
3. Lower arm
4. Pelvis
5. Femur or upper thigh
6. Tibia or lower thigh
7. Tarsal bones

is very strongly marked it may give rise to knuckling over, in which the forelegs give at the wrists, causing these joints to bend forwards. In the first decade of the present century and before, this extreme form of unsoundness was common. Today it is so rare that few contemporary exhibitors and judges have ever seen it. Let us hope they never will!

The original Standard, it may be recalled, described the chest as deep and narrow. Today we still require depth, but narrowness over the ribs, or in front, is now regarded as among the worst faults a Dachshund can possess. The chest must be both very deep and very broad in proportion to the dog's size; with full, well-rounded ribs carried well back. This formation gives ample space for heart and lungs and enables the dog to

[1] See Fig. 3A, page 42.

remain, without inconvenience, in the vitiated air of narrow underground cavities while continuing to bark loudly and continuously to announce its position in a fox or badger earth. In section the thorax should be oval, coming well down between the forelegs, with its lowest point level with the wrists. That is the ideal. Too deep a keel is as incorrect as is one that is too shallow. In practice it may be even less desirable, for if there is insufficient ground-clearance the dog's activity, both above and below ground, will be impeded and may unfit him for any kind of field work. On the other hand, any suspicion of legginess is rightly condemned as a cardinal fault. The correct sweep of the underline depends largely on the depth and shape of the keel. The ribs should, as has been said, extend well back and the line of the lower breast run in a graceful curve, without any abrupt break, into the line of the abdomen.

A short keel which ends suddenly, as though chopped off, is very unsightly and is evidence of faulty construction of the rib cage.[1] The sternum, or breast bone, should be very prominent, showing as a distinct projection in front just below where the throat merges in the curve of the breast. When this bone is properly developed a deep depression is seen on each side of it. The whole region of the chest in front of the forelimbs should be thrust forward like the bow of a ship. This feature is a characteristic of the Dachshund as are length of body and shortness of leg.

The most controversial point in the official description of the forelegs is that referring to the slight inward slope of the lower arm, giving what is termed the crook. When I first became associated with the breed, some forty years ago, practically every Dachshund seen had strongly crooked forelegs, in accordance with the Standard as it then existed. Today a pronounced crook is looked on as a form of unsoundness and no exhibit showing it has any chance of gaining an award. But the present Standard allows a slight crook, and there is considerable diversity of opinion as to what degree of divergence from the perfectly straight foreleg should be accepted. When dealing with the forefeet the Standard states that these may either point straight to the front or be turned slightly outwards. But it is impossible to have forward-pointing forefeet and a crook. If the feet are dead straight the forelegs must also be straight, for the crook is formed at the junction of these two parts. The perfectly straight front is now preferred by most

[1] See Fig. 3, B, page 42.

judges and it cannot be held to be incorrect. The old idea that out-turned feet were the better for digging is now discountenanced. One of the most accomplished of all natural diggers, the mole, has inturned feet, and neither the fox nor the badger have feet that turn outwards, so there seems to be no good reason for demanding them in the Dachshund.

Unfortunately, the perfectly straight front is often accompanied by small, terrier-like feet which are not what we require in our breed. The Dachshund's forefeet should be large, broad and round, and that type of foot is very difficult, though not impossible, to get with absolutely perpendicular forelegs. The really typical foot is usually found in dogs which show a very slight inward slope from elbow to wrist and turn slightly outwards. Such exhibits are to be preferred to those in which the forelegs are quite straight but the feet too small. To determine how much latitude should be allowed in the outward turning of the feet, think of the dog as standing on the face of a clock with its tail at twelve o'clock and its head at six o'clock. If its forefeet now point to seven and five their position should be accepted as conforming to the requirements of the Standard, but any approach to four and eight should be counted as a major fault.

The foot, besides being large, must be compact, with each toe well arched and with thick hard pads, and the dog must stand equally on all parts. This last point is important. If loose elbows force the feet outwards, or if the crook is too pronounced, the weight will fall on the inner part of the foot. A dog with very loose elbows or weak wrists cannot stand truly. While such a dog is standing still its feet may not look too bad, but when pressure is brought to bear on the withers the elbows will go out and the feet twist as the weight is taken on the inner side. The opposite condition, in which the feet turn inwards, is a very bad fault and indicates wrong angulations somewhere in the shoulder girdle or a twisted forearm. This failing is not common and when seen may be clearly noticeable only when the dog is moved.

In dealing with the back line the Standard asks for a slight depression at the shoulder and a slight arch over the loin. The wording might be improved by the addition of the word "only" before the depression and the arch. The highest point in the back line is over the withers. From there it drops very slightly, then runs straight as far as the pelvis, where there may be a very slight rise before the drop to the set-on of the tail. In nearly all modern winners the arch over the loin is so slight as to be virtually non-existent, as may be seen from the illustrations included in this volume. Anything approaching the well-arched loin described in the old Standard is now taboo. The roach back, in which the top line rises in an arch, then curves down-

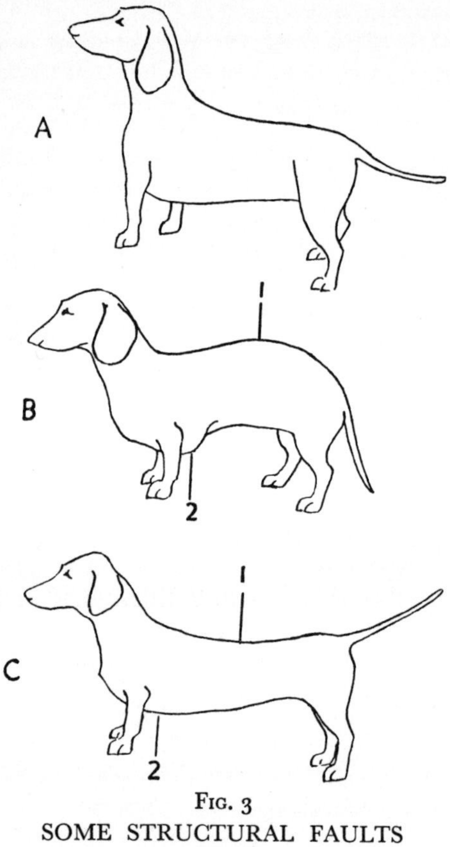

FIG. 3

SOME STRUCTURAL FAULTS

A. Shoulder girdle too far forward
B. Rouch back (1) and too short keel (2)
C. Dipping back (1) and shallow keel (2)

wards to the croup, is one of the worst of all faults, only equalled by a dip in the back. A sagging back is always a weak back and no Dachshund showing the fault in any but a very minor degree should be considered eligible for an award. There are, of course, degrees of roach and dip. Some exhibits which when standing appear quite level, reveal an arched loin when moving; others in which the back is absolutely flat in repose develop a definite dip when made to trot round the ring. In a long-bodied, sporting breed like the Dachshund a strong, firm, level back is of first importance. Exaggerated length from withers to pelvis is not desirable. It usually goes with a tendency to dip, which becomes marked as the dog tires. A correctly proportioned Dachshund should be twice as long as high, the height being taken at the withers and the length measured from the point of the breast bone to the back of the thigh when the dog is standing naturally.

The chief points to be noted about the hindquarters are that they must be broad, with the hocks well let down and well bent. A frequent fault is that the hocks are not sufficiently let down, so that when viewed from behind the dog looks stilted. This arises from the pelvis or the femur, or both, being too short and the tarsal bones too long. The pelvis and the femur, or upper thigh, should be of good length, but the second thigh, or tibia, and the part between the point of the hock and the foot should be short. Provided the dog is well muscled, as he should be, this formation gives a full, rounded shape to the hindquarters and brings the hocks well down towards the foot, so that the whole region looks strong and compact. Adequate width between the hocks is essential. A dog that goes narrow behind shows weakness, as does one in which the hocks turn inwards, producing the condition known as "cow-hocked". On the other hand, a Dachshund may be too wide behind, making it clumsy and ungainly in action. This fault often goes with a tendency to turn the hocks outwards and the toes in when moving—both very objectionable failings.[1]

The subject of colour in Dachshunds is considered at length in a later chapter, so that little need be said about it here. It is surprising that the Standard retains the provision that a red or brown nose, though undesirable, is permissible in a red Dachshund. All our breed judges would, I feel sure, penalize a red exhibit with a nose of any colour other than black; and penalize it so heavily as virtually to exclude it from the awards list. This is so generally recognized by exhibitors that few would so much as think of showing a dog with this peculiarity. The Standards relating to the other Dachshund varieties all insist that a red dog must have a black nose, only in Chocolates is a brown nose allowed. Most of the so-called red Dachshunds that fail to develop black pigment in the nose are genetically bad-coloured Chocolates and nearly all have light eyes. If the

[1] See Fig. 4, page 47.

Smooth Standard is ever revised the clause sanctioning a red or brown nose in an exhibit of any colour but chocolate should certainly be deleted.

The ban on white is of special interest to the few breeders who are now trying to produce all-white Dachshunds. The veto was probably introduced with the intention of discouraging dogs showing extensive white markings, rather than to exclude all-white exhibits from ring competition, for at the time the Standard was drawn up pure-white Dachshunds were unknown. There is no reason to suppose that a white Dachshund would be less suitable for field work than a red or black and tan. Why, then, should it be barred from our shows?

CHAPTER IV

THE SMOOTH DACHSHUND—ITS FAULTS AND VIRTUES

DURING the last three-quarters of a century or so many have essayed the formidable task of producing the perfect Dachshund: of breeding a dog conforming in every detail to the provisions of the Standard. So far no one has succeeded. Individuals approaching the ideal closely in essential points have, from time to time, appeared, but all have shown minor imperfections. What of the modern Smooth? What are its chief failings and how does it compare with the giants of the past?

With very few exceptions, the best of the show winners of the pre-1914 era would have little success in our rings today. Most would be considered coarse, with too much crook and indifferent feet. Many would be passed over because of their backlines; others for heaviness in skull or muzzle. The inter-wars years brought a great improvement right up to 1939. In my opinion the Smooth Dachshund was at its best in the late 1930s. Not only were the principal winners better than any seen before or since, but the general quality of the exhibits of that period was extremely high and very even. Since the holding of championship shows was resumed in 1946, we have, of course, seen many very good specimens of the breed, and in the intervening years there has been marked improvement in several respects among the rank and file, but general quality has not yet caught up with that of the years immediately preceding the outbreak of the last war. All who knew him will, I think, agree that Champion Firs Black Velvet was the best Smooth yet bred in a British kennel; though Champion Firs Cruiser and Champion Dimas Earthstopper were very hard to beat.

Though the Second World War was much less catastrophic in its impact on our breed than was the earlier conflict, it did, nevertheless, inflict a severe set-back, the effects of which are still apparent. I say this without pessimism. We are probably justified in claiming that there are more first-class Smooths in Britain today than in any other country, but it would be foolish to adopt an attitude of complacency towards shortcomings of which many of us are deeply conscious. Of these the gravest and most prevalent concerns hind action.

The Standard of Points is, on the whole, a clear statement of what is required in the ideal Smooth Dachshund. It has, however, one remarkable omission. No mention is made of movement. In extenuation it may be urged that a Dachshund whose anatomical structure accords with the Standard must move correctly. That statement may be true but it is not very helpful. After having studied the Standard diligently a novice may still be left wondering just how a Dachshund should move. Neither is it the novice alone who needs guidance in this matter. Several breeders and exhibitors of long standing frankly admit that they are not sure what constitutes perfect hind action. The most usual cause of bad hind movement is faulty skeletal structure. Before considering the various types of incorrect movement it may, therefore, be helpful to consider how the bony framework of the hindquarters should be put together.

First there is the pelvis, which should be broad, of good length and set obliquely. If it is too narrow the whole of the quarters will be cramped and the dog will be narrow behind. On the correct size, proportions and setting of this part depends the angulation of the hind limb. A pelvis that is set too steeply must result in the femur, or upper thigh, being articulated with it at too wide an angle, so that, unless the femur is too short, the dog will be high behind. This formation is likely to be accompanied by a long shank, or second thigh, set at an acute angle with the femur, cramping the whole of the lower leg and causing the hocks to be too strongly bent, thereby bringing the feet too far under the body. Reference to the Standard shows that the upper thigh should be fairly long, to accommodate the large muscles needed to propel the hindquarters, and articulate with the pelvis at an angle of 90 degrees. The lower thigh must be short and, if the back is to be level and the feet correctly placed, the tarsus, that is the part between the joint of the hock and the foot, must also be short.

When moving, a Dachshund should go forward with long, easy strides, sending each hind leg straight ahead, the two limbs moving parallel to one another *throughout their length*. The italics are important. Many exhibitors seem to think that provided the portions of the hind limbs below the hocks are parallel all is well. That is a mistake. A dog that moves with its hocks parallel may still fall in hind action. A rather common fault is a formation in which the upper parts of the hind legs converge, giving the thighs a bowed outline as seen from behind. This usually brings the hocks too close together and the dog is criticized as "going narrow behind". If, despite the converging of the thighs, there is sufficient room between the hocks, the dog's movement will be lumbering; its gait tending to become a waddle and the hindquarters looking unbalanced.

The condition known as being cow-hocked, in which the joints of the hocks turn inwards, is a very bad fault, as it always indicates weakness. It often arises from incorrect articulation of the upper and lower thigh bones, and a badly set pelvis. Cow-hocked dogs are usually narrow behind and too high in hocks. At one time this fault was very common. Today we

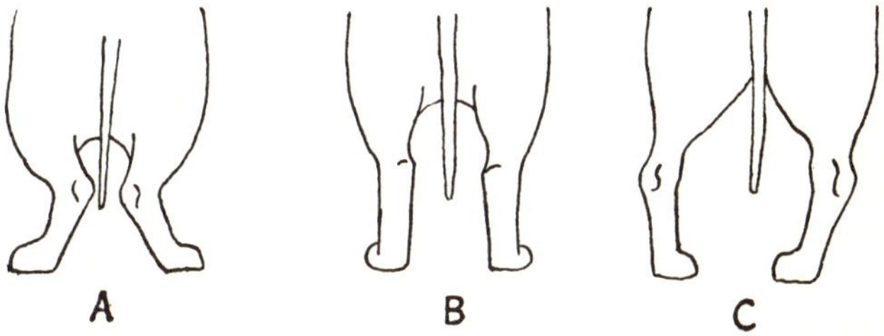

FIG. 4

HINDQUARTER FAULTS

A. Cow-hocked B. Correct C. Bandy-hocked

rarely see it in its most obvious form, but we still find exhibits which, though they do not show the failing when standing still, reveal it in a greater or less degree when moving at a brisk trot. The reverse condition, in which the hocks turn away from each other, causing the feet to come inwards, is by no means rare. It, too, is a bad and very ugly departure from the ideal. The inward slope of the tarsus may cause a slight inturning of the feet, making the dog pigeon-toed. The gait is very ungraceful, with a more or less pronounced tendency to roll. In bad cases the dog looks bandy behind.

A Dachshund that is either cow-hocked or bandy soon tires and would be incapable of standing up to a long strenuous spell of field work. Both failings must be regarded as forms of unsoundness. If a Dachshund is walked over soft muddy ground, so that imprints of its pads are shown, the distance between the marks left by the two front feet and that between the prints of its hind feet should be equal, or very nearly so. Assuming, of course, that the forequarters and fore-feet are correct. If the hind pad-marks are closer together than the fore the dog is narrow behind; if further apart he is too wide.

The proportionate length of the upper and lower thighs has a direct bearing on the length of the tarsus. As has been said, that part should be short, as it must be if the hocks are well let down. The majority of our Smooths are too high in hocks and too short in the upper thigh, which makes them look stilted behind. When moving the stride is too short and the hindquarters seem to lack that strong propelling thrust that should send the hind legs forward like well-powered pistons. High-set hocks are a frequent cause of faults in hind action. They make for weakness, for they go with light or thin musculature of the femur and may eventually lead to a dog's becoming cow-hocked or bandy. High hocks often lack flexibility. Many of our exhibits do not get their hocks far enough back when moving. In making the forward stride the hind feet are brought well under the body with the hocks strongly bent, as they should be, but as the dog moves forward the hocks are not sufficiently extended backwards, so that the feet do not reach to the rear. The stride is, therefore, very restricted, which, besides detracting greatly from the efficiency of the gait, makes the hind action look cramped and awkward. When the hind foot is brought back on the completion of a stride the pads should be clearly visible from behind.

To sum up, then, in the hindquarters we require a broad, rounded rump, full-muscled thighs and hocks well let down. When moving, the hind limbs should be absolutely parallel to one another from hip-joint to foot. The gait should be free and swinging, the stride long, and the whole action should give the impression of calling for no conscious exertion, so that one feels the dog could keep going almost indefinitely without tiring.

I have devoted considerable space to this matter of hind action because faulty movement is at present so general among Smooths that it calls for urgent attention. Lasting improvement can only be achieved by breeders making a serious attempt to understand the details of anatomical structure that govern correct hind action in the breed, and setting out to breed for movement in the same way as they breed for long heads, level back lines and sound fronts. Bad action, either fore or aft, may, of course, result from bad rearing, but the faulty movement of which we now see so much is, for the most part, caused by anatomical imperfections that are congenital.

Faults in the construction of the forequarters will be

reflected in the front action. Upright shoulders, loose elbows, too much crook and out- or inturned feet make it impossible for a Dachshund to move as it should. Upright shoulders give a stilted or mincing gait. Loose elbows or weakness at the wrists may cause a dog to plait—that is, to cross its forefeet when trotting. Exhibits with perfectly straight forelegs and small feet sometimes have a high-stepping front action which, though some owners consider it attractive, is wrong in a Dachshund. A dog showing this eccentricity will tire quickly, for it wastes a lot of energy and has a short stride.

Next to bad hind movement, perhaps the most prevalent fault in our modern Smooths is lightness of bone. In proportion to its size a Dachshund should be heavier in bone than almost any other breed. A lightly boned dog cannot stand up to such strenuous work as badger hunting involves, and to carry the long, and comparatively heavy, body the leg bone in particular must be thick, close-textured and strong. The legs of many present-day exhibits look too thin to bear the weight of the trunk. Some of these individuals have excellent length, impeccable top line, good ribbing, and may be thought to show great elegance, but they would be useless for field work. In this matter of bone the modern Smooth compares unfavourably with the best of the pre-war winners. Where heavy bone is achieved it is often at the cost of grace or refinement, the head, body and quarters all being unduly heavy, making the dog look coarse, clumsy or cobby. What we want is great substance allied to good length of head, neck and trunk, to give the appearance of strength with elegance and perfect balance. The qualities requisite in the show Dachshund may be summarized as the three S's and the three L's, which stand for Soundness, Substance and Symmetry with Length, Lowness to ground and Level top line.

For the benefit of the novice owners it may be stressed that the word "substance" applies to bone, not to flesh. In efforts to counter lightness of bone some exhibitors show their dogs unduly fat. This, so far from disguising lack of bone, makes it glaringly apparent. The body becomes almost cylindrical, with the under line almost as flat as the top line and, though the keel may appear to be deeper than it would were the dog in leaner condition, that illusory effect is unlikely to deceive any competent judge. The weight of the corpulent trunk may cause the elbows to protrude, the feet to splay and the back to dip, so that not only will lightness of bone be accentuated but other major faults may develop to add to the exhibit's original handicap.

The Standard gives the maximum weight as 25 lb. for a dog and 23 lb. for a bitch. That means that a Standard Smooth may weigh anything between 11 and 23 or 25 lb. according to sex; which gives our breed a much wider weight margin than most others. Yet even this is, it seems, too narrow for some breeders. Many of the exhibits now seen would certainly bring the scales down with a loud bump if subjected to a weight test. Up to 1939 the big winners ranged in weight between about 17 to 23 lb. Few, if any, were heavier; some were a pound or so lighter than the lower weight mentioned. Today almost all our winning Smooths are heavyweights. The majority come very near to, if they do not actually exceed, the maximum imposed by the Standard. Dogs are the worst offenders in this respect, but quite a number of our bitches would have to undergo drastic slimming to bring them within the stipulated 23 lb.

This trend towards overweight is, in my view, a most unfortunate development. One of the great attractions of our breed is that it may be had in a variety of colours and in many different sizes, but all weight variations should fall within the limits laid down in the Standard. A Dachshund is supposed to be able to go to ground if required, but some of our present winners would need a burrow of very unusual dimensions to accommodate them. Such oversized specimens may be very handsome and typical in shape, but they would be useless for the work for which the breed was evolved and for that reason should be discouraged. The tendency towards undue size has become so marked of late years that judges look in vain for sound, typical exhibits of medium size and have no alternative to putting up the big ones. The first-class Dachshund, weighing from 16 to 20 lb. or so, seems to be virtually extinct. Most of the light weights that do, from time to time, appear in our rings are inferior in so many other points to the larger competitors that they have to be relegated to the ranks of the also-rans. This has given rise to the complaint that judges are prejudiced in favour of the heavy weights and will not look at the smaller exhibits. This is very far from the truth. Most championship show judges would welcome an opportunity to give high awards to a medium- or lightweight Dachshund if they could find one good enough. There can be little doubt that the non-showing public prefer the smaller type, and unless something is done to bring it back the breed may suffer in popularity.

Since I drew attention to this matter some two years ago there has been more general recognition of the problem of overweight, and it is hoped that in the not too distant future we may again see outstanding specimens of medium size with the active, alert sporting temperaments shown by so many of the best Smooths of the inter-wars period. Champion Remagan Max, Champion Wolf von Birkenschloss, Champion Fernwood Brigand and several of the Firs exhibits were all of this type. Mrs. Huggins tells me that all except two of her Firs champions won in Special Open Classes for Smooths not exceeding 18 lb. in weight. Is there a single champion Smooth today that would be eligible for such a class?

There is, of course, a very real difference between size and weight. A big Dachshund with light bone may weigh less than a more heavily boned dog of smaller size. For that reason it is unwise to insist too rigidly on a particular weight, but the limit of 25 lb. gives full scope for all the substance that can be desired in a dog that is not too large. Despite its heavy bone, full ribbing, broad chest and body length, a Dachshund should give the impression of being a small dog. No one wants to see the practice of weighing exhibits introduced into our rings. A judge should be able to recognize both excess of weight and too large size in the exhibits brought before him without having to make use of scales.

For later information see Addendum 1.

CHAPTER V

THE LONG HAIRED DACHSHUND—A HISTORICAL SURVEY

THE origin of the Long Haired Dachshund is as obscure as is that of the Smooth. The theory that it was produced by crossing the Smooth Dachshund with a small Spaniel lacks confirmation and is, in my view, unlikely. All who have experience of the breed know it to be very constant in type, and no trace of Spaniel characteristics is apparent either in its physical shape or temperament. The Dachshund-like dogs depicted in the crude sixteenth-century woodcuts referred to in a former chapter show feathering on the ears and tail, and many of the early figures of the breed suggest that in the fore-runners of the modern Teckel the coat varied much both in length and texture. Whatever its ancestry, we can claim that the Long Haired Dachshund has existed for upwards of two centuries, and without delving deeper into its genealogy we pass on to consider the history of the breed in this country.

The pioneer of Long Haired Dachshunds in England was Mrs. Allingham, who, at the beginning of the century, had a kennel of them at Marlow, Bucks. Her foundation stock came from Austria and the strain was maintained up to the outbreak of the First World War. Stock bred in this kennel was distributed to many private homes, but none of these early dogs were shown, so that the variety remained unknown to the dog-loving public. I first became interested in Dachshunds as a boy in 1908 and for the next four years visited most of the principal London shows, but when I went to Germany as a student in 1912 I had never seen a Long Haired. My connection with the variety dates from a week or so after my arrival in the University city of Bonn, when I saw a pair of bitches being exercised in the street. These I promptly bought, and during the next two years I visited nearly all the larger shows held within reach of the Rhineland, thereby becoming acquainted with most of the leading exhibitors and their dogs. The outbreak of war forced me to dispose of all my canine possessions and to return hurriedly to England and six years' military service.

When I resumed my show-going in 1920 the Dachshund

was still my favourite breed, but I was also very interested in Scottish Terriers and became very friendly with Mrs. E. S. Quicke, whose Tattenham Kennels were in the forefront of that breed. I tried hard to win her over to Dachshunds, but with little success, till in 1922, on the eve of her departure for a holiday in Germany, I implored her, jokingly, to bring back a brace of Long Hairs. To my astonishment this request was taken seriously and she returned with a dog and bitch, Ratzmann vom Habichtshof and the German Champion Gretel III von Lechtal. Both were deep red and of similar type but not closely related.

I consider Ratzmann to have been the most handsome specimen of his breed I have seen. He excelled in length, head, top line and coat, had heavy bone, excellent feet and that high, proud head carriage which gives such dignity to a Dachshund. His weight was about 23 lb., and though he looked a biggish dog he was extremely active and free from the least suspicion of coarseness. He was released from quarantine in December 1922 and was entered at the Cruft's show to be held the following February. There were, of course, no separate classes for the different Dachshund varieties in those days, for Smooths were the only type of Teckel that had been shown till that memorable occasion. Ratzmann was entered only in the Open Dog Class, and the judge, the late Major P. C. G. Hayward, created a sensation when he awarded the challenge certificate to the lone Long Hair, putting him over some of the best-known Smooths of that day. This win brought the breed a lot of publicity but it also caused a good deal of ill-feeling among the exhibitors of Smooths, who strongly objected to having their dogs beaten by what, they insisted, was not a Dachshund at all! To avoid a repetition of such unpleasantness, Ratzmann was thereafter shown only in variety competition until the variety was sufficiently strong to warrant the guaranteeing of separate classes.

Gretel III von Lechtal unfortunately died before she could be bred from in this country, and to replace her Mrs. Quicke imported Edeltrud von der Waldflur, a small black and tan daughter of Ratzmann and Gretel. Edeltrud was a bitch of exquisite quality, weighing about 15 lb., and had had a brilliant show career in Germany. A week or two before leaving her native land she was awarded the trophy for Best Dachshund Any Variety at the Frankfurt show. Stock bred from her by Ratzmann found a ready sale and a number of people were soon attracted to the breed. Bitches so bred had to be either put back to their sire or mated to their full brothers, and when the next generation arrived the process had to be repeated. As a result of this intensive inbreeding many superlative specimens were bred, but after a time trouble came with the appearance of badly overshot mouths. A few bitches were mated to a dog owned by Colonel E. J. Harrison, Sepel of Combe, but the results were not wholly satisfactory and the need for new blood became acute.

In 1927 some notes I had written on Long Hairs for the canine press brought me a letter from Lt.-Col. W. G. Bedford, saying that he was interested in the breed and suggesting we should meet. When I visited him I found he had a dog which he had bought from the Battersea Dogs' Home, of all places, and liked him so much that he was contemplating starting a kennel. We were able to identify this dog as a son of Ratzmann and Edeltrud, whose owner had gone to live in South Africa; though how he came to the Dogs' Home remained a mystery. This waif was registered as Hengist of Armadale. He was very like his sire in size, colour and general appearance, but, owing to bad rearing, was very rickety. Lt.-Col. Bedford asked me if I could suggest how he might obtain a bitch, but when the difficulties of the position had been explained he agreed that the wise course was to import one unrelated to the stock then in the country. In 1928 he imported Elfe von Fels, in whelp to the German Champion Stropp von der Windberg. Her litter was born in quarantine and included a dog and bitch Rufus and Rose of Armadale, both of which made history.

By 1929 the time seemed ripe to start a Club to foster breed interests. A meeting was held at St. Ermins, Westminster, at which the Long Haired Dachshund Club was formed with Colonel E. J. Harrison, T.D., as President, Lt.-Col. W. G. Bedford as Chairman of Committee and myself as Hon. Secretary. I was asked by the Committee to draw up a Standard of Points and submitted a document which was an almost literal translation of the German version. This was duly adopted and is still the only official Standard of the breed. In 1930 the Kennel Club acceded to our request for a separate breed register and challenge certificates were allocated the following year. Rose of Armadale was the first British champion and her litter brother Rufus the first dog to win the title.

The introduction of a complete outcross into breeding operations is always a gamble, but by great good fortune the blood lines carried by Elfe von Fels and her progeny by Stropp von der Windberg proved wonderfully well suited to infuse into the home-bred stock. Among the most outstanding examples of this blood combination were Champion Captain of Armadale, Champion Chloe of Armadale, Champion Michael von Walder, Champion Daffodil of Dilworth, Champion Golden Patch and Champion Golden Lady of Primrose Patch. Besides these there were a number of lesser lights which went to kennel owners who, though not regular exhibitors, were active breeders, and through them the Habichtshof–von Fels bred stock became widely distributed. The great majority of present-day winners will be found to carry this blood if their pedigrees are traced far enough back.

In 1930 Colonel Harrison told me he wished to import a dark, clear red dog to serve as a further source of new blood. The finding of such a dog proved much more difficult than was anticipated, for high-class Long Hairs of that colour were few and far between even in Germany. Eventually Jesko von der Humboldshohe was located and went to join the Combe Kennels at Dulverton. Jesko was a handsome, medium-sized dog, excellent in bone, ribbing, feet, top line and coat. He was deep, clear setter red and soon became a champion. His colour and attractive temperament made him popular at stud and he sired a number of good winners. The best of his offspring was the dog Jager of Dilworth, bred by Mrs. Midwood and sold as a puppy to Mrs. B. Franklyn, in whose ownership he quickly became a champion and one of the most successful show dogs of his day, and the Canadian Champion Bartonbury Vogue, bred by Mrs. V. Rycroft.

A year after the arrival of Jesko, Lt.-Col. Bedford brought over the black and tan Otter von Fels, a dog that was destined to have an immense influence for good. Otter made his show debut under me at the Windsor show in 1932, where I gave him the certificate and made him Best of Breed, and he won his title at his next few shows. He was a most striking-looking dog, showing all the qualities needed in a really good Long Hair. In head, neck, length, lowness to ground, bone, feet and quarters he was faultless and he was strong, compact and masculine without heaviness or coarseness. His progeny included Champion Karl von Walder, Champion Micheline von Walder, Champion Roderick of Primrose Patch, Nicholas of Armadale and Stephanie of Stutton. Otter was later sold to Mrs. J. M. Stutchbury, who imported a very typical black and tan bitch,

Ursel von der Goldenen Perl, as a mate for him. It is unfortunate that the progeny of this outstanding pair seem to have been lost sight of, for they could have been of great value to the breed. Otter was certainly one of the best Long Hair Dachshunds seen in this country. After leaving the Armadale Kennels he was shown very little and was not much used at stud, but the years that have elapsed since his death have shown him to be one of the main pillars of the breed. His blood is carried by most contemporary celebrities and can be inbred to without fear of undesirable results to almost any degree.

A litter bred from the mating of Champion Rose and Champion Rufus of Armadale included a small brindle bitch, Drusilla of Armadale, which I acquired from her breeder with the object of mating her to Champion Otter von Fels. Before that project could be carried out I was called away from home for a period, and rather than let the opportunity be wasted I transferred Drusilla to Mrs. L. S. Bellamy, then beginning to build up what was to become the famous Von Walder Kennels. The mating produced Champion Karl and Champion Micheline von Walder. Karl was dark brindle, a colour he inherited from his dam. Besides being a great show winner he proved invaluable at stud and his influence on the breed is still strongly perceptible. He sired Champion Magdalena von Walder, one of the greatest bitches of all time, and the dog Champion Nicholas of Brincliffe, of which there will be more to be said later, as well as a host of other very high-class specimens whose names are to be found in the pedigrees of many post-war winners.

Champion Magdalena von Walder was mated to Champion Michael von Walder, a son of Champion Rufus and Champion Chloe of Armadale, and bred Champion Jack Horner von Walder and Champion Miss Muffit von Walder in one litter; a brace which was unbeatable in the years immediately before the outbreak of the last war. Champion Jack Horner von Walder won 13 challenge certificates. His name will be familiar to most readers, as he is the sire of five post-war champions in Christopher of Brincliffe, Royce of Northanger, Rosalinda of Hilltrees, Rhona of Northanger and Roger of Hilltrees. Champion Magdalena von Walder's dam, Knowlton Mädel, was born in quarantine, a daughter of the small black and tan imported bitch Zola von Jungfrauental, by Blucher von Drachenburg. She and her litter brother, the black and tan Knowlton Jochen, were bred by Mrs. Herdman, but later passed into my possession. Each played an important part in moulding type in our modern Long Hairs. Later matings of Mädel to Karl produced several excellent specimens, including two brindle bitches bred by me which were purchased by Dr. Lea and registered as Jerica and Jaglish of Warstock. On the dispersal of the Warstock Kennels these, with others, went to Mr. and Mrs. A. J. Buck to strengthen their Buckmead strain. Jaglish later became the property of Mrs. Howard Joyce and, mated to Champion Jack Horner von Walder, bred the two champions Royce and Rhona of Northanger. Another of Jaglish's sons, Jirfield of Warstock (by Champion Otter von Fels), sired Champion Ballerina of Buckmead, the grand-dam of Champion Jeremy of Buckmead.

Mrs. Smith Rewse was one of the earliest devotees of the Long Haired Dachshund. Her Primrose Patch Kennels, the largest and one of the most successful in the breed, were founded on a very typical brindle bitch Bluebell of Armadale, a daughter of Hengist of Armadale and Elfe von Fels. The mating of Bluebell to Champion Rufus of Armadale produced Champion Golden Patch, the first of the many title-holders to come from these world-famous kennels. About 1935 Mrs. Smith Rewse imported a very good red bitch, Alma von der Glonn, in whelp to the German Champion Ebbo Krehwinkle. Her litter included the dog Krehwinkle of Primrose Patch, sire of the dog Black Knight of Primrose Patch and several others shown under that suffix, and the bitch Walder of Primrose Patch, a big winner and very unlucky not to gain her title. Another of Mrs. Smith Rewse's importations was the bitch Ilse von Jungfrauental, a daughter of German Champion Ebbo Krehwinkle.

The last of the pre-war importations that call for mention here was the small red dog Eberhard von Adlerstein, brought over by the Hon. Mrs. Still. The best of his offspring was Dandelion von Walder, bred by me from Knowlton Mädel, whose daughter Katherine von Walder is the dam of Mr. John Pollard's Tercel-Erlenmark, the sire of three champions.

From the brief sketch given above it will be seen that the blood lines represented in our modern Long Hairs have been contributed mainly by Ratzmann vom Habichtshof, Jesko von der Humboldshohe, Otter von Fels, Knowlton Jochen and Eberhard von Adlerstein, on the male side, and by Elfe von Fels, Zola von Jungfrauental (through Knowlton Mädel) and Alma von der Glonn on the female side. Fortunately all these lines were preserved through the war years, so that the coming of peace found the breed in a strong position.

Of recent years the two most prominent dogs have been Champion Nicholas of Brincliffe, and Champion Christopher of Brincliffe. They are owned, and were bred, by Miss K. Cheaney, whose kennel was founded on the bitch Gretchen von Blenheimberry, by Knowlton Jochen out of Sadie von Walder, a daughter of Champion Karl von Walder and Champion Chloe of Armadale. Gretchen mated to Champion Michael von Walder bred Margot of Brincliffe, which, when put back to her great-grandsire Karl, produced Champion Nicholas of Brincliffe. Gretchen's later litter, to Champion Jack Horner von Walder, included Champion Christopher of Brincliffe. Thus, these two outstanding dogs represent different variations of the same blood combination based on Ratzmann, Elfe von Fels, Otter and Jochen. Champion Nicholas of Brincliffe, born in 1943, is the winner of eight challenge certificates and is the sire of Champion Julietta of Hilltrees, Kyral Kummel, Rosteague Roxana, Brock of Longcroft, Rosteague Rima of Northanger and Robsvarl Ripple, all prominent winners. Champion Christopher of Brincliffe, born in 1944, won 13 challenge certificates. His numerous winning offspring include Champion Anna of Hilltrees, Champion Northanger Rosteague Rogue, Champion Rosemarie of Ferrens, Midas of Brockhurst, Franz of Hilltrees, Rosteague Rinty of Windgather and Rosteague Rollo. Another famous dog bred by Miss Cheaney was Simon of Brincliffe, born in 1938, a brother of Margot. He won two certificates before the suspension of Championship shows and would certainly have gained his title but for the war. It was a great disappointment that he proved to be impotent, for he was, in my opinion, one of the three best dogs of his breed yet seen. The other two are Ratzmann vom Habichtshof and Champion Otter von Fels. His photo indicates his superb quality, great substance and perfect balance.

The Hilltrees Kennels, belonging to Lt.-Col. A. Hodge, D.S.O., M.C., have been among the most consistently successful in the post-war period. They were founded in 1944 with the bitch Rachel of Fenlands, a grand-daughter of Champion Jack Horner von Walder and Captain Courageous of Stutton (by Champion Captain of Armadale). Mated back to Jack Horner she bred Champion Rosalinda of Hilltrees, winner of 14 challenge certificates, and the dam of Champion Julietta of Hilltrees. Rachel's second mating to Jack Horner produced

Champion Roger of Hilltrees, winner to date of seven certificates, and her litter by Champion Christopher of Brincliffe included Champion Anna of Hilltrees, winner of five certificates.

Other prominent exhibitors are Mrs. Van Gutten of the Rosteague prefix; Mrs. Howard Joyce, who has bred three champions in Royce and Rhona of Northanger and Northanger Rosteague Rogue; Mr. and Mrs. Buck, whose Buckmead strain is founded firmly on Otter blood and whose Champion Ballerina and Champion Jeremy of Buckmead have already been mentioned; Mr. John Pollard, whose most successful exhibits have been Mona Lisa von Walder and the three champions Mira Erlenmark of Seton, Mauna-Loa Erlenmark and Kay Erlenmark; Mrs. Ireland Blackburne, whose Robsvarl Rufus is the sire of Champion Robsvarl Sepia and Champion Robsvarl Reseda; Mrs. Gwyer, owner of Champion Royce of Northanger and breeder of Champion Robsvarl Jeneth of Marlenwood; Mrs. H. E. Roberts, who has bred five champions; Mrs. Newton, owner of Brock of Longcroft and Champion Anna of Hilltrees; Mrs. Kidner, who has Champion Julietta of Hilltrees and Jasper of Hilltrees, Champion Tony of Kitenora and Champion Jean of Kitenor; Mr. J. C. Connell, who has a home-bred champion in Highlight von Holzner, a son of Champion Royce of Northanger; Mrs. E. R. Moore, owner of Champion Shadmor Silken Socks; Mrs. E. Meyer with Champion Reanda Satin Lassy; Mrs. W. H. Hollinshead, who has scored well with her Champion Grisbeech Director of Seton; Mr. Jackson with Champion Bella of Selah and Champion Karla of Hilltrees; Mrs. E. Hales with Champion Clayona Christine; Mrs. Griffiths with Champion Rosemarie of Ferrens; Mrs. Mills of the Whipsderry Kennels; Lady Kathleen Hare of the Reedscottage prefix and Miss K. M. Raine whose team of home-bred winners includes Champion Imber Coffee Bean, Champion Imber Café-Noir, and Champion Imber Café-au-Lait.

Other devotees of the Long-hairs whose exhibits have distinguished themselves include Miss D. J. Bennett, Mrs. M. Griffiths, Mrs. G. M. Wildish, Miss K. M. MacPherson, Dr. B. Raven, Mr. and Mrs. H. Jordan and Miss M. R. Mothersill.

For later information see Addendum 2.

CHAPTER VI

TYPE IN THE LONG HAIRED DACHSHUND

THE Standard of the Long Haired Dachshund issued by the Kennel Club reads:

Characteristics. The Long Haired Dachshund is an old fixed sub-variety of the "Teckel," and its history extends back to the beginning of Teckel breeding. The breed is full of character, quick in attack and defence, faithful when properly brought up and very obedient. All the senses are well developed. It has the reputation of being extraordinarily intelligent and easy to train. Its build and temperament fit it to hunt quarry both above and below ground; its eagerness, keen sight and hearing and its sonorous bark make it especially suitable for tracking. In these respects it compares very favourably with any other variety. The thick, soft hair protects it against thorns, enables it to endure both cold and heat and is rain-proof. It is especially suited to water work. In following a trail its highly developed sense of smell stands it in good stead. It is easily trained to retrieve. The long-haired Dachshund can therefore be used in many different ways by the sportsman.

General Appearance. Form, colour, size and character similar in all respects to those of the Smooth Dachshund, except for the long, soft hair. The form is compact, short-legged and long, but sinewy and well muscled, with bold and defiant head carriage, and intelligent expression. In spite of the shortness of the legs the body should be neither too plump nor so slender as to have a weasel-like appearance. Height at shoulder should be half the length of the body measured from the breast bone to the set-on of the tail, and the girth of the chest double the height at the shoulder. The length from the tip of the nose to the eyes should be equal to the length from the eyes to the base of the skull. The tail should not touch the ground when at rest, neither should the ears (i.e., the leather) extend beyond the nose when pulled to the front.

Head and Skull. Long and conical when seen from above, and in profile, sharp and finely modelled. Skull neither too broad nor too narrow, only slightly arched, without prominent stop. Foreface long and narrow, finely modelled. Lips should be tightly drawn, well covering the lower jaw, neither too heavy nor too sharply cut away, the corners of the mouth slightly marked.

Eyes. Medium in size, oval, set obliquely, clear, expressive and dark in colour.

Ears. Broad and placed, relatively well back, high and well set on lying close to the cheeks, broad and long, nicely feathered and very mobile.

Mouth. Wide, extending back to behind the eyes, furnished with strong teeth which should fit into one another exactly, the inner side of the upper incisors closing on the outer side of the under ones.

Neck. Sufficiently long, muscular, showing no dewlap, slightly arched at the nape, running gracefully into the shoulders, carried well up and forward.

Forequarters. Muscular, with deep chest. Shoulders long and broad, set obliquely, lying firmly on well developed ribs. Muscles hard and plastic. Breast bone prominent, extending so far forward as to show depressions on both sides. Upper arm the same length as the shoulder blade, jointed at right angles to the shoulder, well boned and muscled, set on close to the ribs but moving freely as far as the shoulder blade. Lower arm comparatively short, inclined slightly inwards, solid and well muscled.

Body. Long and well muscled, the back showing oblique shoulders and short and strong pelvic region. Ribs very oval, deep between the fore-legs and extending far back. Loin short, strong and broad. The line of the back only slightly depressed over the shoulders and slightly arched over the loin, with the outline of the belly moderately tucked up.

Hindquarters. Rump round, full, broad, with muscles well modelled and plastic. Pelvis bone not too short, broad, strongly developed and set obliquely. Thigh bone strong, of good length and jointed to the pelvis at right angles. Second thigh short, set at right-angles to the upper thigh, well muscled. Hocks set wide apart, strongly bent and, seen from behind, the legs should be straight.

Feet. Broad and large, straight or turned slightly outwards; the hind feet smaller and narrower than the fore. Toes close together and with a distinct arch to each toe. Nails strong. The dog must stand equally on all parts of the foot.

Tail. Set on fairly high, not too long, tapering and without too marked a curve. Not carried too high. Fully feathered.

Coat. Soft and straight or slightly waved, of shining colour. Longer under the neck, the underparts of the body and, particularly, on the ears, behind the legs, where it should develop into abundant feathering, and reach the greatest length on the tail, where it should form a flag. The feathering should extend to the outsides of the ears, where short hair is not desired. Too heavy a coat gives an appearance of undue plumpness and hides the outline. The coat should resemble that of an Irish Setter, giving the dog an appearance of elegance. Too much hair on the feet is ugly and useless.

Colour. Black and tan, dark brown with lighter shadings, dark red, light red, dappled, tiger-marked or brindle. In black and tan, red and dappled dogs the nose and nails should be black, in chocolate they are often brown.

Weight and Size. As a rule Long Haired Dachshunds are classified as follows: Middle weight up to 7·7 kg. (17 lbs. for bitches and 8·2 kg. (18 lbs.) for dogs. Heavy weight over 7·7 kg. for bitches and over 8·2 kg. for dogs. The Middle weights are best suited for badger and fox drawing and the Heavy-weights for tracking, hunting larger animals and for water work. The last named are also very useful for retrieving rabbits and water fowl.

Note. Male animals should have two apparently normal testicles fully descended into the scrotum.

This Standard is essentially that for Smooths except for the length and texture of the coat. This must be long and silky. On the body the coat must be flat, lying close without any tendency to rise or curl. It must be thick enough to form a protection against wet and cold but should not obscure the outline of the trunk. On the ears, side of the neck, front of the neck, front of the chest, underparts, on the back of the forelegs and behind the thighs, it should form long, silky—not fluffy—feathering and be sufficiently abundant on the tail to hang as a flag; longest at the base and tapering to the tip. The Standard states that a slight wave is permissible, but the wave must be flat and the less there is the better. Any tendency of the coat to rise, either in a wave or a curl, is a serious fault. A fluffy or curly coat is an abomination.

Besides being quite flat and silky, the coat should have a natural gloss. Such a coat is much more efficient as a protection against wet than is an open, fluffy coat, though the latter may look thicker and warmer. A good-coated Long Hair needs very little grooming. The hair does not mat, and rain and mud are thrown off instead of penetrating through the hairs. A thick open coat, that is one in which the hair rises in waves or curls, soaks up moisture like blotting-paper and holds mud and dirt tenaciously, so that to keep it clean constant brushing and combing are necessary. One sometimes sees exhibits in which the coat, though flat, looks dull and dusty and, if handled, feels dry and harsh. This lack of gloss is a fault, for the hair lacks the oily covering needed to render it waterproof. A coat of this kind may be improved by diligent and regular grooming and by the use of hair tonics and other dressings, but it is inherently faulty.

Few contemporary Long Hairs grow the long, straight, silky feathering on the ears that adds so greatly to the expression. The Standard says "the feathering should extend to the outside of the ears, where short hair is not desired". That means the long fringes should extend to the ear tips, not be confined to the upper part of the ear flaps. Too often these fringes grow only from the ear bases; the hair on the flaps being comparatively short, so that the lower parts of the ears are almost smooth. This is a matter that should receive attention, for well-set, profusely feathered ears are one of the variety's most attractive characteristics. The hair on the front of the forelegs, below the hocks and on the feet, should be short. Long hair on the feet is not only ugly and useless, as pointed out in the Standard, it is also a handicap to an active hunting dog. It collects mud, which may ball beneath the pads, and picks up thorns and burrs, which may pierce the tender flesh between the toes. In a house dog it is a nuisance, in that it causes clots of mud to be brought into the home whenever the weather is inclement.

A good-coated Long Hair needs no preparation for show beyond grooming with a dandie brush and hound glove. Dogs with too thick and open coats may need to have it thinned, particularly over the back and on the sides of the neck. Surplus hair on the feet should be removed. Unless this is done the feet will look soft and may cause a superficial judge to put a dog down for a fault that it does not, in fact, possess.

From time to time arguments occur as to what extent an exhibit that is out of coat, or short of coat, should be penalized in ring competition. Non-specialist judges, the so-called all-rounders, are apt to pass over such exhibits entirely; holding the view that, since a long coat is the most outstanding characteristic of the variety, no award should be made to individuals deficient in that respect. There is, however, a good deal more to it than that. Length of hair is not the only coat requirement. Besides being long the coat should also be straight, silky and glossy. The table setting out the value to be apportioned to the various points in a Long Haired Dachshund allots ten for coat. This covers length, lie and texture and, if we consider each of these qualities to be of equal importance, an exhibit that is short of coat, but shows the correct texture and lie of hair, should be preferred to one with a longer, but coarser and more open, coat.

The ideal coat is usually slow in growing. Puppies that are full-coated at ten or twelve months old rarely carry perfect coats as adults. It is often the youngster that looks almost smooth until its puppyhood is left behind that eventually grows the best coat. Long Hairs vary much in the degree to which they lose their coats at moulting time. Some dogs shed all their feathering and much of the body hair very quickly, in others moulting is so gradual as to be almost imperceptible. The shedding of the old coat and the growth of the new may be hastened by frequent and regular grooming. From the time the hair begins to come out till moulting is completed the dog should be gone over twice daily with a fine comb and a stiff bristle brush.

Curly coats are not often seen in our rings today, but the perfect coat is rare enough to give a judge a shock of pleasure when he finds it. Many exhibits have coats that are somewhat coarse in texture, are not quite as flat as they should be and lack that bright gloss that is found when the hair is soft and silky. The coat asked for in the Standard adds enormously to the appearance of elegance that we want in a Long Haired Dachshund and which sets it apart from the other members of the Teckel family. It is, perhaps, necessary to point out that length of feathering can be overdone. Occasionally we see an exhibit with frillings blowing about in the wind, like the hirsute drapery of a Collie. That is wrong. The Long Haired Dachshund should look a worker. Too profuse feathering detracts from its workman-like appearance and would certainly impair its utility in the field.

Under General Appearance the Standard states that the Long Haired should be similar in all respects to the Smooth Dachshund, and as a generalization that statement is unassailable. It would, however, be a mistake to assume that to

Ch. Ashdown Skipper
(*Smooth*)

Ch. Ingo and Ch. Rufus von Weyher
(*Smooth*)

C. Urbatz von der Howitt
(*Smooth*)

(*E. G. Waterman*)

Ch. Silvae Lustre
(*Smooth*)

(*E. G. Waterman*)

Ch. Silvae Sailor's Quest
(*Smooth*)

(*C. M. Cooke*)

Ch. Rhinefields Diplomat
(*Smooth*)

Tiger Reinecke (imported)
(Smooth – born 1888)

(Windsor-Spice Ltd.)

Teckelwood Silver Shadow
(Silver Dapple – Smooth)

(Cameracraft, Truro)

Littlenodes Quicksilver
(Silver Dapple – Miniature Long)

(*Malcolm Nicholson*)

Ch. Roderick of Primrose Patch
(*Long*)

Ch. Christopher of Brincliffe
(*Long*)

Ch. Northanger Rosteague Rogue
(*Long*)

convert a first-class Smooth into an equally good Long Hair it is only necessary to give it a long coat. The short, close coat of the Smooth hides nothing of the outline of the body, whereas the fuller covering of the Long Hair must detract, in some measure, from the apparent length of the head, neck and trunk. To counter that we need a little extra length in those parts, to give the impression of length, lowness to ground and symmetry that we require in a Dachshund of any variety. A slightly thick or short head, or a neck just lacking in reach, may be passed in a Smooth without adverse criticism, but in a Long Hair these imperfections will show up as obvious faults. The long hair on the ear bases will accentuate any thickness of skull or shortness of head, and the frill on the sides of the neck will make that part look considerably shorter than it would were the coat short and smooth. The same is true of body length. The ribs must be full and rounded and the chest broad, but if there is the slightest tendency towards shortness in body, or undue height at the withers, the dog will look cloddy. In this variety, therefore, length is of special importance, as is a refined, well-proportioned head with fine, tapering muzzle. Depth of chest, on the other hand, must not be overdone. The ideal, as in the Smooth, is for the lowest point of the keel to be level with the wrists, but while a slight exaggeration here may be pardoned in a Smooth, it is most undesirable in a Long Hair, for the long hair beneath the chest will be brought so close to the ground that it will sweep up mud and dirt like a broom. This formation is very rare in modern exhibits. The opposite condition, in which the keel is too shallow, is much more common. Full feathering may hide that fault from an uncritical observer but a competent judge will quickly discover it and inflict a severe penalty.

Good heavy bone is another essential. Some exhibitors of Smooths have been known to express the opinion that in a Long Hair lack of bone may be offset by coat. That is a fallacy. A lightly boned dog with full feathering looks effeminate and weedy; its failing is much more noticeable than it would be in a Smooth. This is generally recognized by breeders and there can be no doubt that the majority of Long Hairs are better in bone than are any of the other Dachshund varieties. The large, broad foot has also been more generally retained.

The remarks relating to the implications of the Smooth Standard contained in Chapter IV are equally applicable to Long Hairs, so that it is unnecessary further to analyse the wording of the official description here. Anatomically all the Dachshund varieties are, of course, identical. In all, deviations from the ideal, as described in the separate Standards, arise from the same shortcomings in skeletal structure or from bad rearing.

One of the most prevalent faults in Long Hairs is insufficient fullness over the ribs. This makes a dog flat-sided and usually goes with narrowness, both in front and behind. No manipulation of the coat can hide these faults, neither can it disguise a flat chest from the judicial eye or hand. Loose elbows also reveal themselves when pressure is applied over the withers, though so long as an exhibit stands perfectly still this aspect of unsoundness may be concealed by carefully arranged frills. Feet are fundamentally good in the variety. By this I do not mean that faulty feet are hard to find, but most of the exhibits that are penalized for bad feet fail through lack of hard road work, or other errors of treatment, rather than from structural defects. Long Hairs are generally better in hind action than are Smooths. Many are too narrow behind, others are too high in hocks or fail in hind angulation, so that the stride is too short and cramped (*see* page 48), but hind movement is not nearly so universally unsatisfactory as in the other variety. Cow-hocks, once a common failing, are now rarely seen and a Long Hair that is bandy behind is virtually unknown.

Heads, on the whole, are good in shape and fairly well proportioned. There are, of course, exceptions. Some exhibits, mostly dogs, have adequate length of head but are rather too broad in skull. Eye colour is pretty good but large, round eyes are too common. This fault is, I think, on the increase and should receive attention from breeders. The perfect eye, rather small, very dark and set obliquely, gives a most striking finish to a good head. It is well shown in the study of Champion Christopher of Brincliffe (see illustrations). Body length and back lines are satisfactory but we want more length in neck. A reachy, nicely arched neck is necessary if the head is to be carried high to impart the air of aristocratic elegance that is, or should be, a breed characteristic, and which we seem to be in danger of losing. A Long Haired Dachshund which carries its head low looks second rate however good it may be in other respects, and is likely to make a less favourable impression on a judge than one having more faults but a more alert and dignified bearing. Our Long Hairs are free from the wrinkled forelegs that mar many otherwise good Smooths, but some dogs show a slight dewlap under the throat. As a rule this unsightly blemish is confined to the bigger type of male and usually goes with a rather coarse head.

Until 1951 the Long Haired Dachshund Standard made no mention of a maximum weight. In pre-war days the omission caused no comment but of late years there has been a definite increase in the average size of the exhibits seen in our rings, and high awards have gone to one or two dogs which were heavier and larger than a Dachshund should be. This led me to raise the question of imposing a top-weight limit at the Annual General Meeting of the Long Haired Dachshund Club in 1951. Agreement was unanimous that a clause should be added to the Standard making the maximum weight 25 lb., thus bringing it in line with the Standard for Smooths. None of the champion dogs of pre-war days weighed much more than 23 lb. and the bitches were usually a pound or two lighter. Some good winners of both sexes came within the category of middle-weights, weighing less than 18 lb. Today really good Long Hairs of that size are rare, but the desirability of breeding the smaller type is becoming generally recognized and it is hoped that the middle-weight champions will be seen again before long. This should not be taken as suggesting that there is anything wrong with a heavyweight, but it would be a great pity if all Long Hairs were to become standardized at the top limit of weight. Any exhibit weighing from 11 to 25 lb. should be regarded as correct and within those limits no account should be taken of weight in judging.

Taking the breed as a whole, the modern Long Hair compares very favourably with its forerunner of pre-war days. In some respects it is better, as in coat, body length and feet. It loses something in head, expression, dignity of carriage and hind angulation. There is, too, a lack of alertness and verve in many contemporary exhibits. They look bored and dull in the ring, move lifelessly and rarely use their ears. This is due mainly to lack of training in ringcraft, rather than to bad temperaments. Exhibitors would be well advised to give more attention to getting their dogs used to mixing with, and being handled by, strangers in unfamiliar surroundings before subjecting them to the ordeal of the show ring.

CHAPTER VII

THE WIRE HAIRED DACHSHUND IN BRITAIN

THE origin of the Wire Haired Dachshund as we now know it, is a good deal more recent, and therefore less obscure, than is that of the Smooth and Long Haired varieties. Dachshund-like dogs with wiry coats certainly existed way back through the centuries, but as a separate, well-defined breed, the rough-coated Teckel seems to have had its beginning in the second half of the eighteenth century. The old German authority Jester writing in 1797 mentions a rough-haired type of Dachshund and fourteen years later Hartig, in describing the Badger Dog, wrote: "The coat is generally smooth and short but there is also a wire-haired Dachsel not so short in leg but with curved legs like the smooth kind." In 1812 we find Walther referring to the Wire Haired Dachshund as being especially good for work and claiming that its legs are less bent than in the smooth. Through the greater part of the nineteenth century these dogs were bred solely as workers. No pedigrees were kept and there are no pictures to indicate what these first Wires looked like.

In 1888 a Wire Haired Dachshund was exhibited at the Berlin show by a Captain von Wardenburg. This dog, named Mordax, appears to have been the first of its kind to be entered at a show and was awarded a prize. A drawing made of Mordax during his life shows him as a dog of excellent general type, low to ground, with good body length, plenty of bone, deep chest and strong quarters. His back line would not please us today and I believe his coat was soft. No information is available as to how Mordax was bred, but there seems little doubt that most of the Wires of the 1800s arose from crossing the Smooth Dachshund with the German rough-haired Pincher. This cross gave a very harsh, close coat, straight legs and less body length and depth in chest than was shown by the pure-bred Smooth. To obtain greater length and depth recourse was had to the Dandie Dinmont, a breed which, according to Major Emil Ilgner, was taken to Germany from England by the Mecklenburg horse traders. The infusion of Dandie blood, though it improved length and depth of keel, introduced soft coats with a tendency for the long, fine hair on the skull to form a top-knot. This legacy from the Dandie was shown by several of the first Wires bred in this country. The pepper and salt colouration of the modern Wire comes from its Pincher ancestors and is not seen in any other Dachshund variety.

The first Wire to be brought to England was the dog Woolsack, bred by Baron von Gemming in 1888 and imported by Mr. E. S. Woodiwiss, a prominent breeder of Smooths at that time. In his portrait this black and tan looks a strongly built fellow with a good coat, typical head, sound forequarters and feet. He appears a bit leggy and his back line, hindquarters and tail might belong to a Dandie. I do not know if Woolsack was ever shown but he seems to have aroused some interest, for he was used at stud to several Smooth bitches and some of his progeny were registered. A red son of his, Waxwing, out of a well-bred Smooth named Mickleover Rhoda, was shown by Mr. Woodiwiss and qualified for entry in the Kennel Club Stud Book; but interest in the variety was short-lived and no effort was made to form a kennel of Wires or to provide separate classes for them at shows.

The Wire Haired Dachshund first came to England in a big way in 1927 when Mr. H. A. Fisher, who had previously been prominent as an importer of Alsatians, felt the time had come to try to exploit a smaller breed as yet unknown in Britain that was likely to make an appeal to British dog-lovers. At that time the boom in Alsatians was over, prices were slumping, sales were difficult and several breeders were very willing to join Mr. Fisher in his project. On 1st July a meeting was held at the Ulster Chambers, Regent Street, London, at which the fifteen people present agreed to form a Wire Haired Dachshund Club with Major C. E. W. Beddoes as Hon. Secretary and Air Vice-Marshal Sir Charles Lambe, K.C.B., as President. That year saw the arrival of the first batch of importations. All the founder members of the Club were experienced exhibitors in other breeds and fully appreciated the need for importing the best available stock. Their policy was quickly rewarded, for when these first Wires made their show debut they were very well received, gained much favourable publicity and brought a number of new members to the Club. As interest increased further importations were made, more classes were put on at the larger shows and the variety was safely launched.

Mr. Fisher's first imports included Fritzle von Paulinenberg,

Hannes von der Abtscheck, Moritzel von der Abtscheck, Dieter von der Abtscheck, Zitta and Zilla von der Silberberg, Hexe von Maien and Waldmaus von Maien. Of these Fritzle von Paulinenberg went to Mr. C. E. Ratee and became the first champion in the breed, Hannes von der Abtscheck is remembered as the sire of Champion Kingswalden Luke, one of the best-coated dogs ever shown, and Moritzel was bought by Mrs. M. Howard to act as a founder of the now famous Seale Kennels, but unfortunately died before siring a puppy. Dieter von der Abtscheck is of special interest to present-day breeders. He was a handsome dog with a perfect coat and became popular at stud. Mated to Daisy von Fichtenhain of Nunneshall, a lovely bitch imported by Lady Schuster, he sired Barnabas of Nunneshall, whose son Dally of Nunneshall is the great-grandsire of the two champions Boris and Ferdinand of Seale.

The Wires brought over by Mr. Fisher were not the first to come to England in the present century. Some time previously Lady Berwick had imported several from Czechoslovakia and had been breeding consistently for several years when the Wire Haired Dachshund Club was founded. Some of her dogs were shown at the first show at which classes for Wires were provided, in the winter of 1927. Among her most successful exhibits were Maenne von Maien, winner of the Open Class at Crufts in 1928, Carmen von Stradina and the dog Erdmann von Stradina (the last two imported from the Countess Kinsky of Kostolec), Siegmund, Magdalena and Margaret of Attingham.

Daisy von Fichtenhain of Nunneshall, mentioned above, came over in whelp to Puck von Oberbruck, and her litter, born in quarantine, included two bitches Avis and Anna of Nunneshall, both of importance to students of pedigrees, as will be shown. One of Mr. Fisher's later importations was the bitch Brita of Tavistone, the first of her sex to become a champion. She left Germany in whelp to Wicht St. Georg and the resulting litter included Flott of Tavistone, one of the great stud forces of the breed. Mated to Anna of Nunneshall he sired Champion Achsel, bred by Mrs. M. V. Blandy in 1929 and bought as a puppy by Miss Theo Watts, in whose possession he became a champion and the most famous British Wire of all time. In all this great dog won 13 challenge certificates. After having made him Best of Breed at the Great Joint Dachshund Associations show Major Emil Ilgner, the great German authority, wrote: "The Open Dog class with sixteen entries presented something beautiful, rarely seen. I have hardly seen anything similar in our country. I put Miss T. Watts' splendid Champion Achsel on top. . . . His typical body and splendid coat fully justify his many wins." Achsel sired many outstanding winners, including Champion Trix of Tynewydd, American Champion Tess of Tynewydd, and Tim of Tynewydd (all in one litter out of Mookie of Dunkerque, a daughter of Flott of Tavistone), Champion Achja of Seale, Champion Achtoi of Seale, Champion Amelia, Champion Boelcke, Champion Greta of Tippylands, Einar and Justice of Erlegh.

Mr. C. E. Rattee bought the imported bitch Heidi von Feuerberg and mated her to Flott of Tavistone, producing Champion Diana, Champion Dora, Maya, Mira and Mooki, all of Tavistone; names which may be found in the extended pedigrees of many modern winners. Up to the time of his death in 1931 Mr. Rattee had one of the largest and strongest kennels in the breed. When the Tavistones were dispersed Fritzel von Paulinenberg went to Mrs. P. S. Allen, then the owner of the Fernwood Kennels. Flott of Tavistone, Champion Diana, Mira and Moya were acquired by Mrs. M. Howard and Lady Schuster in partnership, and did much to lay the foundations of the Seale successes. Another of Mr. Rattee's breeding, Brownie of Tavistone, proved a most valuable brood. For a time she joined the Seale Kennels on breeding terms and was the dam of such notabilities as Champion Achja, Champion Achso, Achnein, Champion Achtoi, Mookie and Brownie of Seale.

Mrs. M. V. Blandy, already mentioned as the breeder of the incomparable Champion Achsel, was one of the most prominent pre-war exhibitors. She had Anna of Nunneshall, one of the litter by Puck von Oberbruch ex Daisy von Fichtenhain, from which she bred both Champion Achsel and Champion Anetta, a red bitch of exquisite quality and the first British-bred bitch to win the title. Mrs. Blandy bred two other champions in Amelia and Astra, the former by Champion Achsel out of the imported Diestel von Konigshufer and as good a bitch as her sire was a dog, and owned among many other big winners the two imported dogs Champion Milan von Konigshufer and Junker Hans von Konigshufer.

Air Marshal Sir Charles Lambe, K.C.B., the owner of the world-famous Dunkerque prefix, was a leading figure in the breed from 1927 till his death twenty-five years later. He was not present at the historic meeting on 1st July of that year but in his absence was unanimously elected as the Club's first President. On receiving news of his election Sir Charles read through the rules that had been drawn up and found one which stipulated that all members were required to own at least one specimen of the breed. At that time Sir Charles did not possess a Wire. He therefore wrote declining the appointment and explained his reason for so doing. The difficulty was soon overcome; a bitch was presented to the President-elect, who thereupon agreed to serve. The bitch was the imported Mausae, which had been mated to her son. She produced only one puppy, a bitch registered as Wally of Dunkerque.

Wally won several awards but proved a disappointment as a brood. Later Mausae gave birth to a litter of nine of which five were reared, the survivors including Michael and Mookie of Dunkerque. The real foundation of the Dunkerqe strain was laid when Sir Charles imported Hugo von Paulinenberg, whose sire was a Smooth. Mated to Marguerite of Attingham, he sired Dinah of Denford, which, when bred to Michael of Dunkerque, became the dam of Champion Vim of Dunkerque, the first of the Dunkerque champions. A later mating of Michael and Dinah produced Champion Ivor of Dunkerque.

About 1934 Sir Charles felt the variety needed fresh blood and joined Miss Theo Watts, Mrs. Rowley (now Mrs. MacCaw) and Mr. Stanhope Joel in importing the small, very sound dog Sports Mentor II from Sweden. This dog proved of great value to the breed. He was the sire of the two champions Helen and Hero of Dunkerque, the former of which became the property of Miss Theo Watts and the latter went to the U.S.A. soon after winning his title. In 1938 Sir Charles, in partnership with Miss Theo Watts, brought over another dog Loki von der Zeben Berges. The outbreak of war cut short Loki's show career but he was used at stud and his name may be found in the pedigree of several living Wires. Among the many outstanding specimens bred in the Dunkerque Kennels, in addition to those already mentioned, were Champion Hexe of Dunkerque, Olga of Dunkerque, winner of two certificates and considered by her breeder the best bitch he ever had, and the post-war Champion Judy of Dunkerque. Judy is a daughter of Olga, who was by Echo of Dunkerque, a grand-daughter of old Dinah of Denford.

The late Miss Peggy Seton Buckley conferred lasting benefit on the Wire Haired Dachshund when in 1937 she imported the bitch Wizden Sports Primavera from Sweden. Primavera created a sensation when first exhibited, had a brilliant show career, and was the first of her breed to become an International Champion. She came to England in whelp to Sports Troll and her litter included an excellent black and tan dog Petrouchka of Seton, who, like his dam, excelled in front, shoulder placement and back line. In 1939 Miss Seton Buckley made a further raid on the Sports Kennels and brought over the dog Theatre Street of Seton, by Sports Ergo out of the Swedish Champion Sports Spielerin, a litter sister of Primavera.

When war broke out in 1939 the Wire Haired Dachshund was firmly established in British dogdom, with a strong Club to watch over its interests and a band of devoted admirers eager to help their favourite to reach new heights of popularity. The break of six years imposed by war conditions inflicted a set-back much graver than could have been foreseen. The resumption of shows found the breed in a most unfortunate condition. Many of the older breeders and exhibitors had disposed of all their stock and were unable, either through age or personal circumstances, to restart their kennels. The great majority of the pre-war winners were dead or too old to be bred from. Young stock was hard to find and newcomers who might have been attracted to the variety were put off by the difficulty of getting started. Miss Seton Buckley and Mrs. M. Howard alone had kennels of any size and were among the few who continued to breed, so that most of the exhibits seen in the rings came from one of those sources. The Wire Haired Dachshund Club was, however, active, and as a result of its efforts the Wires slowly began to show signs of revival. The last two years have witnessed a most gratifying increase in interest in the breed. Many new adherents have been won, breeding has gone ahead with fresh energy and the classes at all the larger shows at which the breed has been scheduled have been very well filled.

Of the kennels that have contributed most to the revival of the Wire Haired Dachshund in recent years those of Miss S. N. Evans of the Wylde prefix deserve special mention. Miss Evans started her strain by mating Trix of Dunkerque, a daughter of Sports Mentor II and Echo of Dunkerque, to the Smooth Wylde Rory, a son of Champion Firs Black Sheen, and bred the outstanding bitch Champion Wylde Enchanter and the dog Champion Wylde Encore. Enchanter was mated to Champion Midas of Seton, whose sire, I.K.C. Champion

Paganini of Seton, was by Petroucka of Seton and whose dam, Sports Silence of Seton, was imported. Her litter included Champion Wylde Caprice, Champion Wylde Cantata and Wylde Canoodle. Mercury of Seton, litter brother to Champion Midas, mated to Enchanter, sired Champion Wylde Surmise, a particularly lovely bitch now in the U.S.A. Champion Wylde Caprice, now owned by Miss Dodds and Mrs. Rice Evans, is the sire of Champion Retann Caprine and Champion Medmount Retann Clarino, bred by Mrs. Allnatt out of the Dunkerque–Seale bitch Demerara of Doms. Another of the Wylde Rory × Trix of Dunkerque litter was Wylde Enthusiast, the dam of Champion Wylde Boomps a Daisy. Miss Evans owned the largest kennel of Wires in England and stock of her breeding is widely distributed throughout the country. Much of the credit for the breed's present satisfactory position must go to her. But for her steady faith in its future through the dark days of the war the Wire might have virtually disappeared from our shows. Eight post-war champions have been bred in the Wylde Kennels.

Mrs. M. Howard, who has been one of the most successful breeders of Wires since 1927, has figured prominently in post-war awards lists with exhibits from her Seale Kennels. Her home-bred litter brothers Boris and Ferdinand of Seale, born in 1948, are both champions; the former is the only dog of the breed to be an International Champion. Others of her breeding are Champion Dusty Shoes of Seale and her brother Irish Champion Brown Boots of Seale, Twinkletoes of Seale, the dam of Grunwald Rita, the mother of the litter brother champions Gerhardt and Georg of Wytchend, Champion Osborne of Seale and Champion Honey of Seale.

Among the best known of the younger generation of post-war exhibitors are Miss Dodds and Mrs. Rice Evans of the Moat Kennels, whose show team includes Champion Wylde Caprice, his daughter Champion Retann Caprine and Mrs. M. Allnatt the breeder of Champion Retann Caprine, Champion Medmount Retann Clarino and Retann Corno, all Wires of the highest class. Mr. Douglas Hodges is the owner of Champion Medmount Retann Clarino and is building up a strong team in his Medmount Kennels. Mrs. Z. Donovan has an exquisite bitch in Champion Dusty Shoes of Seale and Mrs. H. Pead has an outstanding winner in her home-bred dog Champion Oklahoma of Shennis. Major and Mrs. Ellis Hughes are the breeders of Champion Gerhardt and Champion Georg of Wytchend and have done much to foster the interests of the breed in Wales. Mr. and Mrs. G. A. Lloyd bred Grunwald Rita, dam of the two champions last mentioned and of Champion Grunwald Graduate, now owned by Mr. G. F. Farrand, whose other big winners include Champion Coq d'or of Seton and Champion Coral of Seton. Mr. E. E. Gross has scored many triumphs with Champion Wylde Boomps a Daisy. Mrs. Hollinshead has the dog Wylde Canoodle, with two certificates, and the brood bitch Sports Silence of Seton, and Mrs. Mary Jones has collected many prize cards with exhibits bearing her Marfre prefix. Mrs. MacCaw, whose "of Clouds" Wires were well known before the war, has the imported dog Hobel aus dem Lohegau, which promises to prove a valuable addition to our stud force. He represents a complete outcross to all British-bred stock. Miss Theo Watts of the Tynewydds is still an occasional exhibitor, but she is now best known for the great services she renders the breed as Chairman of the Wire Haired Dachshund Club and Secretary of the Great Joint Dachshund Association, whose annual show, under her inspired management, is the premier event in the Dachshund year. Her Brudena, Tuppence and Tim of Tynewydd are direct descendants of her old favourite Champion Achsel. Mrs. V. Collins is the principal breed devotee in Scotland and owns in partnership with Mrs. Dolan the champion bitch Wylde-Will-She-Win, and Mr. F. McSally's Craigmere prefix is well known to all show-goers. Miss E. Hoxey of the Tumlow Kennels, Mrs. B. C. Taylor of the Bluefelts and Mrs. Glover, whose prefix is Cliftonhill, are all consistent winners; while Dr. T. Rigg, a leading exhibitor in the Variety has bred among a long line of winners such celebrities as Champion Simonswood Sabina, Champion Simonswood Stiletto, Champion Simonswood Sheba and Champion Simonswood Sulphur.

Mrs. B. Farrand and Group Capt. and Mrs. W. A. J. Satchell must also be named as among the variety's most consistent and successful exhibitors.

For later information see Addendum 3.

CHAPTER VIII

TYPE IN THE WIRE HAIRED DACHSHUND

THE Standard of Points for the Wire Haired Dachshund drawn up by the Kennel Club is as follows:

Characteristics. The Dachshund should be clever, lively, courageous to the point of rashness, sagacious and obedient. He is especially suited for going to ground because of his low build, very strong forequarters and forelegs, long, strong jaw and the immense power of his bite and hold. His loose skin enables him to manœuvre with ease for attack or defence. His deep, loud bay indicates his position to those working him. He is also well equipped for field work on account of his good nose and sound construction. He can force his way through cover so dense that it would stop even the smallest gundog. Because of his nose, voice, good sight and perseverance he makes a good tracking dog.

General Appearance. Low to ground, short legged, the body long but compact and well muscled. The head should be carried boldly and the expression be very intelligent. Despite his short legs, compared with the length of his body, he must not be awkward, cramped, crippled or lacking in substance.

Head and Skull. Looked at from above or from the side, the head should taper uniformly to the tip of the nose and be clean cut. The skull is only slightly arched, being neither too broad nor too narrow and slopes gradually, without marked stop, to a finely formed, slightly arched muzzle, the nasal bones and cartilage (Septum) being long and narrow. The ridges of the frontal bones are well developed giving prominence to the nerve bosses over the eyes. Jaw has extremely strong bones, is very long and opens very wide. It should not be too square nor yet snipy. The lips are lightly stretched, the corners just marked and the upper lip covers the lower jaw neatly.

Eyes. Oval, medium in size, set obliquely, lustrous and expressive. The colour should be dark except in the case of Chocolates, when they may be lighter, and of Dapples, when one or both wall eyes are allowed.

Ears. Broad and rounded, the front edge touching the cheek. They are relatively well back and high and are well set on. The length is such that when the ears are pulled forward they reach a point approximately half-way between the eyes and the tip of the nose.

Mouth. The powerful canine teeth fit closely. The correct bite is a scissor bite, any deviation being a fault.

Neck. Sufficiently long, muscular, clean cut, not showing any dewlap, slightly arched in the nape, extending in a graceful line into the shoulders and carried erect.

Forequarters. The shoulder blades are long, broad and placed firmly and obliquely upon a very robust rib cage. The upper arm is the same length as the shoulder blade, set at right angles to it and, like the shoulder blade, is very strong and covered with hard but supple muscles. The upper arm lies close to the ribs but is able to move freely. The forearm is comparatively short, inclined slightly inwards to form the crook, when seen in profile is moderately straight and must not bend forward or knuckle over, a state which indicates unsoundness. A correctly placed front leg covers the lowest point of the breast bone.

Body. The breast bone is strong and prominent enough to show a dimple at each side. Looked at from the front the thorax should be very oval allowing ample room for the heart and lungs; seen from the side it should intersect the forearm just above the wrist. The top line, very slightly depressed at the shoulders and slightly arched over the loin, is parallel to the ground. The whole trunk should be long, well ribbed up and underneath should merge gradually into the line of a moderately tucked up belly. The rump is full, round and wide with strong and pliant muscles.

Hindquarters. The pelvis is strong, set obliquely and not too short. The upper thigh, set at right angles to the pelvis, is strong and of good length. The lower thigh is short, set at right angles to the upper thigh and is well muscled. The hocks are well developed. The legs when seen from behind, are set well apart, straight and parallel to one another.

Feet. The front feet are full, broad in front, straight or turned just a trifle outwards. The four toes forming the foot are compact, well arched and have tough pads. The fifth toe (dewclaw) is usually left on. The nails are strong and short. The dog must stand true and equally on all parts of the foot. The hind feet are smaller and narrower than the fore feet and placed straight. There should be no dewclaw. In all other respects the hind feet and toes are similar to the forefeet and toes.

Tail. Continues the line of the spine; is but slightly curved, must not be carried too gaily or reach the ground when at rest.

Coat. With the exception of the jaw, eyebrows and ears, the whole body is covered with a completely even, short, harsh coat and an undercoat. There should be a beard on the chin. The eyebrows are bushy. The hair on the ears is almost smooth.

Colour. All colours are allowed but a white patch on the chest, though not a fault, is not desirable. Except in the case of Chocolates, when it may be brown or flesh-coloured, the nose should be black.

Weight and Size. It is recommended that dogs should weigh 9–10 kg. (20–22 lbs.) and bitches 8·2–9 kg. (18–20 lbs.)

Faults. PRIMARY FAULTS: An overshot or undershot jaw. Out at elbow. Knuckling over. Toes turned inwards. Splayed feet. Cow hocks. A bad coat. SECONDARY FAULTS: Very light eyes. A narrow chest. Breast bone insufficiently prominent. A dip behind the shoulders. A hollow back. A roach back. Rump higher than withers. Weak loins. Excsssively drawn up flanks. Bad angulation of forequarters or hindquarters. Legs too long, too close in front, or behind. Toes turned too much outwards. Bowed hind legs. A sluggish, clumsy or waddling gait. Poor muscle. Too long a tail. MINOR FAULTS: Ears too high, too low, sticking out, folded or narrow. Too marked a stop. Head too wide, too narrow or too short. Too pointed or too weak a jaw. Short neck or swan neck. Dewlaps. Goggle eyes. Too short a tail.

Note. Male animals should have two apparently normal testicles fully descended into the scrotum.

This full description is on the lines of the other two Standards printed earlier. Except for its coat, the Wire Haired Dachshund is similar to the other varieties and the reader is referred to Chapter IV for a detailed explanation of anatomical vagaries.

The coat of the Wire Haired Dachshund is unique. Briefly, it should be so distributed and arranged that at a short distance the dog looks smooth except for a growth of harsh whiskers and wiry tuft above the eyes. To the touch the hair should be harsh, strong and pliant. When rubbed the wrong way the coat should fall back into place immediately it is left undisturbed. If it does so, the hair forming the top coat will be of the right length and texture. If, on the other hand, the coat stays ruffed up after being stroked against the lie of the hair, it is too long, or too soft, or both. The Standard states plainly that the body coat should be completely even. There should be no appearance of roughness or raggedness. The only parts on which longer hair is required, or permitted, are the jaws and the eyebrows. At the sides of the neck, on the front of the chest and at the back of the forelegs the top coat appears to be longer than elsewhere because there ridges are formed by the coming together of hair growing in opposite directions on contiguous parts. The coat must be double. Beneath the wiry top coat there should be a close, dense under coat. This may be seen by raising the top coat, when it will appear as a rather softer, shorter, paler covering, so dense that the skin cannot be seen through it. A double coat of this kind is completely weather-proof and is an efficient protection against thorns. A good-coated Wire will go through the thickest undergrowth without hesitation or injury and will finish a day's work in a muddy earth, or by a stream-side, as clean and dry as when he started.

One sometimes sees a winning exhibit described in a judge's critique as "a rugged little dog". But a dog that looks rugged is not a good Wire. An exhibit that can be justly so described probably has an over-long or open coat and needs tidying up. The coat should lie quite flat on all parts of the body. Even the tufts above the eyes and the small beard should be harsh and, though standing out from the shorter coat on other parts, should not be exaggerated into drooping fringes. The eyebrows and beard are needed to protect the eyes and muzzle as the dog pushes through thorny undergrowth or narrow, rocky tunnels in pursuit of its quarry. To serve that purpose they must be harsh, close and fairly short. The hair on the forelegs is usually rather longer than on the trunk, but, though some latitude may be permitted here, it must not be overdone. Wires which appear to have their forelegs encased in leggings are nearly always soft in coat. Too much hair on the forelimbs, especially if it is at all soft, is a handicap to a working dog, for it tends to collect mud and may be a serious inconvenience on wet or boggy ground.

The ideal coat needs no trimming, but this perfect covering

is, and, it must be confessed, always has been, rare. Many Wires with good harsh coats of the right length grow a sort of ruff on the sides of the neck. This should be thinned prior to a show, otherwise the neck will look short and heavy. There may also be a superfluity of hair where the neck runs into the shoulders. This, too, should be thinned to bring out the slight arch at the nape and to make the back line clean and sharp. Bunchy hair above the withers detracts from the appearance of length in both neck and body and may cause the shoulders to look loaded. This is all the trimming a Wire should need and the tidying up should be done a fortnight before the show, to give the coat time to settle.

No amount of trimming will convert a bad coat into a good one. The ideal harsh, short, flat, double coat must be bred for, and breeders should arrange all their matings with this in mind. At present there are many Wires that fall far short of what is required in the matter of coat and need a good deal more than tidying up to fit them to take part in ring competition with any hope of success. The coat may be too long, not as harsh as it should be, or the undercoat be rather woolly. Such a coat must be taken in hand six weeks to two months prior to the date of the show for which the dog is to be prepared. The whole of the top coat should be stripped out. The best way to do this is to pluck the hairs out between the thumb and forefinger. It is a long, tedious job, calling for much patience and care. The operation need not be performed at one sitting. It is better to spread it over several days. This saves the dog from too great an ordeal and is less likely to lead to the plucking being done hurriedly and unevenly. A quicker method is to remove the hair with the aid of a stripping knife with a serrated blade, but some experience is necessary in the use of such an appliance to get satisfactory results. When all the top coat has been removed the dog should be groomed daily with a stiff bristle brush to stimulate the growth of the new coat.

Individuals vary in the time taken to grow a coat of the length desired after being stripped, but from six to eight weeks is usually necessary. Stripping may have to be done two, three or even four times a year if the natural coat is very long and soft. Repeated stripping usually has the effect of causing each new growth of hair to be slightly harder than its predecessor, so that, in time, a permanent improvement in texture may be brought about; but there is nothing one can do permanently to convert a long coat into a short one. Some exhibitors seek to avoid the tedium of stripping by clipping an over-long coat. This practice is to be strongly deprecated. A clipped coat is likely to grow longer than if it were left uncut and the undercoat may be entirely spoilt by such treatment.

Even worse than a long, soft top coat above a thick undercoat is the covering from which an undercoat is altogether absent. Exhibits with single coats of this kind may be trimmed to look quite presentable, and in some cases have a short, fairly harsh top coat which, until handled, appears to approach the ideal. The lack of undercoat is, however, discovered immediately the top hair is turned back. A single coat should be very severely penalized. It affords no protection against either weather or undergrowth and must be regarded as among the worst faults a Wire Haired Dachshund can possess. When the top coat becomes dry and dead at the approach of moulting time it should be removed entirely by the thumb-and-forefinger method. This will speed up the growth of the new hair and the dog will be out of coat for a considerably shorter period than would be the case were the old coat left to fall out naturally.

An experienced judge can always tell if a coat is in its natural state or whether it is only partially grown following stripping. However expert the trimmer, a trimmed Wire when placed against one with the correct natural coat looks glaringly artificial, and the contrast becomes additionally evident when the coat is handled. When judging Wires it is essential to run the hand over and through the coat to assess its length and texture. If an exhibit has been stripped within a week or two of a show, the top coat will not have grown sufficiently for its texture to be felt. I have known bad-coated dogs to be shown in this condition; the owners hoping the judge will regard such exhibits as being "out of coat" and give them the benefit of the doubt as to what their top coats would be in respect of length and texture when fully grown. Because of the impossibility of forming any reliable opinion on the nature of the top coat until it is fairly well grown, exhibits shown in their "under-vests" should always be penalized. To assume their coats would be correct if properly grown is grossly unfair to other competitors.

A judge should give credit only for what he can see and assess during the time an exhibit is in the ring. There can be no justification for giving an exhibit that is out of coat full marks because on a previous occasion it has been shown with a perfect coat. In making his awards a judge should be guided by neither prophecy nor memory. On the other hand, it is unfair seriously to fault an exhibit which, though having a harsh, short, double coat, is somewhat short of hair on chin and eyebrows. The ideal coat is slow in growing. Often a Wire destined to have a perfect coat when fully mature will look almost smooth up to a year old, and may be twice that age before it acquires full furnishings. But even while these are growing the texture, length and lie of the body coat and the density of the undercoat may be judged, so that, though a few marks may be deducted for lack of eyebrows and beard, the exhibit should score more points for coat than a competitor shown in full coat of indifferent texture.

Novice breeders are sometimes dismayed to find puppies in litters bred from Wire Haired parents looking quite smooth-coated for some weeks after birth, and wonder what has gone wrong. So far from this being a cause for worry, it is a most encouraging sign, for whelps that show a wiry coat before the age of ten weeks or so are likely to grow into bad-coated adults. Until they are four months old the smoother the pups look the better. After that age close examination will reveal longer hairs beginning to appear on the muzzle, between the toes and on the forelegs. By running the hand along the back against the lie of the hair the coat will be found to be slightly longer and coarser than in Smooth puppies of similar age. Thereafter the coat becomes longer and harsher as the weeks pass, till by the time they are six months old the youngsters will be clearly Wire Haired. In the past many novices have bitterly regretted the impatience that prompted them to dispose of their smooth-coated puppies as pets and to retain the long-coated ones for future breeding and showing.

Apart from those affecting coat properties, the most prevalent faults in our modern Wires are lack of length and bad back lines. We see many very sound, well-ribbed exhibits with good movement and the correct game, alert temperament, which fail to please in general appearance because they look cobby. Heads, necks and bodies all tend to be too short and in some cases the lack of length and elegance is aggravated by tails carried unduly high. These faults are not universal and some improvement has been noticed in the past year, but they are still much too common. Some breeders have had recourse to a Smooth cross to get greater length in the Wires, usually with very satisfactory results. There is nothing against such a cross. It may have a beneficial effect on the coat, besides making for longer heads, necks and bodies. The intercrossing of the two varieties must, however, be done with discretion. Once the cross has been made the progeny should be bred back to the blood-lines of the Wire Haired parent. Indiscriminate crossing of Smooths and Wires could be disastrous; leading to the introduction of faults from which the Wire variety is at present free and to the appearance of litters consisting of Smooth as well as Wire Haired pups (*see* Chapter XI).

Back lines which dip behind the shoulders or rise steeply to the top of the rump spoil many otherwise good exhibits. It is difficult to understand why these faults have become common, for they were not general failings in pre-war Wires. Up to less than two years ago one could go through many classes of Wires without finding a single exhibit with a correct top line. Things are not so bad now, but the fault has not been wholly eliminated. Dipping or rising back lines are not confined to any one type of exhibit. The failings occur in short- and long-backed individuals with equal frequency, and in both sexes. Here, again, a judicious dip into Smooth blood might help. The high set-on tail is very ugly in a Dachshund of any variety. It is particularly undesirable in a Wire, for dogs of this breed are usually fearless and full of spirits and in the excitement of meeting strangers of their own kind in ring competition are apt to carry their tails as high as they can. This detracts both from the apparent length of the body and from the general symmetry of the outline. The sweeping line which, starting at the nose, runs over the head, down the neck and along the back, is cut off abruptly by the almost upright tail and the hind-quarters look as though they had been put on as an after-thought.

Hind movement is fairly good but in front action there is sometimes a tendency for the forefeet to be crossed when the dog trots. This is a bad fault, since it indicates wrong angulation somewhere in the shoulder girdle or weak wrists, and gives a plaiting gait quite unsuited to a working dog. At one time most Wires failed to Dachshunds of other varieties in depth of keel. This has now been remedied and we see few exhibits that can be seriously faulted for being too shallow.

The revival of the Wire Haired Dachshund that has taken place during the past few years has been accompanied by an improvement in general type, but we have some way to go yet before catching up with the best of the pre-war exhibits in that respect. At present type is uneven. This makes judging difficult and accounts, in some measure, for the reversal of placings from show to show. There is, however, no grounds for pessimism. The Wire is climbing rapidly back to its former high place in the esteem of British dog lovers and we may look with confidence for a great advance in general type in the next few years. All who have experience of the breed are loud in its praise; newcomers are joining the ranks of its admirers in a steady stream and the Wire Haired Dachshund Club is stronger today than at any previous time in its history. Despite the difficulties that beset the variety in the years immediately following the war, registration figures are already at pre-war level and the appreciation of the quality of our modern Wires by overseas buyers is such that the demand for stock far exceeds the supply. To all who have worked to put this game little dog back on the map, it is most gratifying to know that we in Britain now hold a stronger hand in Wires than any other country in the world.

CHAPTER IX

THE RISE OF THE MINIATURE DACHSHUND

DACHSHUNDS of very small size, suitable for going to ground after such quarry as rabbits, were bred in Germany before the beginning of the present century. Some were, no doubt, "sports", or runts, which came by chance from normal-sized parents, but others, known as Kaninchenteckel, were intentionally produced by mating lightweight Dachshunds to Toy Terriers or Pinchers. These early Kaninchenteckel were a heterogeneous lot, with little of the show Dachshund in their shape. The majority had round skulls, goggle eyes, short ears and were high on the leg and shallow in chest. They were valued solely for their adroitness in the field and were kept almost exclusively by owners of working kennels. In 1909 a few were brought to England by a Herr Heermann, an Austrian, who thought to popularize them in this country, but their importer died the following year and nothing is known of what happened to his dogs. By 1910 German Dachshund breeders had become very dissatisfied with the Kaninchenteckel and the feeling became general that if a Miniature Dachshund was required it should be a small version of the Standard, not a cross-bred nondescript which was a Teckel only in name. Thereafter a much better type was bred, but for long the Dwarf Teckel, as it was then called, showed the shallow chest, short head and full eye that had characterized its predecessor.

I have found no record of any dwarf Dachshunds being shown in Britain up to the outbreak of the 1914–18 war, but soon after shows got going again Miss F. E. Dixon, owner of the Kar Kennels of Smooths, exhibited a Smooth Miniature named Klein Kurio, born in quarantine from German parents, which created quite a sensation. This little red dog was a typical Dachshund in miniature and came as a revelation to show-goers who had previously known only full-sized representatives of the breed. He was by far the most notable of the Smooth Miniatures brought over in the late 1920s and early 1930s by Miss Dixon and a few others. Shortly after Klein Kurio's arrival Miss Dixon and Major G. Maitland Reynall imported a team of Long Haired Miniatures. These, too, aroused much interest and were very favourably received, so that when stock bred from these first representatives of their breeds became available it found an eager market. The many admirers who were attracted to the Miniatures soon arranged for special classes to be provided for their favourites, and it quickly became clear that the diminutive Teckel was destined to achieve great popularity.

At first some hostility was shown by certain exhibitors of Standard Dachshunds, who castigated the newcomers by describing them as toys, freaks and degenerates, but their antagonism was short-lived, for the little dogs proved to be fearless, game and hardy; as well able to stand up to a day's field work as their larger relatives. Indeed, before long several of those who had achieved distinction with other varieties were numbered among the Miniature's staunchest supporters. When in 1935 the Miniature Dachshund Club was formed, its first President was Colonel G. Spurrier, D.S.O., one of the best-known figures in Standard Smooths, and among the members chosen to serve on the Committee were Miss D. Spurrier, owner of the famous Querns Smooths, Mrs. M. Howard of the Seale Wire Hairs and Mrs. Herdman, then one of the most successful breeders and exhibitors of Standard Long Hairs.

From the first the Long Haired Miniature got off to a flying start, leaving the Smooth lagging far behind. Perhaps the main reason for this was that the number of Long Hairs brought over by Miss Dixon and Major Maitland Reynall was larger than that of the Smooths imported, so that breeding operations could be carried out immediately on a larger scale. Another factor may have been that the Long Haired Dachshund Club, of which I was then Hon. Secretary, took the Miniature Long Hair under its wing and did all in its power to encourage owners to breed and exhibit. Until the Miniature Dachshund Club was brought into existence, nearly all the chief protagonists of the Miniature Long Hair were members of the Long Haired Dachshund Club, which guaranteed classes, offered special prizes and generally fostered the interests of the smaller variety. The Smooth Miniature, on the other hand, was given no such welcome by any breed club prior to 1935 and the difficulty of obtaining breeding stock further militated against its popularity. Entries at shows were far below those of the Long Hairs and the quality of the exhibits left much to be desired.

The Long Haired Miniatures introduced by Miss Dixon and Major Maitland Reynall were from the Fleezensee Kennels. They were small, game, attractive-looking dogs but showed several very obvious faults. Their coats were of good length but curly and inclined to be fluffy. Heads were short, rather round in skull and snipy in muzzle, eyes were round and full, ears were small and bodies lacked length. If the truth is to be told, it must be admitted that these early Long Haired Miniatures showed several indications that Papillon blood had been introduced in their ancestry in the not very distant past. The best of them was Halodri von Fleezensee, a sound, well-ribbed little dog. He was used a good deal at stud and both he and his progeny did a lot of winning in their day. His name may be found in the pedigrees of many present-day Miniatures if they are traced back far enough.

The best Miniature Long Haired dog of pre-war days was undoubtedly Knowlton Chocolate Soldier, bred from Halodri and an imported bitch by Mrs. Herdman. He was very much better in every way than anything seen up to that time and was, I think, unbeaten in his sex. He was perfectly sound with good length, irreproachable back line, excellent coat and front, reachy neck and typical head with plenty of bone. At stud he proved a great asset to the breed and his blood is carried by many of the most successful of Long Haired Miniatures now living.

Before the arrival of the Miniatures a few very small specimens had been bred, both Smooth and Long Haired, from full-sized parents, but as these were not looked on with favour by judges they had usually found their way to private homes as pets. When weight-restricted classes were put on for Miniatures some of these chance-bred sports were entered and some exquisite specimens were seen. Among the most outstanding were Miss Muffet of Querns, a Smooth belonging to Col. G. Spurrier, the Long Haired Phillipine of Dilwood owned by Mrs. L. Midwood, and Gretel of Mornyvarna, bred and shown by Mrs. Portman Graham. All were extremely typical little Dachshunds which, but for their very small size, would have won high honours in Standard competition, and served to demonstrate just how good a Miniature could be. None of these Standard-bred little ones was bred from, for at that time breeders considered it was too great a risk: believing that such bitches, though mated to the smallest available pure Miniature dog, would be sure to breed puppies too big to be whelped.

Thus these superlative specimens, which might have done so much to improve and fix type in Miniatures prior to 1939, were wasted. But despite such missed opportunities, type did improve steadily, if slowly, and when the coming of war put an end to showing, the Miniature Dachshund was in a strong position numerically, with the Long Haired variety still in the lead. Apart from the few that had been bred from Standards already referred to, almost all the pre-war Long Haired Miniatures failed in head, eye and coat, and many lacked body length. The most prevalent faults in the Smooths were lightness of bone, toyish heads and narrow, stilty hindquarters.

Among the principal supporters of the Smooth Miniatures in the pre-1939 period were Mrs. M. Howard, who had many successes with exhibits bearing the Seale prefix, one of the best of which was the very typical red Arabis of Seale; Mrs. Whitley, the President of the Miniature Dachshund Club, who also favoured Smooths and whose Bletchingham strain made a valuable contribution to the building up of the variety in its post-war form, and Miss Parker Rhodes, whose Partridge Hill prefix may be found in the pedigrees of several contemporary winners.

In Long Hairs Major G. Maitland Reynall was the pioneer and the most consistent exhibitor, Mrs. Herdman did very well with her Knowlton Chocolate Soldier and some of his offspring. Dr. Edward Hindle was the first Hon. Secretary of the Miniature Dachshund Club and for a time a leading breeder and exhibitor. Mrs. Smith Rewse of the Primrose Patch Kennels and Mrs. V. Rycroft of the Bartonbury's were also prominent.

It is unnecessary to try to trace the influence of the pre-war blood-lines on our modern Miniatures, for the Miniature Dachshund as we now know it is, to all intents and purposes, a post-war product. Though many of our present dogs go back in part to the early imported Smooth and Long Haired Miniatures, that original blood has been so intermingled with contributions from other sources that little trace of it remains. We have already seen that the older breeders refrained from introducing Standard blood into their Miniatures on the assumption that such a course must result in the death of the bitch, or in the production of puppies which would grow too big to come within the stipulated weight limit.

The first to challenge this generally held belief and to put it to a practical test was Mrs Smith Rewse, who for long owned the largest kennels of Standard Long Hairs in Britain, and probably in the world, and bred on a very large scale. In the many litters born in her Primrose Patch Kennels very small specimens, from time to time, appeared. Some of these were mated to the smallest Miniature-bred stock then in the country. It was found that the small Standard-bred bitches whelped without trouble and that the pups showed no more variation in size than do those bred from two pure-bred Miniatures. The progeny of the cross were mated to pure Miniatures, again with the most satisfactory results.

The stock thus produced showed great superiority in type over that of the pure-bred Miniatures and proved consistently successful in the ring. Mrs. Smith Rewse's results induced others to follow her example and no tragic consequences were reported.

It is fair to say that the astonishing progress that has been made in general type in the Long Haired Miniature in the last few years is due, in large measure, to the experimental work carried out by Mrs. Smith Rewse in blending the best of the blood carried by her Standards with the pre-war blood lines of the Miniatures. She both showed the way and made available stock on which other breeders could build. The successes won by dogs of her breeding and their progeny has been phenomenal, and their beneficent influence on the breed will be apparent for many generations.

Breeders of Smooth Miniatures were slower to turn to the Standard blood in their efforts to improve and stabilize type, and for some time the variety made little headway. Of late years, however, they, too, have awakened to the benefits to be derived from a judicious use of Standard-bred stock, with results that have surpassed the most sanguine expectations. Some use, too, has been made of the best of the Long Hairs to improve bone and ribbing in the Smooths.

An important milestone in Miniature history was reached in 1948 when the Kennel Club acceded to a petition put forward by the Miniature Dachshund Club and granted separate breed registers for both Long Haired and Smooth. Challenge Certificates were made available the following year. Till then Miniatures could only win certificates in competition with Standards, and though two Long Haired Miniatures, the bitches Miss Mouse of Primrose Patch owned by Mrs. Smith Rewse and Adrelson Golden Orchid belonging to Mrs. W. Bailey, had been awarded the highest honours over their larger relatives, the little ones were so heavily handicapped that it was almost impossible for them to achieve the title of champion. Their elevation to separate breed status had an immediate effect. More classes were provided, more owners were encouraged to exhibit, breeding operations were extended and given a new impetus, ring competition became keener and a great improvement in quality soon became very noticeable. The progress made by both Smooth and Long Haired Miniatures since 1949 has been truly amazing. All the most glaring faults shown by the pre-war stock have been virtually eradicated, so that exhibits in both varieties are now able successfully to compete not only with Standard Dachshunds but with any other breed. On several recent occasions the award of Best in Show in all-breeds competition has gone to a Miniature Dachshund.

The Standard of the Dachshund (Miniature Long-Haired) is:—

Characteristics. The Miniature Dachshund should be gay, alert, bold and highly intelligent. Despite its small size it should be strong, extremely active, hardy and game. Movement should be free and gay. Both fore and hind feet should move straight forward without plaiting or crossing in front, and without any tendency to throw out the hind feet sideways.

General Appearance. In conformation the Miniature Dachshund should be in all respects similar to the Dachshund of Standard size. It should be compact, short-legged and long in body, well muscled and strong, with bold and intelligent expression. The body should be neither so plump as to give an impression of cobbiness nor so slender as to impart a weasel-like appearance. Height at shoulder should be half the length of the body measured from the breast bone to the base of the tail, and the girth of the chest double the height at the shoulder. The length from the tip of the nose to the eyes should equal the length from eyes to base of skull.

Head and Skull. Long and conical when seen from above, sharp in profile and finely modelled. Skull neither too broad nor too narrow, only slightly arched and without prominent stop. Foreface long and narrow, finely modelled. The lips should be tightly drawn but well cover the lower jaw; neither heavy nor too sharply cut away. The corners of the mouth slightly marked.

Eyes. Of medium size, neither prominent nor too deeply set, oval in shape, placed obliquely. They should be clear and expressive and dark in colour, except in Dapples and Chocolates, in which wall or light eyes are permissible.

Ears. Broad and placed relatively well back, high and well set on, lying close to the cheeks and very mobile. The leather of the ears when pulled to the front should not extend beyond the tip of the nose.

Mouth. Wide, extending back to behind the eyes. Teeth sound and strong, the inner side of the upper incisors closing on the outer side of the under ones.

Neck. Long and muscular, showing no dewlap, slightly arched at the nape, running cleanly into the shoulders carried well up, giving the dog an alert, defiant appearance.

Forequarters. Muscular, with deep chest. Shoulder blades should be long and broad, set obliquely and lying firmly on well-developed ribs. The breast bone should be prominent, extending so far forward as to show depressions on both sides. Upper arm equal in length to the shoulder blade, which it should join at an angle of 90 degrees, well boned and muscled, set close to the ribs but moving freely. Lower arm short, inclined slightly inwards, well boned and free from wrinkle.

Body. Long and well muscled with oblique shoulders and short, strong pelvic region. Ribs well sprung and extending far back. Chest oval, well let down between the forelegs, with the deepest point of the keel level with the wrist-joints. The line of the back level or only slightly depressed over the shoulders and slightly arched over the loin, with the belly moderately tucked up.

Hindquarters. Rump full, round and broad. Pelvis bone not too short, broad, strong and set obliquely. Thigh bone strong, of good length and jointed to the pelvis at an angle of 90 degrees. Second thighs short, set at right angles to the upper thighs and well muscled. Hocks well let down, set wide apart, strongly bent. Seen from behind the legs should be straight, with no tendency for the hocks to turn inwards or outwards.

Feet. Broad and large in proportion to the size of the dog, straight or turned only slightly outwards. The hind feet smaller than the fore. Toes close together and with each toe well arched. Nails strong. The dog must stand equally on all parts of the foot.

Tail. Set on fairly high, not too long, tapering and

without too marked a curve. It should not be carried too high and never curled over the back.

Coat. The coat should be soft and straight or only slightly waved. Longest under the neck, on the under parts of the body and behind the legs, where it should form abundant feathering, and on the tail, where it should form a flag. The outside of the ears should also be well feathered. The coat should be flat, resembling that of the Irish Setter, and should not obscure the outline. Too much hair on the feet is not desired.

Colour. Any colour. No white is permissible except for a small spot on the breast and even this is undesirable. The nose should be black except in Dapples and Chocolates, in which it may be flesh-coloured or brown. In all cases the coat colour should be bright and clearly defined. In black and tans the tan should be rich and sharp. Dapples should be free from large, unbroken patches; the dappling being evenly distributed over the whole body.

Weight and Size. The ideal weight is 4·5 kg. (10 lbs.) and it is of the utmost importance that judges should not award a prize to any dog exceeding 5 kg. (11 lbs.) in weight. Other points being equal the smaller the better, but mere diminutiveness must never take precedence over general type and soundness. Any appearance of weediness or toyishness is to be avoided at all costs.

Faults. Round skull. Round or protruding eyes. Short ears. Shallow chest. Narrowness in front or behind. Short body. Long legs. Splayed feet. Cow hocks. Mouth under or overshot. Nervous or cringing demeanour.

Note. Male animals should have two apparently normal testicles fully descended into the scrotum.

The Standard of the Dachshund (Miniature Smooth-Haired) is identical with the Standard of the Dachshund (Miniature Long-Haired) with the following exceptions:

Coat. In Smooths, short, dense and smooth, adequately covering all the parts of the body; coarsest on the under-side of the tail.

Weight and Size. The ideal weight is 4·5 kg. (10 lbs.) and it is of the utmost importance that judges should not award a prize to any dog exceeding 5 kg. (11 lbs.) in weight. Other points being equal the smaller the better, but mere diminutiveness must never take precedence over general type and soundness. Any appearance of weediness or toyishness is to be avoided at all costs.

Faults. Woolly or curly coat.

The Standard of the Dachshund (Miniature Wire-Haired) is identical with the Standard of the Dachshund (Miniature Long-Haired) with the following exceptions:—

Coat. With the exception of the jaw, eyebrows and ears, the whole body is covered with a completely even, short, harsh coat and undercoat. There should be a beard on the chin. The eyebrows are bushy. The hair on the ears is almost smooth.

Weight and Size. The ideal weight is 4·5 kg. (10 lbs.) and it is of the utmost importance that judges should not award a prize to any dog exceeding 5 kg. (11 lbs.) in weight. Other points being equal the smaller the better, but mere diminutiveness must never take precedence over general type, and soundness. Any appearance of weediness or toyishness is to be avoided at all costs.

These Standards differ in no essential from those of the larger Dachshund varieties except in the paragraph dealing with Weight and Size. Here the maximum is fixed at 11 lb. In 1935, when the Miniature Dachshund Club was founded, the weight limit imposed was 12 lb., but this was reduced to 11 lb. in the following year, and it has not since been changed. An ideal weight of between 7 and 9 lb. was first mentioned in the Standard drawn up in 1948. The reason for retaining a maximum weight some pounds above what is recognized as the ideal is to ensure that general type and soundness shall be more highly valued than very small size. A Miniature that shows grave breed faults, or that is unsound, should be excluded from winning high awards no matter how small it may be. Only when two exhibits are equally good in all other respects should size be allowed to affect a judge's decision. The majority of our best Miniatures today weigh between about 9 and 10½ lb., but some excellent specimens weighing little more than 8 lb. are also seen. There is, therefore, nothing much wrong so far as weight is concerned. The retention of what is generally admitted to be a generous top limit has undoubtedly been instrumental in eliminating toyishness and weediness and in encouraging the production of the good bone and ribbing that characterize our modern Miniatures.

CHAPTER X

THE MINIATURE DACHSHUND UP TO THE FIFTIES

THE Miniature Dachshund as seen in our rings today has been created by the enthusiasm, intelligence, skill and determination of British breeders. As a breed the Dachshund is rightly acknowledged to be of German origin, but the Miniature as a true-breeding variety of correct Teckel type is a British product. In no other country are there, or have there ever been, so many or such good Dachshunds under 11 lb. in weight, either Smooth or Long Haired, as are now to be found in Britain.

From the first the ideal placed before breeders by the Miniature Dachshund Club was a dog conforming in all respects to the Standards by which the full-sized Dachshund is judged but of a size which brought it within the stipulated weight limit. Several modern exhibits approach that ideal closely. The importance of keeping constantly before breed devotees the principle that the Miniature is not a Toy but a small, hardy, game, sporting dog has never been lost sight of, with the result that very few indeed of our Miniatures fail in temperament.

All that has been written in the chapters on Standard Smooths and Long Hairs applies equally to Miniatures, so that it is unnecessary to deal further with structural details here. Until very recently the Long Hairs were much better in general type than Smooths, but the latter are now showing marked improvement.

Long Hairs still have the advantage in bone, heads, feet and action. The faults most noticed in this variety are a tendency to be too high at the withers in proportion to the body length. As in the Standard Long Hair, a little extra length in body is needed to offset the effect of the longer coat, and if an exhibit is too high the back will appear shorter than it really is. Eyes might be improved in some cases, but on the whole heads and expression are fairly typical. In many small exhibits the muzzle or foreface is rather weak; a formation that is often accompanied by round and slightly bulging eyes. It seems to be very difficult to get Miniatures below about 8½ lb. that are wholly free from these defects, and most of the very small ones are also too short in body and too high on the leg.

Few breeders now breed for very small size. The tiny Miniatures which appear from time to time, for the most part come accidentally from matings made primarily to improve type. It is earnestly to be hoped that this sound policy will continue to be followed by all breeders who have the best interests of the Miniature at heart.

In Smooths there is a general lack of bone and rather too much "legginess". These faults are often associated with narrowness in front and behind and make the dog look spidery, which is the reverse of what the Standard demands. Heads tend to be rather small, the skull is often domed and the muzzle is pinched in front of the eyes. Feet, too, are far from good. They are usually too small and may be too thin. In efforts to improve these points some breeders have mated Smooths to Long Hairs with very satisfactory results. There is nothing to be said against this inter-breeding between the coat varieties. The progeny are Smooth and will never breed Long Haired pups so long as they are mated back to pure-bred Smooths. The long coat will, however, appear if a Smooth bred from the Smooth–Long Haired cross is put to a mate similarly bred or to a pure Long Hair. The first-mentioned mating may be expected to give one Long Haired pup in a litter of four; the second equal numbers of Smooth and Long Haired whelps (*see* Chapter XI).

In the last chapter I mentioned the great improvement in type that followed the use of Miniatures bred from full-sized parents to mates derived from the stock imported by Miss Dixon, Major Maitland Reynall and a few others. Now that there are so many Miniatures available in both coats there is no reason to experiment further by introducing Standard blood-lines, except in very exceptional cases when an experienced breeder may decide to try an outcross of that kind to correct a prevalent fault or strain weakness. The indiscriminate mixing of Standard and Miniature blood-lines can bring nothing but evil.

Before buying foundation stock or selecting a stud dog

the novice should obtain accurate information as to the size and weight of the ancestors for two or three generations. In litters of Standard Dachshunds, as in most other breeds, one pup is sometimes much smaller than the others. This may be a runt, weakly and weedy, that remains small because it neither thrives nor grows normally, and as an adult may weigh something under 14 lb. Should this weedy specimen be a bitch her owner knows that it will be unwise to mate her to a full-sized dog but may consider it quite safe to put her to a Miniature. Such a procedure is quite unjustifiable. The bitch, being a weed, should not be used for breeding at all. Because of her ancestry she is likely to throw at least one or two pups too large to be whelped normally, whatever the mate selected for her. If put to a Miniature dog some of her pups may be small enough to be sold as Miniatures but, though small as puppies, they will probably exceed the maximum weight of 11 lb. when full grown and their value for breeding purposes will be problematic.

Miniature puppies vary much in the age at which they reach their full size and weight. Some are not much smaller than Standard pups at birth and for a time grow quickly till about fourteen to sixteen weeks old, when growth is suddenly arrested and from then on they grow very little if at all. Others are very small at first and seem to increase little in weight from week to week, but they continue to grow slowly for long after four months old and may, as adults, weigh more than the pups which looked much larger in the nest.

The puppy that is smallest when very young is not necessarily the smallest when full grown, and it is always something of a gamble to pick a Miniature for size before it is at least four months old. Knowledge and experience of a strain may help in enabling a breeder to form a rough estimate of the weight a young puppy is likely to reach at maturity, but even the most knowledgeable and experienced can and do make mistakes.

When selecting a puppy, weight and size must be judged in conjunction with such qualities as bone, ribbing, breadth and length. By choosing the smallest the novice may be landed with the weed of the litter, which, though it may be well within the weight limit as an adult, will be valueless either for showing or breeding.

The belief that Miniature bitches are difficult to whelp is

(*Ramsay & Muspratt*)

Ch. Rosalinda of Hilltrees
(*Long*)

(*Diane Pearce*)

Ch. Swansford Brigg of Truanbru
(*Long*)

Ch. Imber Café Russe of Voryn
(*Long*)

Ch. Achsel
(*Wire*)

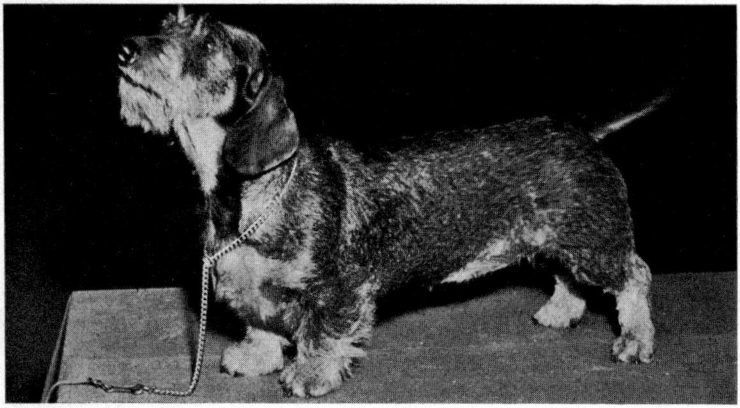

(*C. M. Cooke*)

Ch. Retann Caprice
(*Wire*)

Ch Wylde Caprice
(*Wire*)

(*Clement Burge*)

Ch. Dusty Shoes of Seale
(*Wire*)

Ch. Wylde Surmise
(*Wire*)

(*H. J. Fountain*)

Ch. Tan Trudi of Thornton
(*Wire*)

Ch. Stephan of Montreux
(*Miniature Smooth*)

(*B. Thurse*)

Ch. Minivale Miraculous
(*Miniature Smooth*)

Ch. Minivale Melvin
(*Miniature Smooth*)

wholly fallacious. As in all breeds, the puppies vary in size at birth, but all who have had experience in breeding both Standard and Miniature Dachshunds agree that the latter have fewer whelping complications than the former. Matings must, of course, be arranged with due regard to weight and breeding and very small bitches should not be bred from. As a general principle I consider it unwise to breed from a bitch weighing less than 8 lb. On the other hand, bitches that are overweight for showing though bred from Miniatures, can be most valuable for breeding if mated to small dogs.

Among those who have contributed to the rise of the Miniature Dachshund Mrs. M. Howard deserves special mention. The owner of the Seale prefix is one of the few pre-war exhibitors who is still showing and breeding and has rendered great services to the breed both as Hon. Secretary of the Miniature Dachshund Club and as breed delegate to the Kennel Club Council of Representatives. The zeal which she has brought to the task of directing the Club's policy has been an important factor in putting Miniatures in the very satisfactory position they now occupy. In Smooths Mrs. E. A. Winder of the Minivale prefix is the most successful exhibitor. Her Champion Minivale Miraculous was the first of his variety to win a challenge certificate and the first to become a champion. He is the sire of Champion Minivale Miranda, Champion Minivale Marte of Silwood and the dog Champion Minivale Melvin, generally accepted as being the best of his kind yet seen. This kennel also includes Champion Minivale Rusty Boy of Kellett, that great stud dog Minivale Majestic and several others which seem certain to win their titles in the near future.

Mr. A. Negal has made his prefix of Montreux famous by breeding such exquisite specimens as Champion Contessina of Montreux, the first bitch champion and a daughter of the imported Kisska von der Howitt, Prince John of Montreux a son of Contessina and sire of the lovely Champion Livia of Montreux, whose dam Monique of Montreux carries the Schneid and Von der Howitt blood, and the outstanding young dog Champion Stephen of Montreux, a son of Prince John and Champion Contessina.

Flight-Lieutenant Peter Townshend's little red bitch Champion Tallula of Gladsmuir was the second of her sex to win the title and is dam of a beautiful son in Ch. Querns

Tango of Gladsmuir. Mrs. M. W. Willows has had many successes with exhibits bearing her Rushton prefix and Mrs. Bassett's Merryweathers, Mrs. Littmoden's Wendlitts, Mrs. Wakefield's Sillwoods, Mr. and Mrs. F. G. Fox's Shepherdsdenes, Mrs. B. Weatherly's Bewletts, Mrs. J. A. Borley's Rossdenes, Dr. Blakiston and Miss New's Taschens, Mrs. I. G. Head's Daxheads, Mr. and Mrs. W. E. Hickling's Embassys and Mr. and Mrs. Sauvage's Saumindas are all well known.

Tribute has already been paid to the pioneer work done by Mrs. Smith Rewse in building up the Miniature Long Hairs. Her first Miniature was Zwerg Golden Primrose, which, mated to old Knowlton Chocolate Soldier, bred the two bitches Goldlein and Roselein of Primrose Patch. Goldlein was the dam of Meadow Sweet of Primrose Patch and Roselein of Black Watch of Primrose Patch; both well-known names in the pedigrees of many present winners. The mating of Bluebell of Armadale, Mrs. Smith Rewse's first Standard Long Hair, to the imported Mürks von Eldenwerder produced Golden Gorse of Primrose Patch, a dog to which our modern Miniatures owe much of their excellent type. Among the many post-war winners that have come from these kennels special mention may be made of Champion Primrosepatch Jasper, Champion Primrosepatch Juliette, now owned by Mrs. Marsh, American Champion Primrosepatch Diamond, the first Miniature to become a champion in the U.S.A., Champion Primrosepatch Daffodil, Primrosepatch Honey Gold, now in America, and Primrosepatch Tinyteckle. On Mrs. Smith Rewse's retirement from active participation in show competition her prefix was taken over by Mrs. A. Sidgwick, who continues to add to the number of celebrities which have borne the world-famous name.

Captain and Mrs. R. Portman Graham's Mornyvarna Kennels are also famous wherever the Long Haired Miniature is known. Their Champion Marcus of Mornyvarna has won more challenge certificates than any other exhibit in his variety. He was the first Miniature of either coat to become a champion and has proved a tower of strength at stud. This wonderful little dog is the sire of Champion Tina of Mornyvarna, Champion Little Gretchen of Mornyvarna, Champion Primrosepatch Jasper, Champion Grafin Lieselotte, Champion John of Mornyvarna and Champion Highbury Pal, besides a host of other big winners. Marcus was sired by Otto of Mornyvarna, a son of Otto von Tanzenwerde and Meadow Sweet of Primrose Patch, out of Mitzie of Mornyvarna, a daughter of Black Watch of Primrose Patch and Bluebell of Alfenberg (by Golden Gorse of Primrose Patch). Besides winning the highest honours in Britain, stock from the Mornyvarna Kennels has gone to many countries to establish the breed overseas.

Mrs. M. Ireland Blackburne, M.B.E., is one of the oldest and most consistent breeders. Her Champion Robsvarl Red Robin is famous both as a great bench winner and as a prolific sire of small puppies of the highest type. His numerous winning offspring includes the celebrated Champion Chloe von Walder, bred and owned by Mrs. L. S. Bellamy. Robsvarl Raven is the sire of Champion Wylands Countess Vanity, bred by Mrs. J. D. Wyatt out of Primrosepatch May Queen, Robsvarl Martin, and of Mrs. Bailey's Champion Adrelsan Golden Orchid, one of the few Miniatures ever to win a challenge certificate in competition with Standards. Other notable exhibitors include Mrs. L. S. Bellamy of the Von Walders; Mrs. F. Gwyer of the Marlenwoods; Mrs. H. L. Waddington of Smokyhole fame; Mrs. Dove of the Bordaks; Mrs. A. R. Greenwood, breeder of Champion Grafin Lieselotte and Champion Tina of Mornyvarna; Miss M. C. Sherer, owner of Champion Wylands Countess Vanity; Mrs. Marsh, who has Champion Primrosepatch Juliette; Mrs. M. F. Commeline, owner of Champion Hurlington Huffy; Miss M. Fletcher (Hoylins); Mr. and Mrs. S. G. Christmas (Esspeejay); and Miss J. Fardell (Farick).

Of recent years a few very good Wire Haired Miniatures have been imported and several excellent specimens have been bred in this country. Most of those that have been shown are descended from the small Wire bitch Kiwi of Dunkerque, belonging to Sir Charles Lambe, who mated her to a Smooth Miniature dog, but one or two excellent little specimens not exceeding 11 lb. in weight have been bred from full-sized parents.

To encourage owners to show these small Wires the Wire Haired Dachshund Club guaranteed classes for exhibits up to 12 lb. in weight at several of the larger Championship shows, an extra pound being added to the usual maximum weight for Miniatures to widen the field from which entries may be drawn. Among the best individuals that have been shown are Mrs. E. Gale's Jodima Turquoise, a most typical little bitch bred from Standard parents; Mrs. A.

Molony's Nutmeg of Dunkerque, a daughter of Kiwi of Dunkerque by the Smooth Miniature Teckelholme Minola Song Bird; Mrs. B. C. L. Taylor's Lou of Dunkerque and her offspring Alberich of Teki and Welgunda of Teki by the Smooth Miniature Black Knight of Montreux. All these are very attractive and have aroused much interest. The demand for diminutive Wires is increasing and there seems good reason to hope that before long the Wire Haired Miniature may be as widely bred and exhibited as the other varieties. Among those who are most active in espousing its cause are Mrs. Molony, whose Huntersbroad strain is founded on imported stock, Mrs. Waddington of Smokyhole fame and Group Captain and Mrs. Satchell. The name of Miss M. F. Rhodes must also be mentioned as being prominent among those who of recent years have worked tirelessly to further the cause of the third member of the Miniature Dachshund group.

Since the above was written, it is gratifying to know, the hopes entertained by its admirers for the future of this charming variety of the Teckel family have been fully realized. As its many attractive qualities have become more generally known, the Miniature Wire-Haired has increased steadily in popularity. It now has a numerous and enthusiastic following and has been adopted by several of the best-known breeders of other varieties. Type shows marked improvement and, what is even more important, is very much more uniform than it was a few years ago. The variety was elevated to championship status in 1959 and the first of its representatives to gain the title was the bitch Jane of Sillwood, owned by Mrs. R. Wakefield, who may justly claim to have made breed history. The first dog to become a champion was Mrs. M. F. Rhodes' Coobeg Ballyteckel Walt Weevil. Today the best specimens of the variety compare favourably with their larger relative the Standard Wire. The main points to watch are fronts, coats which are apt to be too soft and ragged, and feet which, in some cases, might be tighter, neater and harder with advantage.

For later information see Addenda 4, 5, 6.

CHAPTER XI

COLOUR BREEDING IN DACHSHUNDS

THE Standards of Points as issued by the several Breed Clubs all state that a Dachshund, whether Smooth, Long Haired or Wire Haired, may be of any colour provided it does not show any considerable area of white. Reds of diverse shades, black and tan, chocolate, brindle and dapple are the colours usually seen. A few blue and tans have appeared from time to time and pure-white specimens have been bred on the Continent. In the past little attention was paid to colour-breeding in this country. Most people were indifferent to the colour shown by the puppies they bred so long as they were good enough in other points to be able to win in the show ring. Today that attitude is changing. Many breeders are now interested in the production of stock of some particular colour and it has become a general plaint that none of the volumes written on the breed gives any guidance on this subject. There is nothing mysterious in the inheritance of coat colour in Dachshunds. It follows the Mendelian principles, and if these are understood there is no reason why difficulties should be encountered in predicting with confidence what colours will result from any given mating.

Every puppy arises from the union of two sex cells, one of which is contributed by each of its parents; and every characteristic, or point, it shows must have been represented in some way in one or other of those germ cells. Thus a chocolate puppy receives one unit for the development of the chocolate coat colour from its sire and one from its dam. All its body cells, therefore, contain two units, or genes as they are called, for the expression of the chocolate colour. When the puppy becomes mature it will, in turn, produce sex or germ cells; sperms if a male or ova (egg cells) if a female. But in these cells the units, or genes, received from its two parents separate, so that each of its germ cells contains only one gene for each character represented in its body cells. Our chocolate Dachshund, whether dog or bitch, will produce germ cells all of which carry a single gene for the development of chocolate colour, and so long as it is mated to other chocolates it will breed pups of that colour only. If we mate a chocolate to a black and tan, the body cells of the resulting puppies will contain one gene for chocolate and one for black and tan. Their germ cells will, therefore, be of two kinds: one type carrying the gene for chocolate and the other the gene for black and tan. A Dachshund bred in that way is black and tan; that colour being dominant to, or masking the presence of, chocolate, but, unlike the pure-bred black and tan, it will not breed true for its own colour. Its offspring will vary in colour according to the partner to which it is mated.

The Table which follows shows the colour expectations from the pairing of dogs and bitches of the various colours occurring in Dachshunds. Pure-bred individuals are designated by colour only. Those which are impure for colour are indicated by the inclusion, in parenthesis, of the hidden, or recessive, colour they carry. It should be understood that the ratios given cannot be relied on to appear exactly in a single litter.

COLOUR BREEDING EXPECTATIONS

Colours Mated	*Offspring*	*Remarks*
Red × Red.	All Red.	
Red × Black and Tan.	All Red (carrying Black and Tan).	Red is dominant to Black and Tan in Dachshunds.
Red (carrying Black and Tan) × Black and Tan.	50 per cent Red (carrying Black and Tan), 50 per cent Black and Tan.	
Red (carrying Black and Tan) × Red (carrying Black and Tan).	25 per cent Red, 50 per cent Red (carrying Black and Tan), 25 per cent Black and Tan.	
Black and Tan × Black and Tan.	All Black and Tan.	
Chocolate × Chocolate.	All Chocolate.	
Chocolate × Black and Tan.	All Black and Tan (carrying Chocolate).	Black and Tan is dominant to Chocolate.
Chocolate × Black and Tan (carrying Chocolate).	50 per cent Black and Tan (carrying Chocolate), 50 per cent Chocolate.	
Black and Tan (carrying Chocolate) × Black and Tan (carrying Chocolate).	25 per cent Black and Tan, 50 per cent Black and Tan (carrying Chocolate), 25 per cent Chocolate.	

COLOUR BREEDING EXPECTATIONS (*continued*)

Colours Mated	*Offspring*	*Remarks*
Chocolate × Red.	All Red (carrying Chocolate).	Red is dominant to Chocolate.
Chocolate × Red (Carrying Black and Tan).	50 per cent Red (carrying Chocolate), 50 per cent Black and Tan (carrying Chocolate).	Red and Black and Tan are both dominant to Chocolate.
Black and Tan (carrying Chocolate) × Red (carrying Black and Tan).	25 per cent Red (carrying Black and Tan), 25 per cent Red (carrying Chocolate), 25 per cent Black and Tan (carrying Chocolate), 25 per cent Black and Tan.	
Black and Tan (carrying Chocolate) × Red (carrying Chocolate).	25 per cent Red (carrying Black and Tan), 25 per cent Red (carrying Chocolate), 25 per cent Black and Tan (carrying Chocolate), 25 per cent Chocolate.	
Red (carrying Chocolate) × Chocolate.	50 per cent Red (carrying Chocolate), 50 per cent Chocolate.	
Brindle × Brindle.	All Brindle.	
Brindle × Red.	All Brindle (carrying Red).	Brindle is dominant to Red.
Brindle × Black and Tan.	All Brindle (carrying Black and Tan).	Brindle is dominant to Black and Tan.
Brindle (carrying Red) × Red.	50 per cent Brindle (carrying Red), 50 per cent Red.	
Brindle (carrying Red) × Brindle (carrying Red).	25 per cent Brindle, 50 per cent Brindle (carrying Red), 25 per cent Red.	
Brindle (carrying Red) × Black and Tan.	50 per cent Brindle (carrying Black and Tan), 50 per cent Red (carrying Black and Tan).	Brindle and Red are both dominant to Black and Tan.
Brindle (carrying Red) × Brindle (carrying Black and Tan).	25 per cent Brindle, 25 per cent Brindle (carrying Red), 25 per cent Brindle (carrying Black and Tan), 25 per cent Red (carrying Black and Tan).	

COLOUR BREEDING EXPECTATIONS (*continued*)

Colour Mated	*Offspring*	*Remarks*
Brindle × Chocolate.	All Brindle (carrying Chocolate).	Brindle is dominant to Chocolate.
Brindle (carrying Red) × Chocolate.	50 per cent Brindle (carrying Chocolate), 50 per cent Red (carrying Chocolate).	Brindle and Red are both dominant to Chocolate.
Brindle (carrying Black and Tan) × Chocolate.	50 per cent Brindle (carrying Chocolate), 50 per cent Black and Tan (carrying Chocolate).	Brindle and Black and Tan are both dominant to Chocolate.

COLOUR EXPECTATIONS IN BREEDING DAPPLES

The dapple pattern desired for show purposes represents the intermediate state arising from crossing dapple and white with one of the solid colours. The dapple and white colouration is incompletely dominant to solid colour, the progeny being devoid of white markings, or nearly so. Expectations are, therefore:

Colours Mated	*Offspring*	*Remarks*
Silver Dapple and White × Black and Tan.	All Silver Dapple, without White.	
Chocolate Dapple and White × Chocolate.	All Chocolate Dapple, without White.	
Dapple × Dapple.	25 per cent Dapple and White, 50 per cent Dapple, 25 per cent solid colour.	
Silver Dapple × Black and Tan.	50 per cent Silver Dapple, 50 per cent Black and Tan.	
Chocolate Dapple × Chocolate.	50 per cent Chocolate Dapple, 50 per cent Chocolate.	
Silver Dapple × Chocolate.	50 per cent Silver Dapple (carrying Chocolate), 50 per cent Black and Tan (carrying Chocolate).	

Having shown the results expected in mating the various colours, it is necessary to add a few explanatory remarks to cover cases which may appear to be contrary to the general rule. First a word or two on Dominance. In the Table red is stated to be dominant to black and tan. That is, if a pure-bred red is mated to a black and tan, all the resulting litter will be red. But the shade of red shown by the progeny will probably differ somewhat from that of the red parent. That is because, though red is dominant to black and tan, it is not completely so. The presence of the gene for black and tan appears to exert a modifying influence, so that, instead of being clear red, the pups will show some admixing of black hairs in the coat. The extent to which the black hairs are developed may vary in individuals. Some of the pups may be definitely shaded, or show something approaching a "trace" along the back, whereas others may have to be closely examined before any black hairs are apparent. Similarly, though brindle is dominant to red, the Red × Brindle mating is likely to give pups of a lighter, or less strongly striped, kind of brindle than that which comes from the pairing of two brindles. The matter may be further complicated by the occurrence of ancillary genes which modify the depth of pigmentation.

Among Dachshund breeders the belief that it is inadvisable to continue to mate red to red indefinitely, or to breed chocolate to chocolate, has for long been widely held. All the older breed writers upheld these views; holding that the constant mating of red to red results in the weakening of pigment, so that the colour becomes pale and dull, possibly with the appearance of white patches on the chest and feet. The mating of two chocolates was said to produce washy colour with a preponderance of pink noses and very light eyes. There is, however, no reason why such undesirable results should occur provided both the selected mates are rich and deep in colour. A dark red put to a mate of similar colour should, however many generations of red to red breeding may be behind each, give litters of the same strength of pigment as the parents show. A red may, however, carry a modifying gene, the presence of which is responsible for the development of pale colour, and if put to a mate similarly constituted will be likely to breed pups much poorer in colour than itself. In choosing a mate for an individual whose pigmentation shows any indication of weakness it is, therefore, advisable to select one of particularly rich, deep colour. For that reason the dictum that a pale red should be mated to a black and tan is sensible, though a really deep red mate would probably serve as well. The mating together of chocolates is on the same plane. There can be no objection to it so long as both partners are of rich, dark colour. But immediately colour shows signs of paling, recourse should be had to a black and tan cross to neutralize the effects of the modifying factor, the presence of which is becoming apparent. Such a cross will, of course, give only black and tan pups, if the black and tan mate is pure-bred for that colour. Reference to the Table will show that from pups so bred chocolates may be produced by putting them either to chocolates or to black and tans which, like them, carry chocolate in their genetic make up.

Another much-discussed subject is whether it is safe to mate a chocolate to a red. Red, as has been said, is dominant both to black and tan and chocolate, so that if the red parent is pure-bred for colour, all the whelps resulting from such a mating will be red. If the red parent carries black and tan as a recessive, the litter may be expected to contain both reds and black and tans, but no chocolates. Dark eyes are dominent to light eyes and black nose to brown or pink nose, so that in the Red × Chocolate mating all the pups will show the dark eyes and black nose which, we will assume, their red parent possesses. There is nothing against the mating so far. Trouble is likely to come when the offspring of the cross are bred from. If put to mates which carry the gene for chocolate there is a risk that light eyes or brown noses may occur in some of the pups which are of colours other than chocolate, since these characters may be inherited separately from the chocolate coat colour. Breeders who contemplate mating reds to chocolates should, therefore, bear in mind the necessity of ensuring that the offspring of such matings are put to mates free from chocolate blood.

The brindle, or striped, coat pattern is rarely seen in Smooths, but a few specimens have been shown in recent years and have attracted considerable interest. The colour is, of course, quite common in the Long Haired variety and from the information I have it seems very probable that all the brindle Smooths bred in this country owe their coat pattern to Long Haired ancestors. There should be no difficulty in fixing the colour in Smooths. Brindle is dominant to all other colours, so that a Long Hair that is pure-bred, or doubly dominant (DD), for brindle will breed whole litters of its own colour to any Smooth to which it is mated. The puppies will be Smooth and if mated to other Smooths of different colours will breed brindle pups in the proportion of fifty per cent brindle to fifty per cent other colours. By repeatedly mating the best brindles in the litters thus produced, either *inter se* or to other colours, a stock of brindles could quickly be built up and, by selecting the best to mate together, a true-breeding strain of typical brindle Smooth Dachshunds might be established in a few generations.

The breeding of dapples and of white Dachshunds presents special problems which call for fuller treatment, so that it has been deemed desirable to devote a separate chapter to the subject. (*See* page 109.)

In the inter-breeding of the different coats, Smooth is dominant to Long Hair and Wire is dominant to both Smooth and Long Hair. The expected results, therefore, are shown in the table on page 108.

In the Smooth × Long Haired cross the Smooth coat appears to be completely dominant. I have seen many litters bred in that way but I have never been able to detect any suggestion of additional hair length, or of softness of coat, in the progeny. Similarly, Long Haired specimens bred from two Smooths each of which carries the gene for the Long Haired coat, are indistinguishable from Long Hairs bred from two individuals of that variety. The appearance of an odd Long Haired puppy in a litter bred from Smooth parents, both of which are known to have been Smooth-bred for many generations, is often a source of great astonishment to breeders. The explanation of the occurrence should now be clear. The Long Haired coat is recessive to Smooth and can, therefore, be shown only by individuals carrying two genes for its development. A Smooth carrying a single gene for Long Hair if mated to a pure-bred Smooth can never produce a Long Haired puppy. The character may remain hidden in its carriers for innumerable generations without its presence being suspected. If, however, the carrier is mated to another Smooth which also carries the recessive Long Hair gene, a proportion of Long Haired pups is likely to appear, no matter how many generations have succeeded one another since the Long Hair blood was introduced on each side. In other words, the Long Haired coat can only be developed if the gene which governs its production is present in the genetic make-up of both parents; or, to put it more plainly, it must occur on both sides of the pedigree, though how far back it occurs is immaterial.

The dominance of the Wire coat over the Smooth is sometimes somewhat imperfect. Dogs bred from this cross may have rather shorter, harsher coats than pure-bred Wires, which is

EXPECTATIONS IN INTER-BREEDING DIFFERENT COATS

Coat Crosses	*Offspring*	*Remarks*
Smooth × Long Hair.	All Smooth (carrying Long Hair).	Smooth coat is dominant to Long Haired coat.
Smooth (carrying Long Hair) × Long Hair.	50 per cent Smooth (carrying Long Hair), 50 per cent Long Hair.	
Smooth (carrying Long Hair) × Smooth (carrying Long Hair).	25 per cent Smooth, 50 per cent Smooth (carrying Long Hair), 25 per cent Long Hair.	
Wire × Smooth.	All Wire (carrying Smooth).	Wire Hair is dominant to Smooth coat.
Wire × Wire (carrying Smooth).	50 per cent Wire, 50 per cent Wire (carrying Smooth).	
Wire (carrying Smooth) × Wire (carrying Smooth).	25 per cent Wire, 50 per cent Wire (carrying Smooth), 25 per cent Smooth.	
Wire (carrying Smooth) × Smooth.	50 per cent Wire (carrying Smooth), 50 per cent Smooth.	
Wire × Long Hair.	All Wire (carrying Long Hair).	Wire Hair dominant to Long Hair.
Wire (carrying Long Hair) × Wire (carrying Long Hair).	25 per cent Wire, 50 per cent Wire (carrying Long Hair), 25 per cent Long Hair.	
Wire (carrying Long Hair) × Long Hair.	50 per cent Wire (carrying Long Hair), 50 per cent Long Hair.	

all to the good. A judicious introduction of Smooth blood into the Wire Haired variety can do much to improve both coat-texture and general type. Some of the most successful exhibits of pre-war days were bred in this way. The Wire × Long Haired cross is not advised as, though the offspring show the Wire type of coat, it is usually too soft, full and fluffy.

CHAPTER XII

THE DAPPLE AND THE WHITE DACHSHUND

THE dapple is one of the oldest of Dachshund colours. It is, indeed, probably as old as the breed. The German authority Jester, writing in 1797, refers to the dapple Dachshund as being equally esteemed with the red and the black and tan; the only other colours he mentions. Exactly when the first dapple reached this country is uncertain. The earliest of which we have knowledge is a dog named Tiger Reinecke, born in 1888 and imported from Germany by Major Harry Jones in 1890. This dog created great interest and was widely used at stud. Until 1896 all the most successful dapples appear to have been descended from him. In 1896 Mr. G. R. Krehl imported the silver dapple Unser Fritz, born in 1893. He, too, proved very successful both in the show ring and as a sire and did much to sustain interest in the colour. In 1901 Mr. A. Tooth brought over a very beautifully marked dog which was registered as Wengel-Ermannsheim. Other dapples were, no doubt, imported between 1890 and 1914, but the three dogs named were the most important and left their mark most strongly on the variety.

The First World War, as we have seen, wrought sad havoc among Dachshunds of all colours. Its impact on the dapple was especially tragic. At the end of the conflict only one dapple remained, a dog named Pied Piper, owned by Mrs. Saunders. In 1923, when ten years old and almost blind, he was mated to a bitch, Kardotta, and sired two outstanding puppies, one chocolate and the other silver dapple. The dapple became Champion Foxsilver, generally considered to have been the best of his colour bred in this country. He had a long and brilliant show career, in the course of which he won five challenge certificates and over one hundred prizes in competition with all colours. Every existing dapple owns this remarkable dog as an ancestor and owes its colour to him.

Today the dapple is not receiving the support it merits. Perhaps the chief reason for this is that few modern exhibitors know what a good specimen should look like. Even many of our judges seem to have very little knowledge of what is required, and no detailed description is given in the Standard. Briefly, a perfectly marked silver dapple should have the whole ground colour of the coat bright silver grey, made up of a mixture of black and white hairs in about equal proportion. This gives a roan effect, similar to that seen in a light blue-roan horse. On this light ground irregular shaped patches of black should be evenly distributed, in much the same way as are the dark markings of a harlequin Great Dane. The patches should vary in size from small to medium, but no part of the head, body or limbs should show any large, unbroken area of black devoid of silver roaning. As a rule, tan markings are shown on the head, chest and legs, as in black and tans. In chocolate dapples the ground colour consists of a mixture of chocolate and silver-white hairs and the patches are chocolate. No white is permissible in the show dapple except for a small spot on the chest. The red dapple is like the chocolate, except that the coloured hairs in the ground colour and the solid patches are deep red. In silver and red dapples the nose must be black; in chocolate dapples it is brown. Eyes may be brown or wall, that is blue or whitish.

Often one eye is brown, the other wall. This also is correct. For perfection the eye colour should tone in with the hue of the surrounding area. If that part of the head in which the eyes are set is of solid colour, the eyes should be brown, but if the eyes are surrounded by a silver or roan area they should be wall. A blue or whitish eye set in a head which is almost wholly black or brown gives a dog a staring expression which is very unattractive.

The breeding of show dapples has always been regarded as a gamble, but it need not be so. It is as easy to ensure the production of whole litters of dapples of the colour desired for show purposes as it is to breed all red or all black and tan litters. I have already explained that the show dapple, which must not show white markings, represents the intermediate stage between the dapple and white, the dominant form, and the black and tan or chocolate which is recessive to it. That means that to get whole litters of show dapples it is necessary to mate a dapple and white to one of the whole colours. All the progeny will be free from white and will, of course, carry the genes for both dapple and white and the whole colour in their genetic make-up.

Years ago, when dapples were more widely owned than at present, double dapple matings were frowned on by breeders on the grounds that they almost invariably gave a proportion of white-marked puppies, which were then regarded as useless either for showing or breeding. All such mismarked whelps were destroyed at birth or given away as pets. To avoid the appearance of these "wasters" the mating of dapples to black and tans or chocolates became the accepted practice. But this mating cannot be relied on to give all dapple whelps. The theoretical expectation is fifty per cent dapple and fifty per cent whole colour, but often fate is unkind and the result is a litter of black and tans with, perhaps, one lone dapple.

Many breeders appear to regard black and tans bred in this way as especially valuable in future breeding operations, on the supposition that, being dapple-bred, they must carry the factor which produces the dapple coat pattern and will, therefore, breed a larger proportion of dapple pups than will black and tans which have no dapple ancestors. This is a fallacy. No black and tan, whatever its breeding, can carry the genes that give the dapple markings. Any Dachshund which inherits the dapple factor from either of its parents will show it in its coat pattern. If the gene is received from only one parent the individual concerned will be silver or chocolate dapple (DR); if the genes are contributed by both parents the dog will be dapple and white (DD). The development of a whole-coloured coat, whether black and tan, chocolate or red, proves conclusively that no factor for the dapple pattern is present. This point may at first seem of little practical interest, but when we turn to deal with the problem of improving type in our dapples the realization that the dapple-bred whole colour has no value as a potential source of coat pattern is of the greatest significance.

At present very few dapples are capable of winning the highest honours in competition with other colours. Most breeders will agree that the main obstacle in the variety's path to greater popularity is the need of improving its general type. All the dapples known to exist in this country trace back to a common ancestor and most, if not all, show the same sort of failings in make and shape. The most obvious way to effect improvement would be to out-cross to the most perfect line-bred specimens of other colours. But in the past breeders have been very unwilling to adopt this course, believing that it would lead to deterioration in markings, if not to the total disappearance of the distinctive pattern. In selecting whole-coloured mates for their show dapples they have tended to keep rigidly to individuals possessing dapple ancestors, thereby restricting their operations within a very limited field. The appreciation of the fact that a whole-coloured bitch, bred from a long line of whole-coloured ancestors whose pedigree is innocent of dapple blood, is capable of producing the same proportion of dapples in a litter bred to a dapple dog as is one which comes from an inbred strain of dapples, at once opens the way to rapid progress in the upgrading of type. If this principle is firmly grasped the day of the dapple Champion should not be far off. It is high time for the practice of the old-time breeders to be operated in reverse. Instead of cherishing the whole colours which crop up in dapple-bred litters and discarding the dapple and whites, the whole-coloured pups should be got rid of and the best of the white marked dapples put to the best out-cross solid-coloured mates that can be procured. This would give whole litters of dapples (without white markings) and the puppies might be expected to show some, at least, of the desirable qualities of the whole-coloured parents and to carry factors for other excellencies which, though not apparent in their own physical make-up, they would be capable of transmitting to their progeny if suitably mated.

The chocolate dapple has always been admired and most breeders of dapples are eager to revive it. This need present no special difficulties. In all dapples coat colour depends on two quite separate factors. On the one hand there is the gene complex which governs the ground colour and on the other that which gives the broken pattern. In Dachshunds chocolate is recessive to other whole colours but dapple is, as we have seen, dominant to the unpatterned coat. Bearing these two facts in mind the chances offered by various matings of producing chocolate dapples may be readily forecast. In the absence of chocolate dapple stock the most suitable mating would be silver-dapple-and-white × whole-chocolate. This would give a litter of silver dapples. The pups will all be dapple because that coat pattern is dominant to solid colour and they will be silver dapple because black and tan is dominant to chocolate. Silver dapples bred in this way will, if mated together or put to solid chocolates, breed a good proportion of well-marked chocolate dapples. Another suitable mating would be silver dapple to chocolate. Here the expected result would be fifty per cent silver dapple and fifty per cent black and tan. The dapples could be mated together or to chocolates to produce a proportion of pups of the desired colour.

Attempts have been made on the Continent from time to time to establish true-breeding strains of white Dachshunds. All have failed. Recently several British breeders have embarked on the task but little progress can yet be reported. The most likely way to breed a pure-white specimen is to mate two dapple and whites. Such a mating usually gives a litter in which one or two pups are almost devoid of markings, and by inbreeding these all-white specimens might be bred in a generation or two. Whites bred in that way would, however, have blue eyes and pink or butterfly noses which it would be very difficult to breed out. The production of a white Dachshund with dark eyes and black nose is a task which calls for great patience, a good knowledge of genetics and a good deal of luck. The few that have been bred on the Continent are believed to have owed their immaculate coats to a terrier cross. This method may give quicker results so far as the fixing of dark eyes and nose are concerned but with the loss of Dachshund type, which it would take many generations of very careful breeding to get back. Except through the appearance of an unpredictable sport or mutation, the coming of the true-breeding dark-eyed, black-nosed white Dachshund in our lifetime is in a high degree improbable.

CHAPTER XIII

PRINCIPLES OF BREEDING

BEFORE dealing with the care and selection of breeding stock and the rearing of puppies, it is advisable to glance briefly at the fundamental principles which the breeder should understand before arranging the matings intended to produce litters of future winners. The particulars given of the history of the different Dachshund varieties in previous chapters show that the number of blood-lines represented in any variety is small. From this it follows that almost all the dogs and bitches in any one breed are related in some degree. A novice without much breed knowledge, who confines the examination of pedigrees to three or four generations, may see little evidence of this, but if the family trees are extended the truth of the statement becomes apparent. Thus it is virtually impossible to breed good Dachshunds without employing consanguineous matings.

Dog breeders are prone to draw a sharp distinction between what they call inbreeding and line-breeding. By the first they mean the mating of such near relatives as brother and sister, sire and daughter, or dam and son. The term line-breeding is used to describe the pairing of more distant relatives. Such a distinction is, however, based on a wholly wrong conception of genetics. Much is heard of the evils of inbreeding and the desirable results to be expected from line-breeding, but if the one is condemned it is completely illogical to uphold the other, for the same results may be achieved by each method. Whether those results are good or evil will depend not on the relationship of the individuals mated but on their inherited qualities. This may be demonstrated by a simple example. Let us suppose that a pure-bred red dog is mated to a black and tan bitch. The litter will contain only red puppies. If from that litter we mate a brother and sister, we may get a litter of reds and black and tans in the proportion of three to one. That result would be obtained were we to pair two totally unrelated specimens bred the same way for colour as were our litter brother and sister. The same principle applies to all the various points, good and bad, that a Dachshund can possess.

Those who hold up their hands in horror before the bogey

of inbreeding base their aversion on the supposition that the mating together of close relatives invariably leads to loss of stamina, impaired intelligence, impotence, sterility and general weakness. How or why this should occur is not explained. When challenged, these antagonists of inbreeding seek to justify their prejudice by claiming it to be based either on their own experience or on that of people known to them. If such results come with inbreeding the responsibility rests not with the system but with the breeder, who has employed unsuitable breeding stock. Inbreeding of itself can create no new characteristics. All it can do is to sift out and intensify points or traits, both good and bad, already present in the strain in which it is practised. The danger is that it will bring out, or emphasize, hidden faults as well as latent virtues.

When sketching the early history of the Long Haired Dachshund in this country I recalled how the intensive inbreeding of Ratzmann von Habichtshof with his daughters and grand-daughters, made necessary by the absence of any other representatives of the breed, gave rise to the appearance of badly overshot mouths in the second and subsequent generations. Both Ratzmann and his daughters out of Gretel III von Lechtal had perfect mouths and there was no reason to expect the fault to occur in their inbred progeny. That the fault did occur showed it was carried by the parent stock, though in a hidden, or latent, form. Had this Ratzmann stock been bred to unrelated mates, the existence of the fault might have remained unsuspected for many generations. It was not created but only rendered visible by inbreeding. Had there been another blood-line available and the Ratzmann stock been mated to it, the overshot mouths would not, in all probability, have appeared in the first generation of the cross, and had the progeny of that cross been bred back to the non-Ratzmann line the fault might not have cropped up for years. But when, in subsequent breeding operations, the Ratzmann blood was introduced on both sides, the trouble would have become manifest as surely as it did in the early stages of inbreeding. Yet in that case the overshot pups would have been produced by line-breeding, which shows that the same results may come from that system as from inbreeding, though it takes longer for them to become apparent.

It is impossible in the space here available to deal with the genetics of dog-breeding in detail. For a full explanation of the principles governing canine inheritance, and how they may be applied by the practical breeder, the reader is referred to my *Dog Breeder's Manual*, in which the subject is considered at length. The brief explanation of the nature and behaviour of dominant and recessive characteristics given in the last chapter will, however, suffice for our present purpose. There it was explained how the development of red coat colour or of a Smooth coat may be the expression of the presence of the genes which control the appearance of those features in either single or double doses. What we call the pure-bred red or the pure-bred Smooth carries the appropriate genes in duplicate (DD), whereas the impure red or the impure Smooth carries them only in the simplex state (DR). The various show points required in a Dachshund are, with hardly any exceptions, expressions of the doubly dominant condition and nearly all faults are recessive. A long-bodied dog mated to a short-bodied bitch may sire puppies having longer bodies than their dam but with less length than their sire. That is because, though the genes which produce length of body are dominant, they are not completely so; the DR condition being more or less intermediate between the DD and the RR, that is between the pure-dominant and the recessive. This appears to apply to most characteristics in our breed. If we mate two of the offspring of this breeding we may expect to get one pup in four as long in body as its grandsire, two of the other three of about the same length as their parents and one resembling its grand-dam in this respect. This is the Mendelian ratio, explained in the last chapter, of 1 DD, 2 DR, 1 RR.

The breeder of pedigree stock is, of course, dealing not with one but with several hundred, possibly thousands, of individual characteristics, but all depend for their development on the way in which genes are brought together in mating. The ambition of most breeders is to breed litters consisting entirely of puppies that, with good rearing, will grow into adults capable of holding their own in keen ring competition. Genetically that means that all matings must be arranged with the object of ensuring, so far as may be possible with the breeding material available, the production of animals that are doubly dominant, or genetically pure, for all the qualities demanded by the Standard.

The ideal Dachshund, then, if we exclude the dapple coat pattern needed for show purposes, which is, as has been shown, the expression of imperfect dominance (DR), will be doubly dominant, or homozygous, for all its good points. Such a dog, were it ever produced, would not only be itself faultless, it would pass all its good qualities to all its offspring. This super-dog could only be bred by a system of long-continued in-breeding accompanied by rigorous selection, or culling, in every generation.

In a number of animals of any breed taken at random nearly related individuals are likely to be genetically more similar, in that they have more gene combinations in common, than those bred from parents of totally different blood-lines. Each may be pure, or homozygous, for certain characteristics and impure, or heterozygous, for others, but their genetic make-up will almost certainly be closer than those of unrelated pairs. By mating close relatives the good and bad points represented in their strain will both be accentuated, so that in the first generation their offspring may be as good as, or better than, their parents in some respects but less good in others. But if the best of the progeny be selected and bred back to one of the parents, or paired with its litter mates, the good points will be retained and some, at least, of the faults become less marked. By continuing such a breeding programme and by weeding out all specimens showing definite faults in each generation, a general upgrading of type may be achieved much more quickly and surely than could be effected through the fortuitous mating of unrelated stock.

Perhaps the main reason for the prejudice felt by some breeders against inbreeding is that their opinions are based on results obtained in its initial stages. The first results may be disappointing because of the emergence of faults which had remained latent, and therefore unsuspected, in the strain, as in the case of the overshot mouths referred to above. If inbreeding is continued further, with ruthless culling in the second and subsequent generations, improvement will be progressive and rapid and the value of the system clearly demonstrated.

From what has been said it should be abundantly clear that inbreeding can only be attended by satisfactory results if carried out in a strain free from glaring faults. If the initial stock is faulty its failings will be emphasized and become more strongly fixed in succeeding generations. Provided, however, that the parent stock is suitable and only the best of the progeny is used for breeding, faults will gradually be eliminated and type will become more uniform and stabilized as increasing numbers of individuals are produced of the same hereditary formula. Eventually a genetically pure strain should be built up that can be relied on to breed true for its own type.

The claim that inbreeding must sooner or later lead to loss of vigour, mental degeneration, impotence or any other aberration is without foundation. If such defects appear it is because the original breeding stock carried the taint in its genetic make-up, though it may not have been apparent. The breeding together of two related individuals will bring such failings to light only if they are latent in the strain. The mating of tainted parents, whether they are related or not, will, of course, produce the same results, but inbreeding certainly increases the likelihood of such hidden recessives being brought into prominence. To the thoughtful breeder this is an advantage rather than the reverse, for it indicates the potential as well as the obvious merits and demerits of the strain being used or built up. Knowledge so gained may be of the greatest significance in determining the line to be taken in future matings.

Outcrossing implies the mating of unrelated partners, which are almost certain to be widely dissimilar genetically. It is, therefore, the reverse of inbreeding. The most drastic kind of outcrossing occurs when a dog of entirely foreign blood-lines is imported from abroad and mated to home-bred bitches, or when two different varieties, like the Smooth and the Long Haired Dachshund, are interbred. Lesser degrees of outcrossing are made when a dog and bitch of different British strains are mated, for, though not closely related, they will, as a rule, have some ancestors in common, so that their blood-lines merge in part somewhere in their pedigrees. Just as continuous inbreeding makes for uniformity of type, so outcrossing tends to bring about wide variation. It is almost impossible to forecast with any certainty the results of mating unrelated animals, and for that reason outcrossing is always something of a gamble. The immediate results may be highly satisfactory but type may deteriorate alarmingly in the second and later generations unless rigid control is exercised. Nevertheless there are times when the need to outcross becomes urgent.

As has been shown, it is the height of folly to inbreed with stock which is itself faulty or which comes from a strain carrying glaring faults. If the foundation stock is mediocre, type must be improved by a system of outcrossing and careful selection until a general level of quality has been reached that justifies inbreeding. The way to do that is to examine the animals to be mated, both from the view-point of their own good and bad points and of those represented in their genetic make-up, and to put them to mates which excel in those points in which their partners fail and are known to come from strains in which those excellencies are fixed. The pups may be expected to show combinations of the good points of their parents in varying degrees. Should that be the case, the best of the offspring should be mated together or to a relative of either the sire or the dam, according to which is nearer the type it is desired to fix. The second generation will give a surer indication as to whether the outcross has been successful than will the first. If results are satisfactory the blending of the blood-lines represented should be continued, but if the grandchildren of the original parents are faulty a further outcross must be tried. By following this system with determination, and breeding only from the best individuals in each generation, a line may be built up on which a programme of inbreeding may be safely based.

Recourse must also be had to an outcross when a fault or weakness has emerged and become fixed with the desirable points in an inbred strain. In deciding on the outcross to be used in such cases care should be taken to select an individual possessing as many of the merits of the strain into which it is to be introduced as possible. This is best ensured by using a dog which is of similar, though not identical, blood-lines, if that is possible. The less drastic the outcross the better, provided it will give the required results. Having made the outcross and corrected the strain-fault, the breeder should revert to inbreeding, by mating the outcrossed progeny to genetically pure members of the original strain and exercise very careful selection in the resulting litters.

Line-breeding may be said to represent a system intermediate between inbreeding and outcrossing. The animals mated are less closely related than in inbreeding, so that a larger number of gene combinations must be expected to occur in their progeny. The attainment of type-uniformity is, therefore, less certain and must take longer to achieve. The only advantage it offers is that faults are less quickly brought to light and fixed. Good qualities are also stabilized more slowly, so that variation in general type is likely to persist. Thus, though line-breeding may be attended by fewer dangers than inbreeding when practised by an inexperienced or casual breeder, it can achieve nothing that cannot be obtained with greater speed and certainty by carefully controlled inbreeding.

To sum up on the vexed question of inbreeding, I would again stress that such a system can only be satisfactory if applied to typical stock possessing a high degree of genetic purity, and that it must be attended by rigorous selection in each generation. Mental as well as physical traits are fixed in a strain by inbreeding, so that culling must be carried out with due attention to such failings as lack of intelligence, nervousness, impotence and sterility, as well as to more obvious show points. The belief that inbreeding is the cause of weakness or degeneration is quite wrong. Any aberration that may be revealed by it must be latent in the strain concerned, and is not created by the mating of close blood relatives.

Since the great majority of inborn faults seen in Dachshunds are recessive to the points desired, it is clearly foolish to mate two animals showing the same imperfection, for all their offspring will be certain to show it. To correct a fault in a bitch it is not sufficient to put her to a dog that is free from that fault; care must also be taken to see that he comes of a strain that is without that particular weakness. That is where pedigrees are valuable. To many these documents represent little more than lists of names and give no real information as to the breeding potentialities of the dogs to which they apply. That is why the present practice of issuing pedigrees covering only three generations has been accepted without much comment. Such brief particulars are next to useless to anyone without enough breed knowledge to know what lies behind the names mentioned. The prospective buyer of stock, or patron of a stud dog, should insist on a six-generation pedigree being provided. Having secured this it will be well worth while to trace the ancestry back still further if serious breeding is contemplated.

But however many generations a pedigree may cover, it can be of little significance unless something is known of the dogs recorded. The novice should, therefore, set out to acquire all possible information about the ancestors of the stock on which it is proposed to found a kennel, noting each item as it is collected against the name of the dog to which it relates. If that is done conscientiously an immense amount of breed knowledge may be obtained which will be of inestimable value when the time comes to arrange matings. Knowledge of pedigrees, however profound, is not of itself enough to indicate the results to be expected from the pairing of two individuals. That knowledge must be supplemented by the examination of the animals concerned, for only in that way can an assessment be made of the degree in which the good and indifferent qualities carried by their forbears have been inherited by each and are likely to be combined in their offspring. With information gathered from both sources a breeder should be able to make a reasonably accurate forecast.

As from 1 January 1977, it is no longer permissible to register a Dachshund that is the result of a mating of two Dachshunds of different varieties. It is, however, still possible to register "recessives"—such as a Long bred by chance from two Smooths—under the variety they resemble.

J.V.C.

CHAPTER XIV

SELECTION OF BREEDING STOCK AND MATING

THE success of a kennel will depend in large measure on the quality of its foundation bitches. That truism is often completely overlooked by the novice breeder. A mediocre bitch is unlikely to bear outstanding puppies however she is mated, and should she produce progeny much better than herself they will be unreliable as breeding material. In choosing a brood both pedigree and appearance must be taken into consideration. Good looks without good breeding are as valueless as is a high-sounding pedigree attached to a weedy, unsound animal. That does not mean that it is necessary to limit the choice to bitches that have won honours in the ring. A sound, healthy bitch which, though not superlatively good in all points, shows no bad faults and comes from a strain known to produce a high proportion of winning specimens, is to be preferred to one with an imposing show record but of indifferent breeding. The would-be purchaser should look for a sound, typical, robust bitch with a pedigree which suggests that her immediate ancestors were a good deal better than she is. Bitches of this kind are not hard to find if patience and thought are brought to the task. Too often the beginner is so eager to make a start that he, or she, is tempted to buy the first bitch offered and later learns by hard experience how unwise was the purchase.

It is probably true to say that none of the many illusions common among dog-breeders has caused more disappointment or contributed more heavily to kennel losses than that which holds the sire's influence to be all-important in determining the quality of a litter. Each parent contributes equally to the genetic constitution of their offspring. The idea that any sort of bitch mated to a super-dog will breed winners is sheer nonsense. The influence of the dam may, indeed, be the greater. The nature of the contribution made by each depends entirely on their genetic make-up and how their hereditary units come together in fertilization. Great care should, therefore, be bestowed on the choice of the brood bitch.

The ideal brood is perhaps one of from two to three years

old that has had at least one litter and proved herself an easy whelper and a good mother. If typical and well bred, such a bitch will, of course, cost a good deal more than a younger, untried maiden, but the additional outlay is well worth while. A year-old bitch shortly due in season for the second time is the next best. The danger is that she may prove difficult to mate, sterile, a difficult whelper or an unsatisfactory mother. If, however, she is healthy, well ribbed, with good breadth fore and aft, and comes from a line of fecund ancestors, there should be little risk. Young puppy bitches are less expensive, but they are also more chancy. For a novice to buy a puppy from the nest to lay the foundation of a kennel is like buying a ticket in a lottery. Up to the age of six months or so Dachshunds are very difficult to assess and the younger the puppy the more difficult the task. Whatever the age of the bitch she should be as good as can be procured with the funds available. It is wiser to pay a high price for one really good bitch of the right breeding than to use the same amount to purchase two or three inferior ones. Low-priced bitches usually prove very costly bargains in the end.

In a Dachshund bitch required for breeding head points are of less importance than are body properties. Good bone, breadth and depth of ribbing, strong loins and roomy quarters are the main essentials. Shy, timid bitches are to be avoided, as are those which show a tendency towards obesity or sluggishness. An active, alert bitch in hard condition should be chosen in preference to one that is placid to the verge of lethargy and is soft and fat. Young bitches that run to flesh are apt to be irregular in their periods and may prove unreliable as breeders or have difficulty in whelping.

A bitch usually comes in season for the first time between the ages of six and nine months. Some do not experience their first heat till well over a year old, but the majority do so before their tenth month. Delay in the occurrence of the first oestrum need cause no concern. It does not necessarily indicate any abnormality and may not affect the regularity of subsequent heats, which should recur every six months or so; though this interval, too, is subject to considerable variation. A bitch that does not experience her first heat till over a year old and thereafter goes ten or twelve months between seasons may suffer from some form of sexual inertia and should, therefore, be viewed with suspicion until her suitability as a brood has been proved.

A Dachshund bitch should not be bred from till at least a year old. If she does not come in season till after that age there is no reason why she should not be bred from at the first opportunity, provided she is sufficiently well developed. Bitches, like dogs, vary much in the time they take to reach their full growth, and the condition of the individual concerned must govern the decision as to when a maiden bitch should be mated. Breeding usually stops growth, so that unless a bitch is well grown at her second heat, mating should be delayed till the next period. If, however, she is of full stature and strong but still looks shallow because her keel has not dropped, a litter will improve her. Some Dachshund bitches lack that finish that should come with maturity until they have been bred from. After whelping the chest comes down, the body shows better modelling and in the Long Haired variety the whole appearance is enhanced by the growth of a longer coat with fuller feathering. There should be no danger in breeding from a healthy, well-grown bitch at any time after her first birthday and before she is three years old. Maiden bitches over three are likely to have a bad time whelping, particularly if they have been allowed to get fat.

The period of heat is heralded by a swelling of the vulva and a discharge. At first the discharge is colourless but later becomes reddish, owing to the admixture of blood derived from the breaking down of the walls of the uterus in preparation for the attachment of the fertilized eggs from which the embryos will develop. The coloured discharge usually lasts about ten days, after which it becomes colourless and much less copious. The best time to mate a bitch is within a day or two of the disappearance of the colour from the discharge. Some bitches will accept service at almost any time during their heat period, but as a rule they are most eager at from the eighth to the fourteenth day. To ensure conception and a full-sized litter it is best, whenever possible, to arrange the mating on the tenth or eleventh day.

One satisfactory mating is sufficient. Some breeders like to have two but there is little point in this except where the first is thought to have been ineffective or the bitch is a maiden. Should a second service be considered desirable it should occur within forty-eight hours of the first. If a bitch is mated too early her litter may be smaller than it would have been had service occurred later. The reason is that the ripe ova are released from the ovaries, singly, towards the end of the first week of oestrum. If the mating takes place before the eighth day all the ova may not have been expelled and only those which have reached the oviducts are fertilized. This is not invariably the case, however, for the semen ejected by the dog may remain active in the reproductive passages of the bitch for several days, so that ova dropped after copulation may be fertilized.

The size of the litter depends on the number of ripe ova present in the oviducts and is, therefore, governed wholly by the bitch. The commonly held idea that the dog is responsible for the number of pups born is fallacious. The semen ejected by the male in a normal mating contains many millions of sex cells, or spermatazoa, each capable of fertilizing an egg-cell. In comparison with this prodigious production of sperms the number of ova furnished by the most fecund bitch is very small, so that all should be fertilized by any male that is not impotent. The claim sometimes made by owners of stud dogs that their stallions have consistently sired large litters reflect no special merit on the dogs concerned. It merely indicates that the bitches sent to them have been highly fecund.

The belief that the date of mating influences the sex of the puppies is another delusion. There is no known method of controlling sex in the offspring. The production of a preponderance of progeny of one sex may be characteristic of a strain or of an individual, and special attention to the feeding and general health of a bitch before the onset of heat may help to ensure the survival of a good proportion of dog pups, but in general the average number of dogs and bitches born is about equal.

One of the most common causes of bitches missing today is the too hurried manner in which matings are performed. In the old days, before motor transport was in universal use, a bitch was sent to the owner of the stud dog a couple of days before the date arranged for the mating, so that she had time to rest and settle down in her novel surroundings. After service she was kept for a further twenty-four hours or so before being sent home. The present tendency is to leave matters to the last moment, then rush the bitch over to the dog, effect a mating immediately, then rush her back on the return journey. Such treatment, at a time when the bitch is in a highly nervous condition, must be extremely unsettling, and for a young bitch experiencing her first mating, or for one that is naturally highly strung, must be mentally and physically exhausting.

If the bitch is to be taken to the stud dog by her owner, arrangements should be made for her to arrive at least an hour or two before service. After being rested she should be exercised so that the bladder and bowel may be emptied. When all is ready, the two partners to the mating should be put together in an enclosure large enough to enable them to play and romp together. The bitch will quickly show whether she is willing to accept the dog and, in most cases, if the bitch is at the right period in her heat, mating will occur without trouble and with little or no supervision. During the tie which usually accompanies copulation the bitch must be prevented from sitting down and the dog should be so placed that he stands naturally, with his hindquarters against the rear of the bitch. Each should be held gently but firmly by its owner till separation takes place. The tie may last from ten to forty minutes. On the completion of mating the bitch should be offered a drink and left to rest for an hour before being taken home. If breeders would follow this unhurried routine in all matings many fewer bitches would fail to prove in whelp than is at present the case.

A maiden bitch may be spiteful towards the dog, meeting his advances with vicious snaps. If she has been in season for between ten and fourteen days, such a bitch should be muzzled by having her jaws tied with soft, broad tape. Should she refuse to stand her hindquarters must be supported, by passing the right hand under the abdomen with the fingers between the hind legs, while service is effected. But if less than ten days have elapsed since the first onset of heat, it is better to take the bitch away and try again a day or two later, rather than attempt a forced mating. If the dog appears to have difficulty in effecting penetration the bitch should be examined for stricture by passing a well-greased finger into the vagina. The obstruction may be easily broken down, but care must be taken to use the minimum of force and to ensure that the nails are closely pared, so that no damage may be done to the tender tissues of the vaginal passage. Once the stricture has been dilated a satisfactory service may be secured immediately.

A stricture higher up, at the orifice of the uterus, is more difficult to deal with and a novice will do well to have a maiden bitch examined by a vet. a day or two before she is to be mated, so that any obstruction present may be removed, if necessary by the use of instruments. Conception may be inhibited by an acid reaction of the mucor of the vaginal walls. This destroys the male sex cells before they reach the uterus and is a frequent cause of missing. The acid condition may be neutralized by douches of diluted solution of bicarbonate of soda. The bitch should be tested forty-eight hours before mating, so that the necessary treatment may be given in good time. This douching is so effective and so harmless that it should be carried out with all bitches as a routine safeguard.

In the event of a bitch missing, it is customary for the owner of the stud dog to give a second service free. But the owner of a bitch should clearly understand that this concession cannot be claimed as a right unless a definite agreement to that effect is made. Strictly speaking, the fee paid is for the stud service, irrespective of whether the bitch has a litter or not. Should the owner of the stud dog agree to take a puppy in lieu of the usual fee, a written statement of whatever is arranged should be kept. In some cases first pick of litter may be demanded, in others the second and third choice, or the pick of the pups of one particular sex. Except in special circumstances, it is unwise for a novice to enter into any such agreement, for any one of the pups in a litter arising from a well-planned mating should be worth a good deal more than the stud fee. Unless it is, the mating must be regarded as having proved very unsatisfactory. But if an arrangement of this kind is made the terms agreed to should be clearly stated in writing and should include a clause defining at what age the choice is to be made and delivery of the puppy taken. This is important. I have known several cases in which a breeder has been forced to keep the whole of a litter long after the surplus youngsters could have been sold because the person with the right to take first pick has failed to appear to select and remove his or her puppy.

On returning home the mated bitch should be treated as usual for the first four or five weeks of her pregnancy. Provided her normal diet includes a high proportion of lean meat and she is in good condition, there is no need to offer her extra food at this time. If she is too thin and needs building up, any additions to her menu should take the form of meat or raw eggs. Bitches vary a good deal in their appetites after being mated. Some become ravenous, but the majority show little if any increased desire for food till after the first month. Novices are apt to make the mistake of overfeeding in-whelp bitches. The bitch should be kept in firm, hard condition and given plenty of exercise till her increased girth makes it advisable to control her gambols. Road-work should be given daily; an hour at a time being enough to keep her hard and fit. An in-whelp bitch is not an invalid and should not be coddled. The longer she can be encouraged to keep up her normal routine the better.

At the end of the fifth week a thickening of the flanks and a general rounding of the body will indicate that a litter is to be expected. Such signs may be noticeable after the fourth week or may not be apparent till the end of the sixth, but most Dachshund bitches give evidence of approaching maternity between the thirty-fifth and the fortieth day. From now on the food may be increased. The bitch should be given as much as she will eat, and as she increases in girth it is better to give her smaller meals at shorter intervals than to fill her to capacity once or twice per day. Cod-liver oil, if not included in her usual diet, should now be added; a dessert-spoonful each day is enough for a Dachshund of Standard size. As her time approaches the bitch may be less inclined to take bulky food and should then be given raw egg, milk, bone soup and generous rations of chopped raw meat.

After the sixth week it may be necessary to put some restrictions on the bitch's activity. Some Dachshunds are very foolhardy at this time, indulging in romping and wild play despite their matronly proportions. If kept in the house the mother-to-be must be prevented from ascending or descending steep stairs, from jumping to or from heights of more than two feet and from trying to squeeze through narrow openings. She should also be secluded from too boisterous companions. Less strenuous exercise should, however, be encouraged and the daily road walk continued as long as it causes no inconvenience or distress to the bitch. Adequate exercise will usually keep the bowels working freely, but should there be any tendency towards constipation small doses of liquid paraffin will put matters right.

By the end of the sixth week it is usually possible to detect the presence of the puppies by manual examination. The bitch should be laid on her side and the hand passed along the abdomen, when a number of small, hard, globular swellings may be felt. As the embryos grow they may be located by the same method as the bitch stands on the ground. It is, however, difficult, if not impossible, to be sure of the number of whelps present, as those placed high up in the uterine horns may easily be missed. The only way to make quite certain of the number to be expected is to have the bitch X-rayed. In the

(H. J. Fountain)

Ch. Drakesleat Scarlet Woman
(*Miniature Wire*)

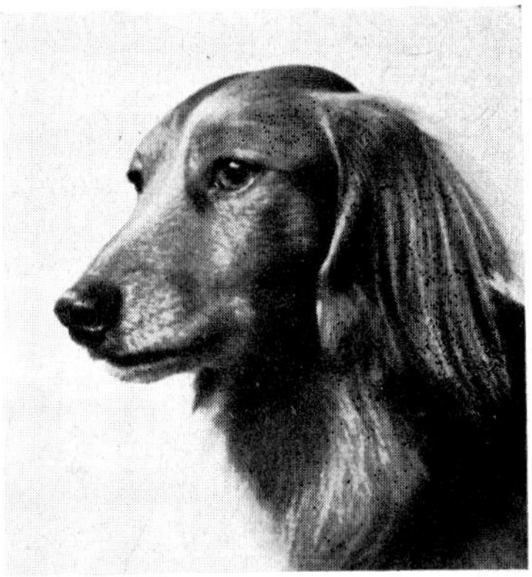

(Donald Allan)

Ch. Marcus of Mornyvarna
(*Miniature Long*)

(C. M. Cooke)

Ch. Primrosepatch Jasper
(*Miniature Long*)

(F. Marshall)

Ch. Robsvarl Red Robin
(*Miniature Long*)

(J. K. Knowles)

Ch. Minutist Mikado
(*Miniature Long*)

(Diane Pearce)

Ch. Glenmoris Sovereign Maid
(*Miniature Long*)

(*C. M. Cooke*)

Ch. Jane of Sillwood at 9 months
(*The first Miniature Wire to become a champion*)

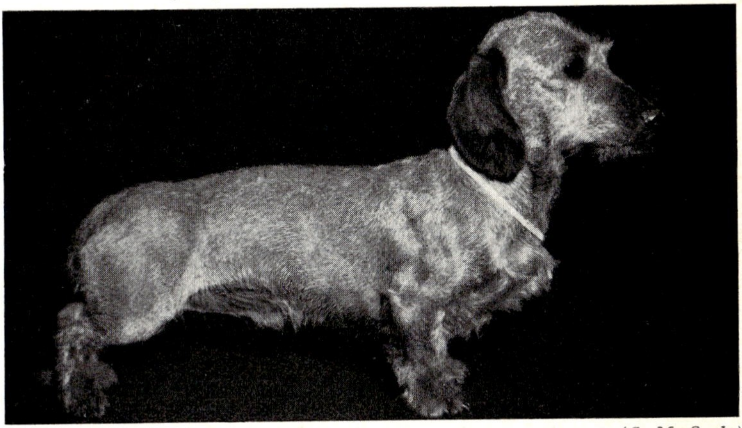

(*C. M. Cooke*)

Ch. Peredur Pimento
(*Miniature Wire*)

(*H. J. Fountain*)

Ch. Drakesleat Ai Jail
(*Miniature Wire*)

(*Anne Roslin-Williams*)

Ch. Limberin Leading Light
(*Smooth*)

Ch. Limberin Loud Laughter
(*Smooth*)

(*Diane Pearce*)

Ch. Jackanordie Val'n'tine
(*Miniature Long*)

case of maiden bitches which promise to have unduly large litters it is wise to have this done. The X-ray plate will show the number and exact positions of the foetuses and enable the vet. to make advanced preparations for dealing with any difficulty or abnormality that may be expected. Many bitches and litters are lost at whelping through veterinary assistance being called at the last moment after parturition has started, so that drastic emergency measures have to be employed.

Little need be said here regarding the treatment of the stud dog, beyond stressing the danger of using a male for breeding before he is fully mature. A dog that is forward and well grown may be used once between the ages of ten and twelve months. Some dogs become restless and fretful at that time if they are kept within sound or scent of a bitch in season, and a mating serves to quieten them and prevents their losing appetite and condition. But not more than two services should be permitted till the dog is over a year old, and he should not be used regularly at stud before he is eighteen months or two years of age. The premature use of a dog for stud purposes arrests development and may cause impotence in later life. A stud dog, like a brood bitch, should be kept in lean, hard condition, fed on a diet of high protein content and should not be overshown.

In choosing a stud dog the breeder should remember that the prepotent male, that is the dog that is likely to transmit his own good qualities to his progeny in fullest measure, looks robust and masculine and shows an assertive demeanour. The effeminate or "bitchy" dog is rarely successful at stud, though his air of ultra-refinement may gain him high show honours. In assessing the suitability of a dog for a particular bitch, due regard must be given both to his appearance and his breeding. Because a dog has sired winning progeny to bitches of one line or strain, it by no means follows that he will do equally well when mated to bitches of different breeding. The value of a stud dog should be gauged by the average quality shown by all his offspring, not by the merits of one or two outstandingly good ones. These may have come from a particularly good bitch and owe their excellence to their dam rather than to their sire. Finally, the novice should be warned against rushing to use the latest champion merely because he is the latest champion. He may be entirely unsuitable for the bitch to be mated and, despite his own good looks, may be of much less value as a potential sire than a dog whose show record is much less impressive but whose pedigree is more satisfactory.

CHAPTER XV

WHELPING AND AFTER

THE full period of gestation in a bitch is sixty-three days but puppies may be born any time after the fifty-ninth day. If parturition occurs earlier the whelps rarely live or, should they do so, require very special attention. Most Dachshund bitches whelp from the sixtieth to the sixty-second day. The whelping box or kennel should be prepared and the bitch accustomed to it at least a week before the family is expected. This is important, for most Dachshunds have very definite ideas of their own and if put into an unfamiliar kennel when whelping is almost due will often make strenuous efforts to break out so that their pups may be born in a place of their own choosing. A bitch may injure herself and her unborn babies gravely in trying to escape from a strange place of confinement to which she has been introduced for the first time only a few hours before her litter is due.

The whelping kennel should be so situated as to afford quiet and a sense of security. A nervous bitch may be greatly distressed by unaccustomed noises, or by the intrusion of strangers or other dogs at this time. The whelping box should be warm, comfortable and free from draughts, and big enough to allow the bitch to stretch out at full length. It should be placed in a dimly lit corner; for Dachshunds prefer to whelp in conditions bearing some resemblance to the dark holes or caverns chosen for the purpose by their wild ancestors. For the actual whelping the floor of the box should be provided with a cushion or small palliasse made of sacking or crash, stuffed with wood-wool or clean, chopped wheat straw. Before whelping starts a loose piece of sacking may be placed on top of the palliasse and removed when all the litter has arrived, leaving the bitch and her newly born family on a clean, warm bed. Sheets of paper are sometimes used in the whelping box, but they are likely to become sodden and messy and may be a great nuisance should parturition be difficult or prolonged. The object of using a coarse material like sacking is to enable a youngster that has been accidentally pushed aside to crawl back to its dam; the rough fabric affording easy purchase for the scrabbling claws.

Parturition often occurs at night or in the early morning hours. If a bitch seems restless when left at night, she should be visited once or twice between midnight and dawn in case labour starts and assistance is needed. Dachshunds vary greatly in their behaviour as their time draws near. Some become very excited and at intervals may be almost hysterical. They may roam from room to room or dash round their kennels, scratching in corners and tearing up their beds, two or even three days before labour begins. Others take matters very quietly until the last moment. A novice who is kept on tenterhooks by the erratic behaviour of a young bitch should have her examined by a veterinary surgeon three days before whelping is expected. At that time it is usually possible to form a reasonably accurate opinion as to whether whelping will occur within twelve, twenty-four, forty-eight hours or longer.

When whelping is imminent a bitch will usually sneak away to her box and lie quiet. She may stretch out at full length with her head on her paws for a time but soon start up whimpering and begin to pant. As labour pains increase she will turn her head apprehensively towards her flanks, perhaps biting or licking herself. Then she may curl up with her hindquarters pressed against the sides of her box. The vulva is swollen and there is a thick mucous discharge. If the labour pains are sustained the first pup may be born within half an hour of these symptoms, but if the pains pass, or are weak and intermittent, birth may be delayed for several hours. Bitches whelping for the first time are usually longer in labour than are matrons. At this stage all unnecessary interference should be avoided.

If left to herself a normal, healthy bitch will manage matters unaided, but if the owner remains fussing over her the mother-to-be may renounce all responsibility and let everything be done for her. On the other hand, an unobtrusive watch should be kept, so that should help be needed it is immediately available. If no pup has been born after two hours from the onset of labour the bitch should be examined. Should a membrane-covered obstruction be visible at the vagina all may be well. This membrane is the envelope in which the puppy is enclosed and its appearance at the genital aperture indicates that matters are progressing normally. But if no such object can be seen, or birth does not occur within the next two hours, assistance may be given by inserting a finger, grasping the puppy behind the head and pulling steadily as the bitch strains. This may be all that is required to bring the puppy through, and when the first has been born the remainder of the litter may follow quickly and without further trouble.

It often happens that the first whelp is considerably larger than the others and cannot be expelled normally. If the bitch is left to exhaust herself by fruitless straining the whole of the litter may be lost. The breeder should, therefore, be prepared to give speedy assistance in cases of this kind, when a veterinary surgeon is not in attendance. Before any manipulation is attempted the vagina should be injected with liquid paraffin and, if difficulty is experienced in getting a hold on the puppy with the bare hand, a piece of soft flannel of suitable size will be found of great assistance in enabling the slippery surface to be grasped. It is important that traction should be applied only when the bitch strains—unless, of course, she is past helping herself at all. In normal delivery the head with the extended forefeet appears first and, once the head is through, the rest of the body follows easily. Where a whelp is wrongly placed, as when the head is bent downwards against the chest or when the hind legs come first or the body lies transversely across the womb, delivery is much more difficult and calls for skilled veterinary aid. Such assistance should, indeed, be within call at every whelping, particularly if no X-ray examination has been made, as even with bitches that have whelped easily on previous occasions it is impossible to be sure that nothing will go wrong.

Delayed parturition arising from the unusually large size of the first puppy may, as has been said, be dealt with successfully by prompt and dextrous manipulation, but that is not always possible. A veterinary surgeon may be able to remove the obstructing youngster piecemeal but such measures are far beyond the powers of the amateur, whose unskilled attempts may cause the death of both the bitch and the other unborn puppies. In some cases it may be deemed expedient to perform the Caesarean operation, that is to open the uterus and extract the young. The operation is safe and does not affect the bitch if carried out before she has been weakened by long, fruitless straining. Within two or three hours of the operation the bitch should be fit to receive and nurse her litter and should settle down to her maternal duties as happily as if she had whelped naturally. A Caesarean section in no way affects a bitch's value for future breeding. Many bitches that have to undergo the operation with their first litters whelp easily and without assistance on subsequent occasions.

Birth may be unduly delayed by the absence or weakness of labour pains. Sometimes a bitch will start to strain but become inactive after a short time and, though the pains may recur, they may be too intermittent or weak to produce the desired result. Uterine inertia of this kind is not uncommon in young bitches. It is usually dealt with by injecting Pituitrin in suitable doses under veterinary supervision. Labour may sometimes be induced or accelerated by the application of hot compresses to the abdomen, or by sustained massage. In the days of horse transport a popular method of speeding the arrival of an overdue family was to take the bitch for a jolty ride in a farm cart!

When the first pup has been born the others usually follow at intervals of from twenty minutes to three hours. In a normal litter of four or five, whelping may be completed in two hours or so, but if the litter is very large the whelps may be born in batches. After the first four or five have appeared, labour may abate for a time before the rest of the family begin to arrive. A bitch that is whelping naturally should be left undisturbed until all the pups have been born, but should she seem exhausted or distressed before parturition has been completed she may be offered a drink of warm milk into which a little brandy has been stirred.

As a puppy is born the mother will rupture the membrane, bite through the umbilical cord and lick the youngster to induce it to breathe. If the bitch is too exhausted to attend to a whelp, the enveloping membrane must be opened above the nostrils and gently worked off the body. The cord should be ligatured with white silk, rather less than an inch from where it is attached to the abdomen, and cut with sterilized scissors. Special care must be taken to ensure that no portion of the afterbirth slips back into the womb, as this may cause inflammation of the uterus or other grave complications. As soon as it has been released, the pup should be dried by rubbing with a piece of soft flannel and made to breathe. Respiration may often be started by opening the puppy's mouth and blowing several times down its throat, or the forelegs may be moved backwards and forwards and the chest and abdomen briskly massaged. Another method is to tap the ribs sharply with a cold wet cloth. In cases of difficulty a drop of brandy on the tongue will generally bring a response even from a pup which seems lifeless. As soon as its first cry has been heard the pup may be placed in a flannel-lined box on a hot-water bottle covered with a blanket.

Under normal conditions it is unnecessary to remove the puppies as they are born. Some breeders prefer to do so, putting each in a warm box or basket as it arrives till the bitch has finished whelping. The object is to prevent the first-born being injured or pushed aside to get cold while the dam is attending to later comers. The precaution is wise when a bitch is known to be clumsy or is whelping for the first time, but as a rule the mother is very careful and may be worried by the removal of the whelps. Should it be considered advisable to move the pups as born, the box containing them should be placed near the bitch, so that she may have ocular and aural evidence that her first-born have not been taken from her. Unless this is done she may try to get out of her bed to search for them while parturition is still in progress.

When all the pups have arrived the dam may be offered a dish of warm milk food, but if she is disinclined to take it no persuasion should be attempted, for during the first twenty-four hours after whelping very little food is needed. She should be made comfortable on a clean, warm bed and left undisturbed with her new family. For the ensuing two days only liquid food should be given, in the form of one of the proprietary milk products specially prepared for dogs or thin gruel. This will enable the stomach to regain its tone, clear the alimentary canal and help to keep the temperature down. On the third day a little wholemeal rusk or fine biscuit meal may be given in broth, beef tea or milk, with a raw beaten egg, boiled fish, stewed rabbit or similar easily digested food. At the end of the week raw meat may be added to the menu. For a fortnight the bitch should receive four meals each day, so that the stomach is not overburdened.

Until the milk flow is well established bulk should be avoided in feeding, but the diet, though light, should be highly nourishing. Cod-liver oil and a little calcium in the form of the precipitated phosphate, lactate or gluconate should be given throughout the time the bitch is suckling, to ensure strong bone development in the pups. Some breeders include calcium in the menu of the bitch during the period of gestation. In my view that is unwise, for it may result in the abnormal growth of one or two of the unborn whelps and give rise to difficulties in whelping. There is no point in encouraging growth unduly prior to birth. Provided they come into the world well formed, strong and lusty, medium-sized pups are to be preferred to very large ones and heavy bone can be obtained by suitable feeding after birth, if the youngsters are bred from the right stock.

The discharge from the vagina should cease after the third day, but there is no need for alarm if it continues for a day or two longer. Should it go on beyond that time the bitch may be syringed twice daily with a tepid solution of ten grains of burnt alum to each ounce of water. If after the third day the discharge is copious and accompanied by a high temperature, veterinary advice should be sought at once, as this condition indicates uterine inflammation, which calls for early treatment. For the first few days some looseness of the bowels is natural and desirable, but if it persists castor oil should be given. The reverse condition, constipation, should it arise while the bitch is nursing her pups, should be corrected by doses of liquid paraffin rather than by the use of chemical purges.

During the early days of maternity the dam is usually disinclined to leave her family even for the short periods necessary for her to relieve herself. She must, however, be taken out for five minutes or so four times each day. After the third day the periods may be increased to a quarter of an hour or longer and at the end of the first week she should be taken for regular walks and encouraged to spend some time in the open. Plenty of free exercise is most essential to stimulate lactation and to keep the bowels working freely. If the bitch is too closely confined at this time her milk flow may be adversely affected. She is also likely to lose interest in her puppies after a time, or may succumb to nursing fits, or parturient eclampsia, from which she may never wholly recover.

A strong Dachshund bitch of standard size will rear up to six puppies without trouble. For a Miniature the maximum should be fixed at four or, at the most, five. Should it be desired to rear all the whelps in larger litters the surplus must be transferred to a foster or fed by hand. The foster may be a bitch of any breed, provided she is about the same size as the dam whose offspring she is required to wet-nurse and has whelped at about the same time. As a rule she will take readily to her new charges. The best method is to mix the two litters in a small box and roll them about together, so that the youngsters to be adopted acquire the scent of the foster's own puppies. The exchange is best made after the bitch has settled for the night. Usually the new whelps are accepted without trouble, but matters must be watched, for the foster may at first show resentment against the newcomers. If she nuzzles them to her and starts licking them all may be expected to go well. In an emergency, as when a bitch dies during or soon after whelping, has no milk or for some other reason is unable to nurse her puppies, and a foster bitch is not available, a cat may be used. A good-sized cat will rear two Dachshund pups up to the time they can be taught to lap, and such a nurse, being very gentle and careful with her charges, is especially suitable for small, weakly or Miniature whelps.

The hand-rearing of puppies is not difficult but involves much labour and calls for immense patience. For the first week the babies must be fed at intervals of two hours through the day and night and must be kept in a temperature of between seventy and seventy-five degrees. If in a kennel, the box in which they lie should be lined with flannel and contain a hot-water bottle covered with a blanket. The most suitable food for hand-rearing is one of the dried milk preparations specially manufactured for puppies. Goat's milk to which a little lime-water has been added is a good substitute. Failing these the yolk of an egg beaten in half a pint of cow's milk may be recommended. Each puppy should receive a small teaspoonful of food at each meal, taking from ten to twenty minutes to swallow that amount. Feeding may be done with one of the special spoons made for the purpose or by means of a fountain-pen filler. Later the pups may be taught to suck the food through a rubber teat at the end of such a pipette. At seven days the interval between feeds may be increased, if the youngsters are feeding well, and at a fortnight a meal every four hours will suffice. After being fed each pup must be cleaned with cotton wool dipped in a weak solution of some non-carbolic antiseptic. Bowel action may be stimulated by massaging the abdomen and rectum with a piece of warm, moist flannel or a wad of cotton wool, in imitation of the action of the dam, which licks her whelps vigorously in these parts after they have fed to induce defaecation. Should this fail, a drop or two of olive oil or liquid paraffin may be dropped on the tongue after a feed.

The bearing and rearing of five or six lusty pups naturally imposes considerable strain on a bitch, so that it is essential to give her ample time to recover strength and condition before breeding from her again. An interval of at least twelve months should elapse between her litters, which in practice means that she should not be mated more often than at alternate heats. That is the maximum. A breeder whose aim it is to breed only strong, healthy puppies, and to retain the services of a bitch as a brood as long as possible, should adopt the system of taking not more than two litters in three years. With such treatment a bitch that is kept in good condition without being allowed to get fat may be expected to remain fecund up to the age of eight or nine years. A bitch that has her first litter when between one and two years old, and is, thereafter, bred from regularly, is likely to have a longer life as a brood than is one that is not mated till later in life and is afterwards used spasmodically. Most Dachshund bitches are at their best for breeding purposes between the ages of two and six years, but there is a danger in mating a maiden bitch after she is three years old. Such a bitch is likely to have great difficulty in whelping and, should the experiment be made, special precautions should be taken for skilled veterinary assistance to be available when her time draws near.

CHAPTER XVI

REARING DACHSHUND PUPPIES

THE rearing of young stock is beset with pitfalls. That is true of all breeds of dogs as well as of other domestic animals, and in none does it apply with greater force than in the case of Dachshunds. The best puppy ever whelped may be ruined for show purposes by bad rearing, while a mediocre one may be improved out of all recognition by skilful attention to such details of nurture as feeding, housing, exercising and grooming. For the first three weeks there is little to worry about if the dam is healthy and her milk flow satisfactory. Difficulties may arise, however, even during this normally trouble-free time. After a meal a pup should look plump, with well-filled stomach, and, having sucked its fill, should relapse into deep sleep. If it refuses to feed for more than a few minutes at a time, is fretful, restless or thin, the milk is probably acid. Acidity may be tested for by moistening a piece of blue litmus paper with a drop of the milk. If the paper turns red a good teaspoonful of bicarbonate of soda should be added to each pint of liquid food or water given to the bitch, or she may be given daily doses of milk of magnesia or citrate of soda. Milk acidity may often be corrected in a few days, but should it persist it may be necessary to feed the pups by hand for a time or to wean them prematurely. Slight acidity, though not sufficiently pronounced to cause the pups to refuse to feed, may give them milk rash, in which the skin becomes dry and scabby in patches. The addition of bicarbonate of soda to the diet of the dam will soon put things right and the bare patches on the pups will quickly respond to treatment with an oily skin dressing. Drugs or medicines administered to the dam may affect her young through the milk. For that reason it is inadvisable to dose a nursing bitch except for giving her liquid paraffin, or some such mechanical laxative, should the need arise.

After having suckled her litter successfully for ten days or so, a bitch sometimes shows impatience when the pups try to feed. This may be due to sore or cracked nipples. Relief may be given by bathing the teats with warm boric lotion. When the parts have been dried they should be dusted with boracic powder or anointed with a healing ointment. This trouble may be caused by the puppies pulling at the breasts with their claws, which grow surprisingly quickly and become needle-sharp. Their nails should be examined each week and clipped if necessary. The dam's nipples should be looked at daily and any soreness or small abrasions dealt with immediately they appear. If the nipples are allowed to become badly cracked and painful the bitch may have to be rested and drained for a few days and the pups fed artificially.

Dachshund pups that are born with dew claws on the hind feet should have these surplus growths removed when three or four days old. At that age the operation is a very slight one. Simply cut the unwanted digits off at the joint with a pair of sharp surgical scissors. The tiny wounds may be dabbed with an antispetic and will heal in a few hours. The eyes begin to open between the eighth and the twelfth day. If they are still closed on the fourteenth day they should be bathed with boric lotion. Until the eyes are fully open puppies should be kept in semi-darkness. In a box placed in full daylight the eyes may remain closed for two or three days longer than is normal, or if opened earlier the pup may suffer from eye strain. The eyes and noses of very young puppies are kept clean by the tongue of the dam. Should there be any discharge it must be kept clear by frequent swabbing with boric lotion. If there is a gummy discharge from the eyes and the eyelids become stuck together a small fragment of golden eye ointment should be inserted in the eye and the lids held together till the salve has been distributed over the eyeball.

At the end of the third week the milk teeth pierce the gums. By this time the pups will have grown considerably in size and strength. They should be well on their legs and crawling about the nest. As they continue to grow they may cause the dam distress by their ceaseless efforts to feed at all hours; dragging at her and giving her no rest. If the nesting box is large it may be now divided into two parts by a board fixed across it from side to side. The board should be low enough for the bitch to jump over easily but sufficiently high to prevent the youngsters from following her. This will provide a refuge to which the dam may retire when she wishes to get away from the importunities of her rapidly growing family. In a room or large kennel a bench raised about two feet from the ground will serve the same purpose.

When the milk teeth are through, the pups should receive their first solid food in the form of fine scraped, lean, raw meat.

A teaspoonful each is enough at first, the meal being given before the dam is returned to the kennel after being out for exercise. The first lesson in lapping should also be given now. Each pup should be taken in turn and placed before a dish of milk food, a little of which should be smeared on its lips and nose. This will be licked off and when the pup has got used to the taste its nose may be gently dipped into the dish. After a few sneezes the puppy will probably begin to lap. Some learn quicker than others, but if the lesson is repeated daily all will be lapping well in a week and from then on one meal a day may be given in this way. The dam may now be removed for longer periods and when five weeks old the puppies should be having three feeds a day, one of raw, minced meat, the other two of milk food, in addition to those supplied by the bitch. At the end of the sixth week four such meals should be given, two of them consisting of raw meat, and in another week the puppies should be weaned, the meals being increased to five and the dam left with the litter only at night.

Puppies that are given small meals of meat and milk food from the age of three or four weeks will suffer no set-back when the time comes to wean them, for they will have been gradually accustomed to solid food. Milk should be given in the form of one of the proprietary products supplied for kennel use. Failing that goat's milk, or the egg-and-milk mixture already referred to (*see* page 136), may be used. Cow's milk by itself is most unsuitable. Compared with bitch's milk it is very deficient in fats and other solids and invariably causes distension of the abdomen, diarrhoea and other digestive disorders. After the sixth week crushed wholemeal rusk or fine biscuit meal may be given soaked in milk, or in broth from which the fat has been skimmed, and a bone or hard dry biscuit is useful in exercising the jaw muscles and to ensure the sound development of the teeth. Cod-liver oil and calcium should be given in small daily doses from about the fifth week and continued till growth is complete.

The amount of food given at each meal must be carefully regulated. It must be sufficient to satisfy the puppy without distending the abdomen and any that is not eaten quickly should be removed. The slovenly practice of leaving food dishes in kennels from one meal to another is a fertile source of puppy troubles. At eight weeks four good meals, of which the first and third may consist of milk food with soaked rusk or biscuit meal and the second and fourth of raw or lightly cooked meat and stale brown bread moistened with good stock or gravy, will suffice. As an occasional change herrings, stewed rabbit or raw eggs may replace the meat at one meal, and a dish of warm milk food may be offered last thing at night to a puppy that seems to need a little extra feeding.

Each puppy should be fed from a separate dish. This is important. Dachshund puppies are usually good trenchermen and if the whole litter is fed from one trough the stronger whelps will get more than their fair share while the smaller, less assertive, or slower feeders will go short, or be tempted to bolt what food they can snatch as quickly as possible, with dire results to their digestive systems. Four meals per day should be given until the pups are four months old, the food being made less liquid as the teeth develop. The meat may be minced at first, then given cut up into small pieces and later in lumps. The rusk or biscuit may be given moist or dry as the puppies grow, but sloppy food should be avoided as soon as more solid meals can be dealt with satisfactorily.

When six months old the pups should be ready to go on to the adult diet and the meals may be reduced to two. Meat should form at least half of the daily food intake, by weight. Many fully adult Dachshunds are fed wholly on meat and do very well under that regime, but some farinaceous food may be necessary to prevent to dog losing flesh.

In general a satisfactory daily menu for an adult may be based on three-quarters of an ounce of food for each pound the dog weighs; from half to three-quarters of this amount being given as raw or lightly cooked meat.

If the dog tends to put on too much weight reduce the farinaceous ingredients; if, on the other hand, it looks too light in condition, increase the bulk and cut down the meat, but not lower than half the weight of the whole. A meat and wholemeal diet supplemented by cod-liver oil will keep an adult Dachshund in health. The only vitamin deficency that may arise is in the B complex. This may be remedied by the use of one of the veterinary yeast products, which are strongly to be recommended for keeping dogs free from skin eruptions, preventing loss of appetite and sluggishness and for improving the coat. This food supplement may be given with advantage from weaning time onwards.

At three weeks old puppies should be treated for round worms. It is impossible wholly to prevent infection by these intestinal parasites, and they should be eradicated before the pups are weaned.

Should the presence of worms be suspected in very young puppies, a few drops of garlic oil given each morning is a safe and satisfactory remedy. Bathing the dam's breasts and underparts with a non-poisonous antiseptic solution before she goes back to her whelps after a spell of exercise will help to minimize the risk of worm-infection.

The permanent teeth erupt through the gums at from the twelfth to the sixteenth week. The milk teeth usually drop out as the second dentition appears, but should some of them remain to obstruct the growth of the later ones they should be drawn, otherwise the mouth may become uneven through the permanent teeth being twisted or displaced. The provision of large bones or hard biscuits will help to loosen the milk teeth, which are not deep-rooted, and aid the development of the second set. In the comparatively rare cases where the cutting of the adult teeth is difficult or slow a puppy may have teething fits, during which it staggers about frothing at the mouth, then collapses on its side kicking violently, or dashes round yelping and screaming. Immediately the first symptoms are observed the puppy should be given five grains of bromide of potassium and put in a quiet, dark place away from companions. For three days following the fit the diet should be light and a dose of bromide should be given each morning for a week to prevent a recurrence.

From the age of three weeks puppies should have all the sunlight possible, but great care must be taken to guard them from draughts. When they are strong on their legs they may be put out in a run or pen, with a box in a sheltered corner to which they may retire to sleep immediately their energy flags. They should be encouraged to romp and play in the open when the weather is suitable and given opportunities of becoming used to new sights, sounds and experiences. Close confinement will slow down their growth and may tend to make them shy, nervous and stupid. The ground on which the pen is placed should be level and free from deep holes, and should contain no box or other object low enough for them to jump on to. Tumbling into holes or jumping on and off a box may injure the legs and shoulders of very young Dachshunds, causing the forelegs to become bent, the pasterns weakened or the feet splayed. The wire surrounding the pen may with advantage be boarded to a height of two feet or so to prevent the youngsters dragging at it with their claws and teeth. All

Dachshund puppies delight in digging. This is a perfectly natural form of exercise and should not be discouraged. If the youngsters have been well reared and are structually sound no harm will come of it and they will derive immense enjoyment from the game. Digging helps to develop the muscles of the forequarters, to strengthen the feet and to foster the hunting instinct.

The lightly boned, rather short-bodied, mediocre puppy is easy to rear. This type rarely goes unsound and can commit all sorts of physical indiscretions without showing much deterioration. It is the heavy-boned, long-bodied youngster that needs the most care. Even with the most vigilant attention it may be very loose in shoulders and rather uncertain in hind action up to and beyond the age of six months. After being plump up to three months old it may get thin as it grows in length, and show no improvement from week to week, so that from being the obvious pick of litter it becomes more and more the ugly duckling. The breeder should not, however, abandon hope. This type of puppy, often a dog, will in all probability eventually come right if fed and exercised with discretion, and allowed to take its own time. Such a puppy should not be parted with lightly. If it has heavy bone and great length, with nicely rounded ribbing and a good top line, its general looseness may be ignored till after its first birthday. It is this type of dog that often grows into an outstanding adult, combining great substance with length, lowness to ground and general quality. A slow developer may not be fit to show till well out of puppyhood and will not be at his best till three years old, but he will last much longer than his more precocious litter mates which are almost fully made up as puppies. A bitch of the type described may look immature and rather light in body till after she has had a litter.

A Dachshund should not be taken for walks until six months old. If kept in a kennel run with a concrete floor its feet should be hard and strong and its shoulders sufficiently set at that age to be able to stand up to regular roadwork. Patience is needed to teach a six-months-old puppy to walk on a lead without pulling or hanging back. If it is nervous or very fractious at first it should be taken out with its dam. The two may be on separate leads or may be coupled together. As a rule, after a few preliminary struggles, the puppy will go where its parent leads and after a few outings will lead well on its own. Violent pulling must be curbed at once, otherwise roadwork will do far more harm than good. The length of road walks must be regulated according to the behaviour and condition of the puppy. At first a quarter of an hour may be sufficient, but as the muscles harden and puppy fat disappears each spell should be extended to half an hour and later to an hour, which should be the minimum amount of hard roadwork given to all adults. To be effective roadwork must be regular. It is far better to take a dog out for half an hour every day than to give it an hour and a half or two hours two or three times a week. Regular exercise of this kind will harden and thicken the pads, keep the feet tight and the nails short, improve the shoulders and strengthen the quarters. If a young dog is inclined to be weak or narrow behind, a daily spell of walking uphill on hard roads may bring about a marked improvement and will also help to broaden the front.

All Dachshunds kept for show purposes need daily roadwork, yet this is one of the details of kennel routine most generally neglected. It is hardly too much to say that a good eighty per cent of the faulty feet seen in our rings could be greatly improved by hard road exercise. When the feet have been allowed to become soft, open or weak, the pasterns will begin to give and the elbows to be thrown out. The long claws tend to cause the toes to lose their arch and the foot looks thin. When that condition has been reached it may take some considerable time to put right. As a first step the nails should be shortened and if the pads are very soft they may be hardened by immersing the feet in a solution of alum for ten minutes daily. After drying, the pads may be dusted with powdered alum. Half an hour's roadwork should be given twice a day and gradually increased as the wrists strengthen and the feet become harder and tighter. No amount of road-walking will turn a badly constructed foot into a good one, but an hour each day will enable the foot faults to be kept to a minimum.

When the puppies have been weaned and are well on solid foods, the breeder may find it necessary to dispose of some of them and will be faced with the thorny problem of which to sell and which to retain. In a previous chapter I said that the selecting of Dachshund puppies before the age of six months is always difficult. In some cases, of course, one or two may stand out as being much superior in every way to the other members of a litter, but if the mating has been well planned the pups should be pretty even in type. The older the puppies the easier the choice, so that it is wise to defer the decision as long as circumstances permit. If it has to be made when the litter is from eight to twelve weeks old the following hints may be helpful. Hold a puppy by the loose skin of the neck and bring its forefeet together. This will enable the width of the front to be seen. That part should be broad, with the breast bone prominent. Next put the puppy down and examine it for ribbing. Here, too, there should be ample width, the ribs being rounded and extending well back. Fullness in ribbing must be accompanied by plenty of body length and good, strong bone. The quarters should be broad, rounded and compact with the hocks well let down. In a dog the head should be of good length with a flat, rather narrow skull. In a bitch the head will be smaller and the muzzle shorter. This is no detriment provided the muzzle is fairly broad and deep, as it will, in all probability, lengthen with age. A weak, snipy muzzle, however, is bad. The mouth should be level and the eye dark. Depth of chest is not to be expected in puppies of this age and shoulder placement is difficult to assess with accuracy. In the Wire and Long Haired varieties there is little to indicate the type of coat that will be carried eventually. A Long Haired puppy shows fringes on the ears but is otherwise almost smooth at two or three months and in a Wire the only roughness shown will be on the muzzle and between the toes, and even there the longer, harsher hairs may be very difficult to detect. Any general fullness of coat in either of these varieties is to be deprecated at this age.

When nine weeks old puppies should be immunized against distemper and at about five and a half months the sexes should be separated. A bitch may come in season before she is quite six months old and dogs may exhibit sexual precocity at the same age, so that unfortunate accidents may occur unless this precaution is taken.

CHAPTER XVII

GENERAL MANAGEMENT AND HOUSING OF ADULTS

IT is not surprising that the Dachshund has, in recent years, become one of the most popular of all dogs, for he has all the qualities most valued in a companion or household pet. His size makes him suitable to the small, modern home and the Miniature varieties may be kept without inconvenience even in small flats. He is alert, fearless, affectionate and hardy, so that he makes an admirable guard; while his high intelligence, loyalty, unfailing sense of humour and adaptability endear him to all who have the good fortune to know him intimately. The great popularity the breed now enjoys is, however, not without its dangers. In the home the Teckel is a lover of comfort and very ready to accept the role of the sleek, pampered voluptuary. But a life of cushioned ease is not good for him. His right place is in the open fields and woods, where his keen senses and lithe, sinewy body may be put to the use for which they were evolved. A soft, fat Dachshund is never happy, for it is never really healthy, and must be an object of pity to those who understand the breed and its true needs. One sometimes hears owners boast that their Dachshunds are good hunters, as though that were something unusual. I have yet to meet a healthy Dachshund that would not hunt with zest if given the chance.

A prevalent fallacy is the belief that to ensure tight shoulders and sound feet it is necessary to keep growing puppies shut up in small runs. The supposition that a Dachshund will go unsound if allowed to romp, dig and hunt is ridiculous. It is, indeed, the reverse of the truth. A dog that becomes unsound when permitted to enjoy its liberty does so because it is structurally faulty and would show its weakness sooner or later however it were treated. Close confinement will, at best, only postpone the appearance of unsoundness and the final result will probably be weakness of a more serious and general type than would have developed under more rational methods of rearing. An owner should not, however, go to the other extreme of allowing a growing youngster to run itself off its feet or to dig and climb without intelligent supervision. Until the bones are set and the muscles hard, reasonable restriction must be imposed. But one does not put a high-spirited child in a cage because it may get into mischief and do itself harm if left to follow its natural inclinations, and children and young Dachshunds have much in common.

Dachshunds are not good kennel dogs. There may be some breeds of dogs which will thrive under a regime which involves their being kept behind the bars of a small kennel run, taken out for exercise at fixed and infrequent intervals and fed at the end of each dreary day on the same dull rations, but the Dachshund is certainly not one of them. Our breed not only enjoys, it actually needs, human companionship and liberty. Its lively intelligence and many-sided character can develop only in an atmosphere of freedom, close contact with its owner and opportunities to exercise that unquenchable curiosity, spirit of adventure and love of hunting which are among the Teckel's most notable characteristics. Undue restraint makes a Dachshund dull, stupid or bad-tempered and may spoil its outline; making it look too heavy through the accumulation of fat or too thin from lack of muscle and failure to thrive. When several dogs are kept it is, of course, necessary to house them in kennels. In my opinion Dachshunds do better when made to sleep out-of-doors than when allowed to spend their lives in overwarm rooms, but some part of each day should be lived away from the kennels and each individual given a chance to develop its own personality.

Dachshunds respond well to training provided it is of the right kind. The Teckel is by nature self-willed and has a strong sense of his own importance, but he is sensitive to correction, anxious to please and very appreciative of praise. All instruction should be given with due regard to the pupil's mentality. Don't start a lesson when the dog is tired and don't prolong it after he shows that he has had enough, or when your own patience is wearing thin. Be sure he clearly understands what is required of him before scolding him for disobedience. Be patient and firm but never harsh. Correction must be given, but undue severity will cow a timid pupil and make a bolder dog sullen. Scolding is much more effective than a blow.

Anyone who sets out to train a Dachshund must first win its confidence and co-operation. Without that the task is almost hopeless. Nothing is more obdurate than an obstinate Dachshund and any attempt to inculcate instruction by force is sheer waste of time. Yet with training based on understanding and affection a Dachshund may be taught to do almost anything and to do it extremely well, as is proved by the great successes achieved in Obedience Trials by representatives of the breed. Mrs. L. Leonard's Firs Kaptor was the first of the breed to win in Obedience Classes in Britain. At his first test, in 1938, after only four weeks' training, he scored full marks and subsequently qualified C.D. (Excellent) at Championship Working Trials in all-breeds competition. More recently Angus of Wilmcourt, belonging to Miss E. M. Lanning, has covered himself with glory at the A.S.P.A.D.S. Championship Trials and the little Wire bitch Nutmeg of Dunkerque, owned by Mrs. A. Molony, claims the distinction of being the first Miniature to be an Obedience winner. Nutmeg qualified when just twelve months old, in competition with Alsatians, Collies and other big breeds, to the loud plaudits of spectators. In America, too, Dachshunds have been conspicuously successful in Obedience Tests, so that there can be no question of our breed's ability to absorb training of a highly specialized type and to respond to the orders of their handlers under the most exacting conditions.

The kennel accommodation provided must be dry, draught-proof and warm. The sleeping bench or box should be raised well above the floor, so that the occupant is clear of floor draughts. In summer Long Haired and Wire Haired dogs may sleep on the bare boards and a thin rug will suffice for a Smooth, but in colder seasons a good depth of clean wheat straw or wood-wool should be provided for a bed. The kennel run should be of concrete, stone or asphalt. This is preferable in every way to gravel or earth. All Dachshunds are persistent diggers and will tear up the most firmly compressed earth run in a surprisingly short time, and may succeed in tunnelling a way out under the kennel fencing. Such runs are difficult to keep clean and in wet weather puddles will form and lie in the hollows. A concrete run of small dimensions should slope slightly away from the kennel, so that water may drain away quickly. A larger run may slope to a central grid-covered drain. Concrete and stone runs may be flushed with disinfectant fluid regularly and will dry rapidly, so that there is no risk of the dogs' suffering from sitting about on damp surfaces. If the kennels are built in ranges the dividing boards should not be less than three feet high. If lower the dogs will get their paws on the top and try to pull themselves up to see what is going on in adjoining compartments. This will inevitably spoil the feet and pull out the elbows.

The aspect of the kennels must be governed by the nature of the ground available, but it should be in the open, away from heavy shade cast by other buildings or trees but screened from east and north winds. In an exposed position detachable wooden shutters, not less than three feet deep, may be buttoned on the lower part of the runs on the exposed sides. Such wind-screens are easily procured and are very effective. For puppy-houses vita glass screens are of the greatest value. When winter litters are reared they are almost indispensable.

Wooden buildings should be creosoted or painted on all exterior and interior surfaces. All benches, boxes and other fittings should be easy to move, so that there may be no un-getatable corners to harbour dust and vermin. The sleeping or inner compartment should have a boarded floor, raised well above the ground and dressed with creosote. This will prevent urine from soaking into the wood and enable the floor to be washed easily and kept free from offensive odours. A generous sprinkling of coarse sawdust over the floor facilitates the removal of faecal matter and keeps the kennel dry. Some Dachshunds have an annoying habit of gnawing the edges of their boxes. This often arises from being shut up too long. It can be prevented by covering all exposed edges with strips of sheet metal. Kennels used to house adult Dachshunds should not be heated, but they must be warm. The walls and roofs of wooden buildings should be lined and if the space between outer and inner walls is filled with sawdust so much the better. In summer open sleeping benches may be used, but in winter the dogs should sleep in covered boxes, so that the heat generated by their bodies may be conserved and they may keep snug and warm through the coldest nights.

In planning the lay-out of kennels special provision should be made for the accommodation of bitches in season and for cases of sickness or suspected sickness. Such quarters should be well away from the other kennel buildings, in a spot that is quiet, secluded and inaccessible to the other dogs. A separate kennel for whelping bitches is also very desirable. This, too, should be well away from the main kennels and if it can be placed near the dwelling house the arrangement will be likely to redound to the comfort of both the owner and the bitch.

Attention has already been called to the danger of allowing a young Dachshund to jump to or from a height. This also applies to adults. The anatomy of our breed is wholly unsuited to this kind of exercise. The weight of the body falling on the short legs produces a jolt which puts a strain on the whole shoulder girdle and if often repeated may do irreparable damage to the front. The heavier the dog the greater the danger, but precautions should be taken to prevent any Dachshund of any age from injuring itself in this way. If a dog is able to jump on to its sleeping box, the box should be raised or fitted with a sloping top, and there should be no shelf or other fixture in the kennel within leaping height. Apart from the harm to shoulders, feet and fronts that may result from continually jumping up and down, an awkward jump from a height may cause a serious lesion in the spiral region which may produce partial paralysis and take months to rectify.

Dachshunds usually have good appetites. They tend to be greedy rather than fastidious in the matter of food. Sufficient was said in an earlier chapter to indicate the principles that should govern the amount and type of food offered. If a dog is well grown and in good condition two meals per day are enough after puppyhood has been left behind. Of these the first may be light and the second more substantial. A diet consisting entirely of meat and bones will keep adults in good health but most owners find it convenient to supplement the meat ration with some kind of farinaceous food such as wholemeal rusks or a cereal. Rusks are prepared by slicing a wholemeal loaf and baking the portions in a slow oven till golden brown and quite crisp. They may be stored in an airtight container till required and will keep almost indefinitely without deteriorating. Theymay be given either dry or soaked in gravy or milk and are far superior in food values, and very much cheaper, than many of the various meals and biscuits marketed for dogs. White bread should not be fed in any form as it is known to be a cause of canine hysteria.

Cooked vegetables are not recommended. Few dogs like them and they contain little nutriment. Grated raw carrot, orange and tomato juice are sometimes included in the diet in the belief that they help to keep the blood cool and the skin free from eruptions. Their value is, however, problematical. Unlike humans, dogs are able to synthesize vitamin C in their own bodies without ingesting it with their food. Vitamins A, B and D are essential and there is some evidence to suggest that if a dog's food is lacking in vitamins of the B complex the synthesis of vitamin C may be weakened or inhibited. Raw vegetable and fruit juices may, therefore, be of use as supplementary sources of vitamin C if the diet is deficient in vitamins of the B group. Such supplements are not necessary if yeast tablets, as prepared for veterinary use, are given as part of the normal, daily menu. Raw eggs are valuable in the feeding of invalids, brood bitches and stud dogs. Most Dachshunds eat them with relish and they are a source of vitamin E, which is necessary to ensure fertility.

Some individuals, usually males, may cause concern by remaining very light in condition despite all their owner's efforts to induce them to put on flesh. Though they may carry good coats and appear perfectly fit, they show little interest in food and look thin and immature. If shown, a dog of this kind is likely to be described as "needing to make up in body". In dealing with such a case the temptation is to increase the number of meals to three or more per day and to try to persuade the dog to eat by offering it special dainties and titbits between meals. This treatment is likely to make the dog even more faddy about food and may destroy what appetite he previously had. A wiser course is to supply but one meal per day and to remove any that is not eaten in half an hour. No more should be offered till twenty-four hours later and any that is left again taken away. This may sound rather drastic, but if the dog is normal and healthy it will be effective after a day or two. Before adopting this treatment it is, of course, necessary to make sure that there is nothing wrong with the dog's digestion and that he is free from worms. He may need a general tonic, for lack of appetite may be of nervous origin. Refusal to feed properly at regular times quickly becomes a habit unless vigorously combated, but petting and fussing a shy feeder will only aggravate matters and make ultimate cure much more difficult. A bad doer may sometimes be cured by feeding it in the presence of a greedy companion; for jealousy and rivalry are strongly developed in almost all Dachshunds.

Much rarer than the shy feeder is the Dachshund which eats well but never carries enough flesh. To increase weight the food should be given in a moist condition and the amount of farinaceous ingredients increased. Two meals of about equal size may be given daily and a good milk preparation added to the diet. A dog that is too fat should have but one meal per day, consisting of meat. Vitamin B should be supplied in the form of yeast tablets. The bowels should be kept active by small doses of salts and the amount of exercise be increased. If this treatment fails to effect an improvement in a reasonable time some glandular deficiency may be suspected and the dog should go to a veterinary surgeon for a thorough overhaul.

A Dachshund's coat is easy to keep clean, bright and free from tangles or mats. A few minutes each day with a hound-glove and soft cloth in the case of a Smooth, or with a stiff-bristled brush and suitable comb in the case of a Long Haired or Wire, is all that is necessary. Exhibitors often boast that their dogs never see a brush till a day before a show, yet are always in good coat. That may well be so, for a Dachshund that enjoys a good deal of freedom in the country will usually keep its coat in good condition without much attention being given to its toilet. Nevertheless grooming should form part of the daily routine in all kennels, for it ensures that each inmate is brought under close scrutiny every twenty-four hours, so that the first indications of ill-health may be observed and dealt with promptly. A little dullness in demeanour, a dry nose, a slight discharge from the eyes, a tendency to shiver or hunch the back, may pass unnoticed when a number of dogs are looked at in kennel runs, but will be immediately spotted if each dog is gone over on a bench or table at grooming time.

Any dog that seems to be off colour should be isolated at once and carefully watched. Its temperature should be taken every few hours for a couple of days and its appetite and bowel action checked. These apparently trivial symptoms may presage an attack of hardpad, or para-distemper, and should be treated with grave suspicion. If such early signs of trouble are overlooked or ignored the dog may appear perfectly fit in a day or two and the next warning may come ten days or more later with partial paralysis, fits and other alarming sequelae, showing that the disease has reached the stage at which hope of recovery is remote. While hardpad continues to be rampant every minor symptom of ill-health must be taken seriously; the animal concerned at once isolated and veterinary advice sought.

A dog that comes in wet and muddy should be dried thoroughly before being put in its kennel, otherwise a chill, rheumatism or, in the case of a bitch in season, metritis may result. Long Haired and Wire Dachshunds do not feel the cold. They are never happier than when gambolling in frost or snow, and grow better coats when housed in well-built outdoor kennels than when allowed to sleep in the house. It is unnecessary and undesirable to provide them with clothing of any kind. Smooths, however, because of their much thinner, finer natural covering, may be the better for a light warm coat or woolly jumper when living in kennels or when left for long periods on a show bench in cold weather. No such protection is needed while a dog is at exercise and if a coat is provided it should cover the whole body and be comfortably loose so that movement is not impeded.

CHAPTER XVIII

SOME HINTS ON SHOWING AND JUDGING

HAVING bought, bred or otherwise acquired a Dachshund which seems to conform to the main requirements of the Standard, the next step is to submit it to the acid test of show competition. If success is to be achieved the novice exhibitor must go to the show with a clear understanding of what will be required of him and of his exhibit. The judge will make his decisions on what he sees of the dogs brought before him during the time they are actually in the ring. His scrutiny of each will occupy only a few minutes and it is the exhibitor's responsibility to see that his exhibit makes the best of itself in that brief period.

It is useless to expect an untutored puppy to deport itself in a manner likely to put it among the prize-winners. A dog which refuses to stand still, will not move without gambolling wildly, or which hunches its back and tucks its tail firmly between its legs when the judge attempts to handle it, is certain to be passed over in favour of more co-operative competitors. As a preliminary to being shown, therefore, a dog must be schooled to assume a stance in which its general make and shape are shown to the best advantage and to move briskly and gaily, but collectedly and under control, when required to do so.

Some Dachshunds will walk well on a lead without special training, especially if, as recommended in the previous chapter, they are taken for their first road walks in company with a well-behaved adult, but others are more difficult. A rampageous youngster may tug furiously against the restraining leash or turn to bite and worry it; while a more timid puppy may sit down, looking tragically miserable, and refuse to budge, or struggle to slink backwards. The best way to overcome such opposition is to get the dog used to the feel of a light collar round its neck before attaching a lead. For this purpose the lighter the collar the better. Put it on while the puppy is playing, then romp with it for a time, so that its mind is distracted from the novel sensation of having its neck encircled. Let it wear the collar at intervals for a couple of days, taking care that it fits snugly, not tight enough to cause discomfort nor loose enough to be scratched or pulled off. When the collar is worn without resentment, a light lead may be attached and left to drag loose over the ground while the puppy is played with. Leave the lead on for an hour or so. The next day while playing with the pupil take the end of the lead in the hand and let him pull against it, but make no attempt to control his movements at this stage. Later, while the end of the leash is being held by an assistant, call the puppy from a short distance, tempting him to come by showing him a morsel of food. He will probably dash forward and the handler follows, keeping the lead taut so that a steady pull is exerted. In this way, with patience and good temper, the shyest or most rebellious puppy may be lead-trained in a week or so, and may be taken for its first walk. No serious roadwork should be attempted till a puppy has been taught to walk freely on a lead in familiar surroundings, for it is much more difficult to induce a wilful youngster to walk sedately when excited by strange sights and sounds than in the less distracting conditions of known ground.

When a dog is going well on the lead his show training may begin. While walking the handler should suddenly halt with the order "Stand". If the dog is brought up without a violent jerk he will usually come to a standstill with his feet well placed and his body extended. Repeat this lesson at intervals for several days, until the pupil learns to understand what the order "Stand" implies and obeys it without being pulled up. Each time he stops of his own volition he should be rewarded and fussed. The instruction should be given regularly, but be careful not to overdo it at first or the pupil may tire and become obstinate or sullen. Having thoroughly mastered this lesson, the pupil should be taught to assume a particular stance when ordered to stand. Each time he halts place his feet in the position that shows off his outline to the best advantage. The forelegs should be perpendicular, with the feet pointing to the front, and the hindquarters so placed that the hind feet are brought well back, with the hocks parallel and the part between hock and foot perpendicular. The head should be held well up and the chest brought well forward. Having placed the dog, keep him in that position for half a minute or so; if necessary by placing a hand under him to prevent him from moving. Should he move a foot, gently replace it in the desired position, at the same time giving the order "Stand".

At first this training should be given away from strangers

or noisy traffic, but when the pupil is responding well to orders he should be put through his lessons in a street or public park, so that he may get used to obeying even when in a strange place amid unfamiliar sights. This is necessary to ensure his good behaviour when taken into a show ring among strange dogs, people and unaccustomed sounds. One often hears exhibitors complaining that their exhibits which behave badly in the ring "show perfectly at home". That, however, is not good enough. What is wanted is the ability to show well under the conditions ruling at shows, whether indoors or outside, to the accompaniment of the blare of loudspeakers, the popping of flash-lights and the clamour of many strange canine voices.

The future show competitor should also be made familiar with the sensation of being handled by those it does not know, and of being in crowded places. If the kennel is located in a secluded district, the dog should be taken from time to time into the nearest shopping town and visitors to the house should be taken to see the dogs and allowed to handle them. Tooth drill is another matter that should have attention. In the course of his examination the judge will ask to see the exhibit's teeth, and the handler will have to turn the dog's lips back to display the teeth in both jaws. Unless a dog is used to this he may object strongly and struggle so violently as to be difficult to control. As a rule, very little training is needed to teach a dog to submit to this examination, but a few Dachshunds strongly dislike having their mouths touched and it may take considerable patience and time to overcome their prejudice.

The show training of dogs should be part of the normal routine in any kennel that aspires to win honours in the ring, yet the sight of exhibits destroying their chances of figuring in the awards lists by their bad ring deportment may be witnessed at almost every show held. The requirements are neither numerous nor exacting. All that is necessary is that an exhibit shall move straight ahead in whatever direction is indicated, with head up and eyes alert, and stand still for a minute or two in a position in which its qualities may be assessed when called on to do so. Movement is of paramount importance in our breed, and unless a judge can see clearly whether an exhibit is correct in fore and hind action he cannot form a fair opinion of the dog's merits. No conscientious judge will take the responsibility of giving an exhibit the benefit of the doubt when matters concerning soundness or movement are involved. If, therefore, a dog refuses to move in such a way as to enable his action to be assessed beyond any shadow of doubt, it must be penalized. When his exhibit is being examined for general outline and proportions, it is up to the exhibitor to see that it stands still in the position in which it may be seen at its best. We sometimes hear it said of a dog that "He cannot stand wrong." But, in fact, almost any Dachshund can stand badly or awkwardly at times, so that it appears to develop faults of which it is normally free. Should it do so while the judge's eye is turned in its direction it is likely to pay the penalty.

The Dachshund is a sporting dog and should be gay, alert and fearless. An exhibit which creeps round the ring with head drooping dejectedly, tail depressed and feet dragging, cannot be held to be typical, however good it may be in physical construction, and a judge who puts such an exhibit down for failing in temperament is fully justified. A Dachshund should not have to be held up to enable its good points to be seen. Nothing looks worse than a line of handlers crouching on their knees, as though taking part in an impromptu prayer meeting, supporting their dogs with one hand under the throat and the other beneath the hindquarters. An exhibit so held invariably looks supremely uncomfortable and as often as not moves at the critical moment, to assume a stance far less attractive than that which it would have taken up if left alone. The need for this undignified posturing can be entirely eliminated by a few lessons in ring deportment given before a show. By watching the most consistently successful exhibitors the novice will see that they rarely touch their dogs while judging is in progress. Their exhibits show well and move freely without being held in a vice-like grip, half strangled by a tight lead or pulled violently about. Such handlers have learned from experience that show-training pays good dividends.

While in the ring the exhibitor should try to take things calmly. When the dog's turn comes he should be led out unhurriedly and persuaded to stand in the position he has been taught to assume. Having examined him the judge will want to see him move. The dog should be led across the ring at a brisk walk in the direction indicated by the judge, *in a straight line*, then taken back, *again in a straight line*, to the spot where the judge is standing. Even in this simple matter many exhibitors err. Instead of walking away from the judge in a straight line they wander all over the place, so that the judge has to hop from side to side in his efforts to get a square view of the dog's action. It is often necessary to ask an exhibitor to take his dog up and down several times before any opinion can be formed of its movement. When the judge has seen him, the dog should be allowed to relax while the other competitors are being examined. Dachshund classes are usually well filled and take some time to go through. If a dog is kept at attention throughout the period of judging it may be too tired to make the best of itself at the check-up that will decide the final placings. The handler, however, must remain on the alert, ready to call up his dog should the judge's eye turn in his direction. A small piece of boiled liver held in the hand and shown to a dog when its attention flags is a help, especially if judging is prolonged, but the liver should be kept back till needed. A fresh, lively exhibit may become boisterous and difficult to handle if shown a much desired titbit soon after coming into the ring.

Dachshunds need very little in the way of special preparation for showing. Regular grooming will keep the coat clean, free from loose dead hairs, and the skin supple. In this breed the claws are very strong and in some cases are not worn down sufficiently however much hard road exercise is given. Cutting is difficult and risky, for, the claws being black, the quick cannot be seen and individuals vary a good deal in the point to which that sensitive part extends. The best method for shortening overlong nails is to use a coarse file, rasping each nail from the side at an angle of about forty-five degrees. When the width of the claw has been reduced by this means the narrow portion may be cut off with a pair of clippers and the nail rounded off with a somewhat finer file.

A well-groomed Dachshund rarely needs washing, but should a bath be considered necessary it should be given at least three days before a show, so that the coat may regain its gloss and natural lie for the occasion. The amount of flesh carried by a show dog must depend on its build. Most Dachshunds look best when well covered, so that the body is nicely rounded and sleek without being corpulent or flabby. A thin exhibit that is long in body is apt to be passed over by a superficial judge as being lacking in ribbing or light in loin. On the other hand, a dog that is full in ribbing and rather short in body should be shown in lean, hard condition, for any surplus flesh will add to its cobbiness.

On arriving at the show venue the exhibit will have to undergo veterinary inspection, after which it should be put on its bench, have its eyes and nose sponged with boric lotion, or a suitable germicide, and thoroughly groomed. A quarter of an hour or so before due to go into the ring the coat should be given a final tidying-up or a polish with a soft cloth. At the last moment a Wire Haired exhibit should have the beard brushed well forward to give a clean finish to the muzzle, and a Long Haired have the ear fringes and feathering combed out.

When a novice exhibitor has attended a few shows he may begin to wonder about what appear to be strange inconsistencies in judging. At one show a certain exhibit may go to the top, at the next be among the cardless majority. A dog that is beaten by two or three other competitors under one judge may be placed over his erstwhile victors under another. There may be several reasons for these reversals. A dog may vary in condition, ring behaviour, coat or in other respects, from show to show. He may show much better in a hall than in a ring in the open, or *vice versa*. If a stud dog he may be upset by the scent left on the ground by a class of bitches that has been judged in the same ring earlier, or he may just be feeling off-colour. Judges do, of course, vary in some degree in their interpretation of the Standard. No exhibit is perfect and a judge's task is to strike a balance between the merits and failings shown by the various animals that come before him. In doing so one authority may give great credit for certain good points and penalize certain faults very heavily, while another may be more strongly swayed by other considerations. Thus one judge may go all out for general type, another for movement. Again, a dog which sweeps the decks at one show may fail to do well at his next outing because he is up against much keener competition than on the occasion of his triumph. For these and other reasons an exhibitor should not expect to win at every show. He will have his good and his bad days, but if his dog is as good as he probably thinks it is it will get its deserts if shown consistently and properly handled.

Dog showing can be a most enjoyable and exciting adventure, but only if it is treated as a competitive sport. Unless one can enjoy a show irrespective of whether one wins or loses it is better not to show at all. Even a challenge certificate may be gained at too high a cost if the strain of waiting for judging to begin reduces an exhibitor to the verge of a nervous breakdown. The wise exhibitor will profit by his defeats. After judging is over a judge will usually be very willing to explain why he was unable to put a particular exhibit higher in the awards. It may well be that his explanation will indicate that what is keeping the dog back is only a minor fault or failing which judicious kennel treatment, training, or better handling may improve or wholly eradicate.

In the fullness of time the novice becomes a seasoned exhibitor and the day may come when an invitation to judge arrives. As the first class parades before him he begins to appreciate some of the trials of those he has been so ready to criticize. If he is wise he will go to the show well primed in all the details of the Standard and with a clear mental picture of the ideal it depicts. His decisions must be based on what he sees and be completely uninfluenced by what he may know of the show records of individual dogs that he may recognize, or by the reputation of the kennels from which they come. He must free his mind from all fads and personal prejudices and make his placings strictly in accordance with the provisions of the Standard. Once a judge was heard to explain that he had not included a certain dog among the prize-winners because he did not like its colour or its light eyes. The dog in question was a chocolate, a colour recognized by the Standard which specifically states that with that coat colour light eyes are permissible. There could, therefore, be no justification whatever for the judge's action. He was either grossly ignorant of the Standard by which he was supposed to judge or, quite wrongly, allowing a purely personal prejudice to sway his judgment. A judge who is also a breeder will often tend to look most kindly on exhibits of the type of his own dogs. That is understandable, for if he did not prefer that type he would not, presumably, adhere to it in his own kennels, but he should not allow that preference to blind him to the virtues shown by exhibits of somewhat different types, or to lead him to ignore faults in dogs of the type he favours.

Every exhibit should be examined with equal thoroughness and tested for the six Dachshund essentials, which are soundness, substance, symmetry, length, lowness to ground and levelness on top. Any exhibit which is free from any grave fault may be put in a corner of the ring. This will facilitate the final placings. After going through a class of twenty or more entries a judge cannot retain a clear mental picture of each competitor, but if those he likes are separated as they are judged he will have at the end of the class perhaps four or five picked exhibits standing together from which to choose his final winners. This may seem simple and straightforward, but in practice various complications are sure to arise. The exhibit whose general appearance is most impressive may move badly;

the soundest dog in a class may be short in back or light in eye. This is where the judge's ability is put to the test. It is easy to fix on one characteristic and let that determine the placings, but it is as bad a system of judging as can be devised, for, though its practitioners may plead consistency, all the awards may go to exhibits which are completely unsound or thoroughly untypical. What is needed is balanced judgment in which no one point is overvalued or its importance underestimated.

That soundness is of cardinal importance no one will deny, but a Dachshund may be sound without being typical and it is as illogical, and as dangerous, to put up dogs merely because they are sound, irrespective of how they fail in other ways, as it is to overlook unsoundness in concentrating on length of body, depth of keel, heaviness of bone or any other breed quality. Once I saw an outstanding Smooth, which excelled in all the salient breed characteristics, passed over completely because of a little looseness in one elbow. Yet it beat all the dogs placed above it in length, lowness to ground, top line, chest formation and general symmetry. That is bad judging. It is bad because it is unbalanced, and because it treats breed type as though it were unimportant. On another occasion, on approaching a ring in which Long Hairs were being judged, I saw a bitch standing apart from the others in a corner. She was of such excellence that I took it for granted that she had been placed by herself as the obvious winner. But when the awards were made she was given no card at all. Later the judge told me that this exhibit had been put down because she was short of coat. Here, again, is a case of unbalanced judging. On no rational system of points allocation could so overwhelming a value be attached to coat length as to nullify all the other virtues in which the bitch referred to excelled. The exhibits that beat her, though in full coats, were all mediocre by comparison. Any method of judging that undervalues merits and too heavily penalizes failings can only lead to the encouragement of exhibits which, though free from glaring faults, are devoid of any outstanding virtues and must react to the detriment of the breed.

CHAPTER XIX

THE DACHSHUND IN SICKNESS

WHEN properly reared, well fed, appropriately housed and adequately exercised, Dachshunds are hardy dogs and less prone to sickness than many other breeds. Scrupulous regard to kennel hygiene and a daily inspection of each dog to ensure that the first symptoms of ill-health may be noted and dealt with promptly will, in most cases, keep a kennel free from serious trouble. Should disease appear veterinary advice should be sought immediately. It is most unwise for the inexperienced to try to deal with any serious illness unaided, and little real help can be obtained through printed instructions. Each case must be considered and treated in the light of knowledge gained from observation of symptoms and the condition of the patient made on the spot. For that reason no attempt is made in this chapter to give detailed directions for the cure of all the forms which canine ills may take. There are, however, some types of sickness or injury which are particularly likely to occur in Dachshunds which seem to call for special notice in a book on the breed. Of these some are easy to deal with if their nature is understood, others demand patient nursing under veterinary supervision. Then there are times when accidents occur which call for emergency measures in the interval which must elapse before skilled assistance can be procured. It is hoped that the hints here given will be of use to the novice owner in dealing with such cases.

Smooth Dachshunds, in common with all dogs in which the coat is very fine and thin, are often affected by what is generally referred to as "*Skin Trouble*". Diseases of the skin may be conveniently divided under two headings, viz. those caused by parasites and those which arise from some constitutional disturbance. Before dealing with these it may be advisable to point out that some Smooths tend to develop bald patches on the flaps of the ears, on the throat, chest, tail and elsewhere at each moulting season. The old hair falls out before the new has grown, so that for a time certain parts are left in a state of hairlessness. The naked skin looks bright and clean and there is no irritation. This peculiarity may be annoying to an owner, for it may keep the dog from being shown for a period each time the coat is changed. Little or nothing can be done about it, beyond regular grooming and the application of a hair stimulant to hasten the growth of the new coat. Some chocolates are rendered unfit for showing while moulting by the fading of the old hair in patches. To the uninformed such a dog may look "mangy" but the condition is perfectly normal. Such seasonal blemishes should not be mistaken for symptoms of skin disease.

Of the parasitic skin diseases the most common is *Sarcoptic Mange*, caused by a mite too small to be seen by the unaided eye. Under a microscope the creature looks like a fat, short-legged, hairy spider. Symptoms are incessant scratching, the appearance of tiny red pustules which soon become surrounded by areas of bare, scabby skin, and a strong, mousey odour. The parts first affected are usually the areas surrounding the eyes, the ear flaps, which may become much thickened, the elbows and the abdomen. The infection gradually spreads till almost the whole body may be covered. The disease, when once it has been recognized for what it is, may be quickly cured if the measures adopted are sufficiently thorough. The dog should be rubbed all over with a mixture of one part black sulphur to eight parts vegetable oil to which a little paraffin has been added. This oily dressing must be worked into the skin, not merely spread over the coat, and every part of the dog must be thoroughly anointed. The treatment should be repeated three or four times at intervals of four days. Three days after the last application of oil the dog should be bathed, using soap and warm water in which a handful of washing soda has been dissolved. This should complete the cure if matters have been taken in hand in good time, but where early symptoms have been neglected and the skin has become much thickened and wrinkled, up to six dressings of oil may be necessary before the dog is bathed. Sarcoptic Mange is very contagious and immediately it appears the affected dogs must be isolated, put into oil as indicated and installed in clean quarters. All bedding must be burned, the kennel fumigated with a formalin candle, and afterwards thoroughly scrubbed with disinfectant. Walls, floors and all boxes and other kennel furniture must be included in the cleansing. Clothing, blankets, collars, brushes, combs and anything else that has been in contact with the dog should be soaked in disinfectant for several hours and then washed. If the dog is kept in the house care must be taken to ensure the thorough disinfection of carpets, curtains, cushions and furniture with which it has been in contact, and all loose hairs must be collected and burned. Unless the disinfection of the dog's living and sleeping quarters, and of everything used by it prior to isolation, is complete, the patient will be reinfected as soon as it comes in contact with them again.

Follicular Mange is much less common than sarcoptic mange and is very much more difficult to cure. It attacks young dogs up to about two years old and is contagious, though it spreads much more slowly than the commoner disease. The first symptoms are one or more small, roundish patches, about the size of a shilling, on the face or muzzle. If the dark greyish patch is examined a number of red pustules will be discovered. If ignored the patches increase in size and the pustules spread and coalesce, exuding pus and blood. As these sores dry up the skin on the affected parts becomes dry and scaly and turns bluish-grey or black. There is little or no irritation, so that the dog does not scratch as in cases of common mange. The mousey odour is stronger and more pronounced than in the sarcoptic form of the disease. The parasite responsible for follicular mange is much smaller than that which causes sarcoptic mange. Under the microscope it looks like a tiny maggot-like grub. It lives deep in the skin in the hair follicles and is difficult to get at. This is a most baffling disease so far as treatment is concerned. Long-continued applications of sulphur ointment with sulphur baths sometimes keep the trouble in check but it is likely to break out afresh, sometimes months after a cure seems to have been effected. A dog suffering from follicular mange should be placed in the hands of a veterinary surgeon immediately the first symptoms are seen. The Bayer treatment is perhaps the most satisfactory method and this can only be carried out by a qualified veterinarian. Unless the disease is treated in its early stages it may well prove incurable.

Ringworm is a contagious disease caused by a fungus. The symptoms are bare circular patches, varying in size from about half an inch to one inch in diameter, on the muzzle, chin, forelegs or elsewhere. The bare skin looks rough and dry and may show a few small, reddish pimples. The dog should be isolated and the patches dressed daily with tincture of iodine. As this disease is contagious to humans the iodine should be applied with a brush or piece of linen that can afterwards be destroyed. Mercury ointment is also effective but it is poisonous and must be used with great care. Once a week the dog should be bathed, using formalin or mercury soap. Efforts should be made to prevent the dog scratching the affected parts, as this causes the infection to spread. The kennel and all clothing, blankets, collars and other appliances must be fumigated and disinfected as for mange. Prolonged treatment may be necessary to effect a cure in cases of ringworm.

Eczema is a non-contagious inflammatory condition of the skin. Symptoms are in some respects similar to those of sarcoptic mange, but the sore, bare patches of skin do not turn blackish. Irritation is intense, so that the dog bites and scratches itself incessantly. The parts most generally affected are the areas round the eyes, along the back, on the chest, the elbows and ears. A skin scraping should be taken and examined under a microscope to determine whether the trouble is mange or eczema. In mange such a scraping will show the mange mites, whereas in eczema no parasites are present. Eczema is of constitutional origin and external treatment alone is useless. Worms may be suspected and measures taken to expel them. A dog cannot be cured of eczema while harbouring these internal parasites. Laxatives should be given and the diet be restricted almost wholly to raw, lean meat. The addition of yeast tablets is of the greatest help. If the dog is in poor condition a good general tonic or a course of condition powders should be given. The sore patches should be dressed with sphagnol ointment and, as the skin clears and heals, it may be dusted frequently with boric and zinc powder. The dog must be prevented from scratching and biting the sores. This may be effected either by putting bags of wash-leather or flannel on the hind feet or, where the patches are distributed over the body, by covering the trunk with a light coat. Where large areas are affected a sulphur bath twice a week may be beneficial.

External Parasites. Dachshunds which hunt over rabbit-infested ground in summer sometimes become covered with fleas or lice. These may be quickly destroyed by rubbing Pulvex into the coat. The dressing should be liberal and every part of the body covered. One good application of the powder will kill all but the eggs, or nits, of the lice. To remove these the coat may be sponged with vinegar or a second treatment with Pulvex given ten days after the first. Kennels and bedding should be sprinkled with the powder periodically and floor and corners kept scrupulously clean. Ticks may be picked up by dogs which run over ground on which sheep are grazed. They may be recognized as swellings the size of small peas protruding from the skin about the head, neck or legs. These blood-suckers should be removed with forceps. A drop of petrol or paraffin should first be dropped on the spot where the head of the parasite is inserted. This will cause the tick to let go its hold and it may be pulled out entire. If the head is broken off and left in the skin an irritating sore may result. Harvesters, or harvest bugs, sometimes cause dogs much irritation in late summer. They are minute, red mites which burrow beneath the skin, usually of the abdomen and the insides of the legs. Close examination will show tiny red spots, each smaller than a pin-head, on the parts attacked. Bathing with T.C.P. or Dettol will quickly allay the irritation and kill the parasites.

ACCIDENTS

Bites and Wounds. In dealing with wounds of any kind the first essential is to see that both outer and inner surfaces are perfectly clean. As a primary precaution they should be bathed with a non-carbolic disinfectant, such as T.C.P. or Dettol, and all foreign particles and hairs removed. If there is much bleeding it may be necessary to apply a tourniquet, but in the majority of cases bleeding may be arrested by pressure of the fingers followed by the use of a wad of surgical dressing or lint. In an emergency, as when one is single-handed or when suitable material for making a pad are not immediately available, bleeding may be stopped temporarily by Friar's Balsam. A wound caused by a bite may be small but deep. After being cleaned such a puncture should be syringed with antiseptic solution and later fomented with warm boric lotion, to prevent it healing too quickly at the surface. Healing must occur from the lowest point of the wound upwards, otherwise an abscess may form. When not being treated the affected part should be well covered with medicated lint. Where the skin and underlying flesh is torn the edges of the wounds, after being thoroughly cleaned, must be brought together and stitched with surgical silk and the injury covered and bandaged. A veterinary surgeon should be called, as the wound will need careful dressing and watch must be kept for suppuration. Should this occur the stitches may have to be removed and special treatment given. If the edges of the tear are ragged or much contused the wound should not be sewn. The injury should be well dusted with iodoform powder or bathed with T.C.P. and bandaged. After a few days, if the wound is clean and free from discharge, boric powder may be used for dusting or a little boric ointment may be applied on a piece of lint. Bandaging should be continued till healing is complete.

Burns and Scalds. Dress the parts with boric ointment, applied by hand, cover with cotton wool and bandage. When the blisters have burst use the same ointment on lint and again bandage. Use the ointment generously and repeat the dressing every four hours. In place of boric ointment carron oil—lime water and linseed oil in equal parts—may be employed. In an emergency burns may be covered thickly with flour or boric and starch powder.

Choking. This is most commonly caused by a dog swallowing a bone which becomes fixed at the back of the throat. The obstruction must be removed quickly or the animal may die from asphyxia. Often the object can be hooked up with the finger but should that prove impossible a pair of long forceps may be used. If the bone is too far down to be pulled up efforts must be made to force it downwards. If it cannot be reached with finger or forceps a lump of meat given to the dog may carry the impediment down the gullet. A bone that has been forced far enough down to enable the dog to breathe normally may become wedged across the lower part of the oesophagus. Should that occur the dog must be fed on liquid and soft foods, when the bone may, in time, soften and move, but it may be necessary to remove it by an operation. Dogs occasionally swallow large stones or other foreign bodies which may cause stomach pains or intestinal obstruction. A large dose of liquid paraffin into which five grains of bismuth sub-nitrate have been mixed should be given and repeated at intervals of four hours. Hot compresses to the abdomen will relieve pain. A bulky meal may assist in some cases by dilating the stomach and intestine. When the dog appears to be in great pain an X-ray examination should be made, so that the nature and position of the offending body may be determined.

Collapse following accident. After being run over or subjected to some other severe shock, a dog may lose consciousness, breathe with difficulty and feel cold to the touch. The animal should be laid on its right side in a quiet darkened spot and given brandy or a similar stimulant. The body should be kept warm with hot-water bottles and covered with a blanket. Veterinary advice should be summoned at once and no attempt made to move or examine the patient for injuries until consciousness has been regained.

Bee and Wasp Stings. Dogs are sometimes stung on the lips, corners of the mouth or on other tender parts and, though little pain may appear to be felt, a large swelling may result. If the sting remains in the wound it should be extracted. The swelling should then be dabbed with T.C.P. or ammoniated tincture of quinine. In the absence of these remedies a dilute solution of ammonia may be used. A sting on the tongue or in the mouth is much more serious. The swelling should be treated as above suggested and veterinary assistance procured at once, for, should the swelling be large, it may impede breathing and even cause death by suffocation.

Poisoning. The symptoms of poisoning are usually abdominal pains, vomiting, a rigid and unnatural gait, difficulty in breathing, convulsions and finally collapse. Which of these is most marked depends on the nature of the poison swallowed, and the treatment must vary accordingly. In all cases vomiting should be induced or encouraged by an emetic, one of the most generally available being salt and water—a heaped tablespoonful of salt to half a pint of warm water. Two or three doses should be given at half-hourly intervals, or oftener if the first is not effective. The dog should be rushed to a veterinary surgeon. Should there be convulsions, ten to twenty grains of potassium bromide should be administered and repeated if necessary in half an hour. Where there is danger of collapse brandy or other stimulant should be given, either through the mouth or sub-cutaneously. If the dog is cold, pack hot water-bottles round it and cover with blankets.

Snake Bite. In districts where adders abound Dachshunds are liable to get bitten by these venomous reptiles. The part bitten swells rapidly, looks red and inflamed and there is considerable pain. If speedy action is not taken respiration is affected, paralysis supervenes and the dog may die in convulsions. If the bite is on the leg or foot ligature the limb tightly above the puncture, then open the part with a sharp knife and swab vigorously with permanganate of potash. When the bite is on the muzzle or on some part of the body it may not be possible to apply a ligature. In that case the swelling should be opened immediately and treated with permanganate. Anti-venom serum is available and its use is strongly recommended. Dachshund owners living in areas where adders are common should keep a supply handy.

MISCELLANEOUS ILLS

Canker. This term is applied very loosely to a number of inflammatory affections of the ear. The trouble may be confined to the ear flap or extend to the tympanic cavity. It often accompanies eczema but may occur in dogs quite free from skin eruptions elsewhere on the body. Symptoms are constant scratching of the ears or shaking of the head. In external canker the ear flaps show pustules and scabs, often with a marked thickening of the skin, and bare patches appear where the hair is scratched off. In internal canker the orifice of the ear usually, though not invariably, shows an accumulation of discoloured wax and there may be a brownish discharge. The cause is generally either water entering the inner ear, through the dog's immersing the head while swimming, being exposed to wet weather or having the ears imperfectly dried after a bath, or from the ear being obstructed by mud or dirt. For external canker the dog should be wormed, then given laxative or tonic treatment as its general condition indicates. The ear flaps should be treated as for eczema and the patient prevented from scratching. For internal canker thoroughly clean out the ear cavity with a swab of cotton wool soaked in dilute surgical spirit or peroxide. If there is a discharge from deep down in the ear, pour or syringe a little of the fluid mentioned into the cavity, leave for a few minutes then dry carefully and blow in boric powder. Great care must be taken to ensure that the inner parts of the ear are properly dried. This treatment should be continued once or twice a day until all irritation and discharge cease. Shirley's canker lotion and powder are very efficacious, as is a preparation of penicillin and boric powder, which may be obtained from a veterinary surgeon or a chemist. Acute irritation of the ear may be caused by parasitic mites. Examination of the aural canal will reveal grey, powdery debris in which the mites may be seen moving. The ear should be syringed with T.C.P., then cleaned out with swabs of cotton wool dipped in that solution and tied to orange sticks, so that they may reach to the base of the channel. Dry the ear thoroughly, then dust with Pulvex. Repeat this treatment daily till irritation ceases. Thereafter clean the cavity once a week to destroy mites hatching from eggs deposited deep down. Unlike non-parasitic canker, this disease is contagious.

Chorea. This is a twitching of the limbs or other parts due to the involuntary contraction of the muscles. It usually comes as an aftermath of distemper or hardpad. Bad cases are incurable but the twitching may become much less noticeable, or almost disappear, after long and patient treatment. Rest, highly nourishing food plus cod-liver oil and yeast tablets, with either sedative or tonic treatment according to the conditions of the patient, are the measures most likely to produce satisfactory results. Even under the most favourable conditions it may be many months before appreciable improvement is made. A dog suffering from chorea should be kept away from boisterous companions and guarded against undue excitement, shocks and exposure to extremes of temperature.

Congestion of the Anal Glands. When a dog is seen dragging itself along the ground in a sitting position it is often assumed to need worming. Usually, however, this behaviour is due to congestion of the anal glands. The skin surrounding the anus will be found to be inflamed and the glands swollen. These parts should be bathed with a warm solution of T.C.P. and the contents of the glands ejected by squeezing. If the condition is neglected an abscess may form. This should be fomented frequently with hot water till it breaks naturally, or becomes soft enough to be lanced, and the pus removed. The wound should be syringed with dilute T.C.P. or boric lotion and fomentations continued for two days, when the parts should be ready for healing. Give liquid paraffin to ease the motions and attend to the general health of the dog.

False Heat. Should a bitch come in season twice in quick succession, with only a few weeks between heats, the first oestrum may be assumed to have been false. If she has been served during that period no offspring will be born and she should be mated again at the appropriate stage of her second heat, when normal conception may be expected.

Hernia or Rupture. Umbilical ruptures in puppies often disappear as the youngsters grow and the muscles of the abdomen strengthen. Should they persist they cause no distress or inconvenience in adults so long as they remain soft and small, but if they become larger than about an inch across and are hard, veterinary advice should be sought. Inguinal hernia sometimes occurs in bitches. This, too, may disappear with maturity but if the condition does not right itself the rupture tends to increase in size. Though it may cause no discomfort at first it is advisable to have it removed by an operation, otherwise it may unfit the bitch for breeding or give trouble as the animal ages.

Hiccoughing, or its variant in which a dog stands with legs flexed and draws air in through the nostrils with a harsh snorting noise, is usually caused by indigestion or worms. The snorting may be temporarily arrested by pinching the nose just behind the nostrils. The dog should be given a dose of bicarbonate of soda and steps taken to ensure that it is free from worms.

Interdigital Cysts. These are swellings which appear between the toes and cause the dog to lick its feet and to go lame. They are caused by infection and seem to be particularly prevalent when roads have been newly tarred. The feet should be poulticed until the swellings burst or are soft enough to be opened with a sharp knife. Swab out thoroughly with tincture of iodine or T.C.P., plug with small rolls of cotton wool dipped in a non-carbolic antiseptic and cover with a sock. Remove the cotton wool each day and bathe with antiseptic. After three days, if the wounds are clean and there is no sign of discharge, anoint them with a healing ointment. Give the dog a dose of castor oil or put on a course of condition powders. Keep the feet free from dirt.

Metritis or Inflammation of the Womb. The acute form is often due to a portion of the afterbirth remaining in the womb and causing blood poisoning. It is a dangerous condition requiring immediate treatment. Frequent douching with dilute antiseptic solution at a temperature of from 40·5–43·3°C. (105–110°F) is the best remedy, but veterinary advice should be obtained as soon as possible. The symptoms are lassitude accompanied by a high temperature, loss of appetite and hard, swollen abdomen. The discharge from the womb is copious and offensive, the milk flow may fail completely or the milk may be so acid that the pups refuse to feed. The litter should be taken from the dam and if necessary the milk drawn off by hand to prevent abscesses forming. Metritis may appear at any time from the first to the fifth day after whelping. The earlier the symptoms are shown the more serious the case if likely to be. Chronic metritis is a disease of elderly bitches, caused by degenerate changes in the womb. It is characterized by a thick purulent discharge, associated with intermittent fever. The only satisfactory remedy is the removal of the womb. If the operation is performed in the early stages of the disease it is usually entirely successful, and the bitch may live in health and happiness for a number of years. Metritis in older bitches is often due to chill contracted during heat, through sitting about on cold, wet ground or from being allowed to lie down while wet.

Paralysis. This is usually the result of an injury to the head, back or loins. The first precaution is to have the dog X-rayed to discover if there is any fracture or displacement of the bones. If no such injury is shown, a lesion of the nervous or muscular tissues in the spinal region may be suspected. The case should be placed in the care of a veterinary surgeon and treatment will depend on his diagnosis of the cause. Rest is the chief essential. If the hindquarters are affected the dog may be unable to urinate, in which case the bladder must be emptied twice daily by pressure on both sides of the flanks, or the water may be drawn off by a catheter. Such an instrument should not be used by the inexperienced, as its manipulation calls for skill and care. The bowels should be kept moving by aperient medicine or, if that is impossible, an enema of warm soapy water must be given. If the dog is in pain morphia may have to be administered. When the animal is helpless it should be turned over every few hours so that it is not left lying too long on one side. Should the limbs be only partly paralysed the dog must be prevented from trying to mount stairs or to scramble on to furniture. Movement should be discouraged until a progressive improvement is apparent and the patient carefully guarded from shocks, jolts or strain until recovery is complete. Great patience is needed in dealing with this distressing complaint but hope should not be soon abandoned, even in seemingly hopeless cases. Recovery may take as long as two years, but with rest, careful feeding and judicious exercise as the use of the limbs returns, eventual recovery may be hoped for, unless there is severe injury to the brain or spinal cord. Paralysis may arise from rheumatism, especially where only the hindquarters are affected. If that is so the dog will give signs of being in pain, particularly when it rises after lying down for some time. A saline purge should be given and the loins and adjacent parts covered with thermogene wool and bandaged. The diet should be light but nourishing: milk and eggs being very suitable, with fish, tripe and stewed rabbit. The dog must be kept quiet in warm, dry, comfortable quarters. Five grains of aspirin may be given three times a day.

Soft Pads. In some Dachshunds the pads remain soft no matter how much exercise is given. Indeed such dogs are unable to stand up to much roadwork without going lame. The best remedy is to soak the feet twice daily in a strong solution of alum. Let the feet remain in the solution for five minutes at a time, then dry and dust the pads and between the toes with powdered alum. The dog should be kept on concrete and exercised on hard roads only until the pads have hardened. Immediate results should not be expected, but if the treatment is continued for some weeks it will prove successful. Cracked pads may be treated in the same way.

Warts. Elderly Dachshunds are sometimes afflicted with warts on various parts of the body. If the growths have narrow bases they should be ligatured tightly with strong silk, when they will drop off in a few days. When the warts are flattened they should be treated with acetic acid or a caustic pencil once a day, great care being taken that only the surface of the wart, and not the surrounding skin, is touched with the caustic.

Wens. These are growths which can be felt as freely movable, smooth, rounded bodies beneath the skin. If small they may be ignored but if they increase in size they should be removed. The operation is very simple and only a local anaesthetic is employed.

ADDENDA

By Amyas Biss (from 1967–75)
and by J. V. Crawford (from 1979)

ADDENDUM 1:
THE SMOOTH DACHSHUND

Since the last revision of this book, many of the same kennels have continued to be paramount in the breed, especially the Silvaes of Mrs. Grosvenor Workman, the Aysdorns of Mr. Crowley, the Turlshills of Mr. Pinches and the Selwoods of Mrs. Peggy Hood-Wright. But Mme. Rikovsky and Mrs. Goodman have died and Miss Spurrier has retired from the show ring. Mr. Pilkington, Miss Hill and Miss Covell are less frequent exhibitors. The outstanding arrival on the scene has been the Womack kennels of Mrs. Rene Gale whose Wrightstarturn has won twenty-five C.C.'s under different judges at the time of writing. Other recent breeders or owners of Champions are Mr. A. W. Hague (Limberin), Mr. and Mrs. G. W. Brown (Droftaw), Mrs. Barbara Pugh (Tarkotta), Miss Rachel Molloy (Mrs. Robert Hood-Wright) (Heidefeld), Miss K. E. Webb (Brackenside), Mrs. B. J. Beaumont (Longanlow), Miss C. M. Edwards (Fieldside), Mrs. Joan Foden (Booth), Mr. and Mrs. Gallop (Rhinefields).

Of considerable interest has been the success of Mr. Pinches's Turlshill Pirate as a sire of Champions—though he himself never acquired that status.

1967

The great and deserved success of Ch. Womack Wrightstarturn has continued and he achieved the highest Dachshund honour for many a long day when he won the Hound Group at Cruft's in 1967—and Best in Show at the Hound Association Show, the latter for the second time running. Mrs. Rene Gale also made up two new Champions in Womack Wroyal Parade and Womack Winterstarlight. Mrs. Peggy Hood-Wright and Mr. Alf Hague also made up two Champions each, while Mr. and Mrs. Crowley, Mrs. Grosvenor Workman and Mr. and Mrs. Gallop each made up one. Mrs. Huet from Ireland, hitherto better known as a Wire breeder, made up her Greygates Trinket and Mrs. Parker made a successful return to the ring with her first Champion since Ardrahan Dorian in the early fifties. Mrs. M. M. Shields made up her Daksmor Desdemona.

1968

Nearly fifty new Champions have been made up since the last edition and many of these bear familiar prefixes such as Womack, Limberin, Silvae, Rhinefields, Tarkotta, Daksmor, Longanlow—not to mention Berndack, a familiar prefix among winning dogs in the more immediate post-war era. There has been no lack of new breeders or old breeders reaching the top. Three Scottish Kennels have done particularly well, Mrs. J. McNaughton (Cedavoch), Miss J. Cook (Deugh) and Miss Stewart (Dargarvel). Mr. Triefus (Mithril), Secretary of the Dachshund Club, bred four Champions, while Mrs. Coxon (d'Arisca) bred two, as did Mrs. Eaton (Eatina,) while a number of others made their initial break-through with a single dog.

There is little doubt that the oustanding dog of the period has been Mr. and Mrs. Gallop's Rhinefields Diplomat who, after Cruft's 1973, had won no less than forty-six Challenge Certificates. He is a most striking dog of exquisite proportion and imposing presence. It is to be hoped that he may succeed the late Womack Wrightstarturn as the stud force of the '70s. *1973*

The decline in registrations of this breed is not much in evidence in the number of Champions being made up, though classes at Shows are inclined to be a little smaller.

Mr. Alf Hague's Limberin Loud Laughter was the outstanding winner of this period – a lovely red dog. Mrs. Peach Lewis came up with a Champion, her first for a good number of years, while Mrs. Grosvenor Workman, Mr. Triefus, Mr. and Mrs. Gallop and Miss Hannay kept their own flags flying with a single new Champion apiece.

Newcomers to the top honours were Mr. Trevor Peak, Mrs. Kelsall, Mrs. Rawson, Sqdn. Ldr. and Mrs. Henson. There is still plenty of new blood (human!) coming into this breed, which is a healthy sign. *1975*

During the 1975–9 period, Smooths have not made very great advances, but several outstanding exhibits have appeared in the show ring. The established kennels of Silvae (Mrs. Grosvenor Workman), Rhinefields (Mr. and Mrs. Gallop), Limberin (Mr. Hague), Cedavoch (Mr. and Mrs. McNaughton), Womack (Mrs. Gale) and D'Arisca (Mrs. Coxon) have continued to be most consistent and provided the basic breeding stock for many other kennels.

Of more recent newcomers to top honours, the Rosenkets of Mr. and Mrs. Rawson, Teilwoods of Mr. and Mrs. Henson, Matzells of Mrs. and Miss Norton and Ralines of Mr. and Mrs. Lockett have been well to the fore as have the Landmarks of Mrs. Heesom – a kennel that has made steady progress since its return from South Africa. *1979*

ADDENDUM 2:

THE LONG HAIRED DACHSHUND

THIS variety has seen many changes among its successful breeders in recent years. Miss Raine's Ch. Imber Coffee Bean, son of the progeny of an all-smooth mating, was the founder of a tremendously successful kennel. Coffee Bean himself has sired a large number of Champions and the breed undoubtedly owes much to the introduction of this valuable outcross. Of the earlier breeders Mr. and Mrs. Buck (Buckmead), Mrs. Roberts (Bolivar), Mrs. Connell (von Holzner), Miss Mothersill (Windgather), Dr. B. Raven (Kennhaven) and Miss Tilney (Clonyard) continue to flourish and produce Champions. *1967*

Later successful competitors in this breed are Mr. Harry Jordan (Danjor), Miss J. Silcock (Sarfra), Mrs. B. Owen (Antrobus), Mr. R. O. Pickup, Miss E. Murphy (Maplecott), Mrs. R. Chatterton (Mooncoin), Mrs. M. E. White (Closegarth), Mr. J. R. Hickson (Wainsford), Mrs. R. S. Simmonds (Minte) and Mr. Barton Emanuel, whose Mountchlowns are mostly of American stock. Outstanding among these more recent breeders has been Mrs. K. Jensen, whose Albaneys have had continuous and remarkable success.

Only three Champions were made up last year—the senior Champions being very hard to beat. Mrs. Connell, one of the doyennes of the breed, made up her Jacqueline von Holzner and a more recent enthusiast, Mrs. Avril Spiers, had her first Champion in Murrumbidgee Black Titan of Albaney, while Mrs. M. White produced another Closegarth Champion in her Crinoline. *1968*

Once again this breed has seen the arrival of quite a number of successful new exhibitors. Of these well established in the breed, Mrs. Jensen (Albaney), Mrs. Spiers (Murrumbidgee), and Dr. Raven (Kennhaven) have held their place with several Champions. Of the relative new-comers in the breed, Mrs Swann (Swansford) has made up three Champions including Swansford Brigg of Truanbru, an extremely successful show dog in 1972, Mrs. J. C. Martin (Mormonstag) bred three Champions, while Mrs. Lloyd Williams (Lynocree) bred two dog Champions and there were again a number of breeders who are just on the verge of big success. Perhaps one might particularly mention Mrs. Tozer (Exeview), who produces consistently good stock in the South West. Champion Kennhaven Caesar was undoubtedly the most successful sire in this variety during the period. *1973*

Seven new Champions were made up during the period and the breed is still largely centred on the stalwarts who have kept it up to its high standard in recent years—Miss Raine, Mrs. Jensen, Mr. and Mrs Swann and Mr. Crawford. Only the two Johnsons are newcomers to the Champion "Club" in this strikingly handsome variety. Let us hope that more intending exhibitors will follow up the good work of the present successful breeders. *1975*

This variety has made good progress in the last four years, having attracted a most welcome number of new kennels – several of which have made-up Champions. The dominant bloodlines are still the Swansfords, Albaneys and Imbers, but many of the newer kennels are producing winners of a consistently high standard—such as the Phaelands of the Misses Gatheral (a long-established kennel that has suddenly come to the fore), the Africandawns of Tony Johnson, the Jamaneans of Mr. and Mrs. Robinson, the Frankanwens of Mrs. Dixon and the Palmyras of Mr. and Mrs. Bishop.

Longs have become one of the stronger varieties of Dachshund and the successes of such dogs as Ch. Imber Hot Coffee (Raine and Crawford) and Ch. Phaeland Phreeranger (Susan Gatheral) with their Hound Group wins typify the present high standard and British breeding also dominates the variety in several overseas countries. *1979*

ADDENDUM 3:
THE WIRE HAIRED DACHSHUND

THERE has been a marked change in the personnel concerned with this breed in redent years. Since the arrival of the Miniature variety, the larger type has suffered somewhat in popularity and a number of breeders have takento the smaller ones as well or have gone over to them entirely. Mrs. Howard continues to breed very successfully, while the Seton affix has been transferred to Mrs. Besson and Mrs. Farrand, who have had great triumphs with Ch. Coral (mentioned on p. 75) and more lately with Ch. Gisbourne Inca—to mention two of their most outstanding Champions. Miss Hoxey has stuck to the larger variety but Group Captain Satchell has transferred his allegiance to the Miniatures. *1967*

Successful breeders and owners of more recent years are Mrs. M. E. Bates, Mrs. M. Flynn, Mrs. A. Wilson, Mrs. N. Shields, Mrs. M. M. Gower, Miss J. Hughes and Mr. and Mrs. Dring.

The great Champion Gisbourne Inca continued to dominate this variety, although he had his sixth birthday last October. Mainly as a result, Miss Hughes with her Trumpeter of Meeching was the only breeder to make a new Champion this year. *1968*

With the gradual withdrawal of the mighty Champion Gisbourne Inca, now an outstandingly successful sire, a number of new dog Champions has appeared. Three of them, not surprisingly, are owned by Mrs. Farrand, while Mrs. Hoxey Harris's Champion Tumlow Fruitcake has been an equally successful sire to Inca. Undoubtedly Mrs. Quick, who owns the Gisbourne prefix, must at this moment stand pre-eminent among Wire-haired breeders. A particularly successful newcomer to this breed is Miss Raphael (Andyc) while Miss Raine, Mrs. Hoxey Harris and Mrs. Gower have continued to produce top-class dogs. *1973*

Only two new Champions were made up during this period, one by Mrs. Farrand and one by Mr. Eric Gross and Mrs. Beynon. Both were sired by the former's successful Ch. Mordax Music Master, who is having a considerable influence on this, the smallest numerically, of the six varieties. This latter fact no doubt accounts for the scarcity of Champions, but logically there must be a fair number of dogs on the verge of top honours.

In spite of the relative decline in numbers being bred, the top quality of this variety is well up to the best standard of past times and this, which is in many ways the most individual of Dachshunds, will continue to attract a small but steady flow of "addicts". *1975*

A steady supply of top exhibits in this variety continues to come from the Mordax kennel of Mrs. Farrand; they are now seldom home-bred, but usually the progeny of her team of stud dogs headed by Ch. Mordax Music Master who is now behind all but a tiny minority of modern Wires and the spearhead of the "Red Revolution" that has brought this colour to the forefront—and with it better angulation at both ends. This variety is also rapidly gaining in popularity and attracting a healthy number of new exhibitors. The leading dog for the period was Mrs. Farrand's Ch. Fraserwood Neon Star—a group winner—and the outstanding bitch was Mr. and Mrs. Pearson's Ch. Tan Trudi of Thornton. It is interesting to note that two famous kennels from other varieties (Silvae and Swansford) each made up a first champion in Wires. *1979*

ADDENDUM 4:
THE MINIATURE SMOOTH DACHSHUND

THE popularity of the smaller varieties has greatly increased of recent years and now registration in all three Miniature coats considerably exceed those of their larger brethren. No doubt the continued urbanization of the country favours the choice of very small dogs—and Dachshunds make splendid flat-dwellers, in spite of their strong sporting instincts.

In Miniature Smooths, the outstandingly successful kennels of recent years have been those of Mr. Negal (Montreux), Mrs. Bassett (Merryweather) and Mrs. Littmoden (Wendlitt)—the first-named especially having produced a steady stream of Champions. Other prominent breeders who have come to the fore of late are Mr. A. W. Hague (Limberin) and Miss G. Barker (Potsdown)—both formerly better known as breeders of the Standard variety. Mr. and Mrs. Newbury (Dalegarth), Mrs. B. V. Samuel (Bettmark), the late Mrs. K. Gordon (Flaunden), Mrs. D. Hague (Berndack) (also well-known in Standards) are others who have made up a number of Champions in the last six years. Other Champion breeders include the Sheperdsdenes of Mr. and Mrs. E. Fox, who continue to breed extensively, Mrs. J. Nunn (Monken), Mrs. J. Foden (Booth), Mrs. M. F. Commeline (Yewden), Mrs. B. Munt (Pipersvale), Mr. and Mrs. J. Varley (Ballygunge), Mrs. J. Cusworth (Banastre), Dr. S. Kershaw (Hobbithill), Mr. and Mrs. Hickling (Embassy—another well-known Standard pre-fix).

1967

Six new Champions won their title in Smooths in 1967. Four of these were owned by well-known breeders, Mr. E. Fox, Miss Georgie Barker, Mrs. Foden and Mrs. Blandford. The two "firsts" were owned by Mrs. M. Gracey with Runnel Petticoat, a lovely bitch who had a very successful year, with 11 Challenge Certificates, and Mr. and Mrs. T. Dunn with their Playboy of Duningham. Mr. and Mrs. Solomon continued to do very well with their Bowbank Champions.

1968

The popularity of Miniatures has continued in all three varieties and registrations continue to go up annually. The Smooth-haired remains outstandingly the most popular and the breeders here are predominantly those who have been successful in the past. Apart from Mr. Negal (Montreux) who has been taking things a little easier lately, Mrs. Littmoden long dominated the dog classes with her Prince Albert of Wendlitt, who won at least forty certificates. Mr. Hague (Limberin), Mrs. Bassett (Merryweather), Mr. and Mrs. Smith (Wimoway), Miss Barker (Potsdown), Mrs. Solomon (Bowbank), Dr. Kershaw (Hobbithill), Mrs. Foden (Booth), Mrs. Samuel (Bettmark), Mrs. Gracey (Runnel', have all made up one or more Champions during the period. Mr. and Mrs. Newbury have made a successful return (from Ireland) with their Dalegarth prefix, which is now a powerful force in the breed once again. Another familiar prefix, that of Flaunden (Mrs. J. Blandford) has made a triple assault in all three varieties with considerable success.

1973

No less than eighteen Miniature Smooth Champions were made up in these two years and twelve of them in 1973. More than half of these were owned by well-established breeders, but as in former years, a number of newcomers achieved success. Mr. and Mrs. E. P. Smith made up three new Champions, but Mr. A. W. Hague has been so busy with his successful Standards that he made no Miniature Champion during the period. New to Champion status are the dogs produced by Mrs. H. Fidler, Mrs. S. Barlow, Messrs. C. V. and P. A. Millard, Mr. and Mrs. R. L. Voaden, Mrs. B. Castle and Mrs. D. Hilton and Mrs. K. M. Evans and Mrs. Angus.

Mrs. Littmoden, so long the Secretary of the Miniature Club and so successful with her Wendlitts, is retiring with her husband to Malta in August. Mr. and Mrs. Smith will be taking over her duties with the club.

1975

Top honours in this variety were shared between a greater number of kennels than previously, but the Cannobio kennel of

Mrs. Castle and the Hobbithills of Dr. Kershaw each produced four Champions, while Mrs. Munt (Pipersvale) made-up five and Mrs. Fidler's Ch. Braishvale Jumping Jack sired five.

Outstanding winners were Ch. Cannobio Schoolmarm, a winner of The Dachshund Club's Jackdaw Trophy for Top Winner all varieties, Mr. and Mrs. Pugh's Ch. Hobbithill Zebedee of Tarkotta who won three Cruft's CCs and Mrs. Bassett's Ch. Willowfield Sweet William who scored well in group competition. *1979*

ADDENDUM 5:

THE MINIATURE LONG HAIRED DACHSHUND

MANY new breeders have come to the fore in Long Haireds. The recent death of Miss M. C. Sherer of the Priorsgate prefix brought to an end a very long run of success for her kennel. Mrs. I. Stevenson (Armorel), Miss T. J. Millburn (Bowerbank), Mrs. N. E. Parsons (Minutist), Mrs. Y. J. Oswell (Mertynabbot), Mrs. B. C. Jolly (Ridgebar), Mrs. S. Gale (Mallards), Mrs. Waddington (Puckridge), Mrs. Hunt (Marpheld), Mr. and Mrs. S. G. Christmas (Esspeejay), Mrs. H. Fielding (Delphik), Mr. and Mrs. F. F. Thomas (Trumond) are leading breeders today. Senior breeders who continue to produce Champions are Mrs. L. S. Bellamy (Von Walder), Mrs. Gwyer (Marlenwood), Mrs. Hickling (Embassy), Miss Fardell (Farick), and Mrs. D. Dove (Bordak). *1967*

In Long-haireds, all seven new Champions were owned by those who had already made up one or more dogs—Mrs. Oswell, Mrs. Hall-Fletcher, Mrs. Green and two each by Mrs. Fielding and Mrs. Fraser-Gibson. *1968*

The Long-haireds have continued to hold most of their old supporters and almost all the "old brigade" have made up one or more Champions during these years. Mrs. Connell, Mrs. Fraser-Gibson, Mrs. Green, Mrs. Hickling, Mr. Oliver, Mrs. Oswell, Mrs. Parsons, Mrs. Sidgwick, Mrs. Fielding, Mrs. Fletcher, Mrs. Waddington, Mrs. Klin, Mr. and Mrs. F. F. Thomas. One of the most successful of the newcomers is Mrs. Dutson with her Rossglen Champions, three of them, while Mrs. Moon (Woodreed), Mrs. Gildersleeve (Meonfalk) and others are now producing excellent stock. There is little doubt that the pre-eminent Miniature of the period was the exquisite Delphik Debbret, belonging to Mrs. Fielding, who had a dramatic show career. I should also add that Mrs. Blandford produced Champions in this variety. *1973*

The Long-haireds acquired nineteen new Champions during the period. Interestingly, the bulk of these (fourteen) were made up by "first timers" in the persons of Mrs. N. Wakefield, Mrs. I. M. P.

Pain, Mrs. Cole-Hamilton and Mr. A. Sharman, with two each, and Mesdames Fishwick, Mather, C. J. Wilson, B. Owen, C. A. Blaxall and B. J. Bayne with one. The "Old Brigade" will have to look to their laurels! *1975*

This variety now consistently provides the largest entry and hottest competition at championship shows, although type is still very varied. The outstanding development in recent years has been the rise in popularity of the dapple colour—the main source being a recessive Min. Long from two Min. Wires in Mrs. Wharton's Littlenodes kennel. Littlenodes Quicksilver, a grandson of this bitch, was the first dapple CC winner in the breed and he sired the first Champion, Mrs. Owen's Ch. Littlenodes Silver Smoke, who in turn sired the next three dapple Champions. This period also saw the crowning of the first chocolate and tan in either size of Long-hairs—Mrs. Wilson's Ch. Ridgeview Dark Brown Tweed.

As can be seen from the list of champions, more Min. Longs were made-up over the four years 1975–9 than any other variety, eight of them by Sunara dogs, four by Delphiks and no less than six bred in the more recent Southcliff kennel. A new name to come to the forefront with three champions was the Rhinestar kennel of Mr. and Mrs. Corn. *1979*

ADDENDUM 6:

THE MINIATURE WIRE HAIRED DACHSHUND

SINCE Championship status was given to Miniature Wire-Haireds, no one kennel has had a monopoly of success in the show ring and a number have made up one or more Champions. These include Group Captain and Mrs. Satchell (Orkneyinga), Mrs. M. F. Rhodes (Coobeg), Squadron Leader and Mrs. E. R. Whitehouse (Granta), Mrs. M. Howard (Seale), Mrs. C. Taylor (Bluefelt), Mrs. K. P. Butcher (Wandleston), Mrs. S. de Bernes (Rigol), Mrs. R. Wakefield (Sillwood), Mrs. E. Quick, Mrs. R. Spong (Peredur), Mrs. M. J. Hone (Kavmar), and Mr. R. W. B. Pinches, who is much better known for his successful Turlshill Standards.

This variety, whose maximum weight is now 11 pounds, has attracted many new breeders and is already well-established and increasing yearly in popularity. *1967*

There were three new Wire title-winners—one each owned by Mr. Jock Lloyd, Mrs. S. de Bernes and Mrs J. Lawley. The latter two, Redenhall Silver Mint and Redenhall Yewberry, were both bred by Mrs. R. J. Colbourne. *1968*

The Wire-haireds have now taken on in a big way and a number of the big names in standard varieties have now entered the field—notably Mrs. Grosvenor Workman (Silvae) and Mrs. P. Hood-

Wright (Selwood). Miss Raphael has been almost more successful in this variety than in the Standards, Mrs. R. D. Spong has added to her successes—as also has Miss Gray and Mrs. Ticehurst. Once again Mrs. Blandford has bred or owned four Champions in this group—and must therefore lay claim to being the pre-eminent Miniature expert! *1973*

Ten new Champions have been made up. Again the success of hitherto less experienced breeders was conspicuous, seven of the above being owned by those who had not achieved Championship status before—Mr. and Mrs. Penswick with three, Mrs. E. P. Blackburn two and Mrs. Z. Andrews and Miss M. E. H. Marshall with one. Mrs. Workman, Mrs. Spong and Mrs. Moate were the only previous breeders of Champions. After a rather slow start, these immensely attractive little dogs are really carving out a niche for themselves through their very individual charms. *1975*

These fascinating little characters have made great strides and attracted many new devotees. The outstandingly consistent Drakesleat kennel of Mrs. Andrews produced six Champions as did the Silvaes of Mrs. Grosvenor Workman—the latter kennel having made-up ten Champions in four varieties during the four years! Miss Raphael made-up four new Champions including Ch. Drakesleat Klunk Klick of Andyc who holds the breed record in CCs. The Dalegarth kennel of Mr. and Mrs. Newbury, previously so successful in Min. Smooths, and the Cratloes of Mrs. Fountain have also come to the forefront by virtue of their own champions and those sired by their dogs. *1979*

APPENDIX A

BREED CLUBS

GREAT BRITAIN

The Dachshund Club

Secretary: Dr. S. Kershaw, 22 Clee Avenue, Fareham, Hants.

The Dachshund Club of Wales

Secretary: Mrs. R. D. Spong, Tynewydd, Henfwlch Road, Carmarthen.

Eastern Counties Dachshund Association

Secretary: Mr. B. Stubbs, 2 Duck Street, Furneux, Pelham, Buntingford, Herts.

East Yorkshire Dachshund Club

Secretary: Mrs. Rosalind Rawson, 202 Grovehill Road, Beverley, Yorkshire.

Great Joint Dachshund Association

Secretary: Mrs. Rhodes, Church House, Durrington, Salisbury, Wilts.

Lancashire and Cheshire Dachshund Association

Secretary: Mr. Jack Hayes, Blanket Hall Cottage, Bull Hill, Darwen, Lancs.

Midland Dachshund Club

Secretary: Mrs. R. W. B. Pinches, The Coage, Hirst Hill, Cosely, Bilston, Staffs.

Miniature Dachshund Club

Secretary: Mrs. A. Smith, Wimoway, Tilehouse Lane, Denham, Bucks.

Northern Dachshund Association

Secretary: Mrs. Anne Reed, 147A Toft Hill, Bishop Auckland, County Durham.

North-Eastern Dachshund Club

Secretary: Mrs. G. Gladwin, 11 Kensington Gardens, Eastbourne, Darlington.

Northern Long-Haired Dachshund Breeders' Association

Secretary: Mrs. K. J. Shaw, Mayfield Cottage, Milnrow, Nr. Rochdale, Lancs.

Scottish Dachshund Club

Secretary: Mrs. J. McNaughton, Balgownie, Ayr Road, Irvine, Ayrshire.

Southern Dachshund Association

Secretaries: Mr. and Mrs. L. Bishop, Garden House, Bury Bank Road, Greenham Common, Newbury, Berks.

West of England Dachshund Association
Secretary: Mrs. J. Hosegood, The Hyall, Lyehole, Wrington, Avon.
West Riding Dachshund Association
Secretary: Mr. Malcolm Olivant, 63 Newlands Drive, Sheffield 122FR.
Wire-Haired Dachshund Club
Secretary: Mrs. D. Moate, 2 Buttermilk Cottages, Leafield, Oxon.

NORTHERN IRELAND
Ulster Dachshund Club
Secretary: Mrs. J. Patton, 31 Ashley Park, Bangor, Co. Down, Northern Ireland.

EIRE
The Irish Dachshund Club
Secretary: Mr. W. Jackson, 4 Maritime House, Blackrock, Co. Dublin.

APPENDIX B

KENNEL CLUB REGISTRATIONS FROM 1945

	STANDARD			*MINIATURE*		
	Smooth	*Long*	*Wire*	*Smooth*	*Long*	*Wire*
1945	2587	437	81	—	—	—
1946	3792	641	42	—	—	—
1947	4489	681	78	—	—	—
1948	4268	615	93	60	29	—
1949	4292	604	112	325	259	—
1950	4038	470	204	395	307	—
1951	3729	526	216	375	401	—
1952	3309	451	166	517	327	—
1953	3132	351	189	652	376	—
1954	3218	439	157	711	469	—
1955	3411	387	238	1028	544	—
1956	3431	401	202	1401	592	—
1957	3395	434	212	1625	685	10
1958	3399	477	242	2051	826	143
1959	3471	521	250	2427	870	179
1960	3465	545	237	2672	1015	236
1961	3375	603	225	2858	1198	287
1962	3016	509	172	3167	1320	328
1963	2583	511	216	3026	1338	337
1964	2292	509	230	2828	1493	348
1965	2178	478	200	2811	1547	357
1966	1753	427	212	2575	1488	417
1967	1745	528	240	2748	1609	390
1968	1733	523	205	2745	1750	423
1969	1679	613	287	2774	1837	516
1970	1565	527	235	2872	1938	513
1971	1244	479	227	2428	2051	545
1972	1441	631	313	2802	2599	579
1973	1231	574	315	2478	2468	765
1974	1118	652	318	2098	2433	744
1975	836	499	261	1648	2103	662

In 1976, the Kennel Club introduced a new system of registration separating those dogs to be shown, worked or used for breeding from other "basic" registrations—so that registrations from that date are no longer indicative of each breed's numbers.

J.V. C.

APPENDIX C

STANDARDS

1. SMOOTH CHAMPIONS FROM 1955 TO 1978

Name	*Sex*	*Sire*	*Dam*	*Owner*	*Breeder*	*Born*
Hawstone Superb	D	Ch. Ashdown Eminent	Hawkstone Syren	Miss N. Hill	Owner	17–12–53
Silvae Keeper	D	Ch. Silvae Bandoleer	Dachscroft Hildegarde	Mrs Grosvenor Workman	Mrs D. M. John	1–5–55
Simonswood Souvenir	D	Ch. Allways Popcorn of Thistleavon	Simonswood Sunny	Dr T. H. Rigg	Owner	10–9–53
Etanin of Streamside	B	Ch. Tugboat of Thistleavon	Polarstar of Streamside	Mrs Grosvenor Workman	Miss A. C. Yardley	22–7–53
Granmede Melody	B	Ch. Hawkstone Matelot	Trasna Memory	Miss N. Hill	Mrs P. Young	17–9–52
Turlshill Rose Marie	B	Ashdown Mark	Brookenville Blackbird	Mr R. W. B. Pinches	Owner	3–11–54
Aysdorn Black Zingaro	D	Ch. Silvae Bandoleer	Aysdorn Black Zara	Miss J. Cook	Mr & Mrs E. G. Crowley	1–5–55
Muscat von Der Howitt	D	Kunz von der Howitt	Martini von der Howitt	Mme P. P. Rikovsky	Owner	21–2–56
Petuchok von Der Howitt	D	Ch. Urbaz von der Howitt	Kachtan von der Howitt	Dr S. Young & Mrs V. Collins	Mme P. P. Rikovsky	17–4–53
Silvae Review	D	Ch. Silvae Bandoleer	Silvae Reline	Mrs Grosvenor Workman	Owner	30–6–54
Craigmere Carmona	**B**	**Craigmere Cornel**	**Craigmere Camille**	**Mr F. McSalley**	**Owner**	**12–8–53**

Name	*Sex*	*Sire*	*Dam*	*Owner*	*Breeder*	*Born*
Grundwald Gitana	B	Ch. Grunwald Gleam	Ch. Grunwald Glenda	Mr & Mrs G. A. Lloyd	Owners	4–10–54
Hawkstone Echo	B	Ch. Ashdown Eminent	Hawkstone Syren	Miss N. Hill	Owner	16–5–55
Praline of Dunlewey	B	Turlshill Pirate	Quinlindt of Dunlewey	Miss M. H. Hannay	Owner	28–2–56
Rhinefields Falka	B	Ch. Rhinefields Lenz	Starboard Jane	Mr & Mrs J. Gallop	Owners	22–4–56
Turlshill Gretchen	B	Turlshill Pirate	Turlshill Ebony Queen	Mr R. W. B. Pinches	Owner	10–2–55
Aysdorn Black Zenith	D	Ch Silvae Bandoleer	Aysdorn Black Zara	Mr & Mrs E. G. Crowley	Owners	1–5–55
Hawkstone Eclipse	D	Ch. Ashdown Eminent	Hawkstone Syren	Miss N. Hill	Owner	16–5–55
Oysterville the Seeker	D	Ch. Potsdown President	Oysterville Wanderer	Miss D. Walsh	Owner	10–5–54
Silvae for Keeps	D	Ch. Silvae Keeper	Silvae Dilys	Mrs Grosvenor Workman	Owner	16–2–57
Tarkotta Black Falcon	D	Petruchka von der Howitt	Tarkotta Black Tarquin	Mrs B. M. Pugh	Owner	23–7–55
Turlshill Lancelot	D	Ch. Silvae Bandoleer	Turlshill Bo Peep	Mr R. W. B. Pinches	Owner	8–8–56
Wellshot Black Bishop	D	Hollyhill Aysdorn Black Knight	Wellshot Black Satin	Dr S. Young & Mrs V. Collins	Dr S. Young	23–6–54
Delysia of Dodwhit	B	Ch. Ashdown Eminent	Embassy Entail	Mrs J. Birley	Mrs A. E. Williams	26–7–57
Hawkstone Treasure	B	Booth Bravado	Hawkstone Trinket	Miss N. Hill	Owner	15–8–56

Turlshill Yvonne	B	Turlshill Pirate	Turlshill Ebony Queen	Mr R. W. B. Pinches	Owner	27–1–57
Ashdown Fernie	D	Ashdown Exponent	Ashdown Barleysugar	Mr R. Pilkington	Owner	3–9–57
Conlystill Guardsman	D	Patrizio von der Howitt	Conlystill Atterton Beatrix	Mrs O. M. Still	Owner	2–11–56
Selwood October Lad	D	Ch. Selwood Sailorman	Selwood Seasaria	Mrs P. Hood-Wright	Mrs W. Bown	6–10–55
Silvae Blueprint	D	Ch. Simonswood Souvenir	Silvae Replica	Mrs Grosvenor Workman	Owner	1–5–56
Turlshill Rob Roy	D	Turlshill Pirate	Ashdown Pol Roger	Mr R. W. B. Pinches	Owner	18–2–57
Booth Brocade	B	Sheumac Something	Booth Laughter	Mrs J. M. Foden	Owner	30–4–57
Selwood Scampari	B	Turlshill Pirate	Selwood Scampi	Mrs P. Hood-Wright	Owner	18–7–57
Turlshill Mona Lisa	B	Turlshill Pirate	Ladylodge Fenella	Mr R. W. B. Pinches	Owner	25–7–57
Withyband of Streamside	B	Ch. Silvae Bandoleer	Withyleaf of Streamside	Mrs Grosvenor Workman	Miss A. C. Yardley	6–9–57
Aysdorn Black Zariba	D	Ch. Silvae Bandoleer	Aysdorn Black Zara	Mr & Mrs E. G. Crowley	Owners	27–6–57
Eastmead Nicholas Nick	D	Ch. Silvae Bandoleer	Eastmead Shandy	Miss B. Covell & Mrs Thomson	Owners	25–3–57
Silvae Outline	D	Ch. Silvae Blueprint	Dachscroft Miranda	Mrs Grosvenor Workman	Mrs D. M. John	18–8–57
Booth Bagatelle	B	Booth Bravado	Booth Piccalino	Mrs J. M. Foden	Owner	4–4–58
Selwood Sunsprite	B	Turlshill Pirate	Selwood Sunshade	Mrs P. Hood-Wright	Owner	16–8–58

Name	Sex	Sire	Dam	Owner	Breeder	Born
Aysdorn Black Zeth	D	Turlshill Pirate	Aysdorn Black Zoreen	Mr & Mrs E. G. Crowley	Owners	23–7–59
Selwood Sea Ranger	D	Ch. Selwood October Lad	Selwood Seapink	Mrs P. Hood-Wright	Owner	28–8–56
Dargavel Mirth of Deugh	B	Ashdown Sinnington	Stroma of Deugh	Miss M. K. Stewart	Miss J. Cook	17–3–60
Rhinefields Mariella	B	Ch. Rhinefields Lenz	Ch. Rhinefields Melanie	Mr & Mrs J. Gallop	Owners	10–5–58
Turlshill Gay Lady	B	Ch. Turlshill Lancelot	Turlshill Ladybird	Mr R. W. B. Pinches	Owner	11–2–60
Turlshill Rosalind	B	Ch. Turlshill Lancelot	Turlshill Rose Marie	Mr R. W. B. Pinches	Owner	30–7–59
Ashdown Stirrupcup	D	Ashdown Exponent	Ashdown Barleysugar	Mr R. Pilkington	Owner	15–6–59
Rhinefields Corsair	D	Rhinefields Catamaran	Rhinefields Mercedes	Mr & Mrs J. Gallop	Owners	27–3–61
Silvae Fieldside Freelance	D	Ch. Silvae Outline	Fieldside Faith	Mrs Grosvenor Workman	Miss C. M. Edwards	28–6–59
Womack Wainwright	D	Turlshill Pirate	Womack Wagonette	Mrs R. Gale	Owner	20–5–60
Dachscroft Polly Peachum	B	Ch. Silvae Review	Dachscroft Hildegarde	Mrs M. Harrison	Mrs D. M. John	21–6–59
Heidefeld Liesel	B	Turlshill Pirate	Turlshill Lorelei	Miss R. de V. Molloy	Owner	16–11–59
Turlshill Gaiety Girl	B	Ch. Turlshill Lancelot	Chesterton Cressida	Mr R. W. B. Pinches	Miss J. F. Jenkins	19–5–61
Heidefeld Lohengrin	D	Turlshill Pirate	Turlshill Lorelei	Miss R. de V. Molloy	Owner	16–11–59
Longanlow Lucifer	D	Longanlow Lodestar	Longanlow Red Ember	Mrs B. J. Beaumont	Owner	5–6–60

Silvae Withyfree	D	Ch. Silvae Fieldside Freelance	Ch. Withyband of Streamside	Mrs Grosvenor Workman	Owner	22–6–61
Tarkotta Red Rubens	D	Ch. Silvae For Keeps	Tarkotta Red Mercedes	Mrs B. M. Pugh	Owner	3–12–61
Turlshill Highwayman	D	Turlshill Pirate	Ch. Turlshill Mona Lisa	Mr R. W. B. Pinches	Owner	28–4–61
Womack Wrightstarturn	D	Ch. Womack Wain-wright	Womack Winterstar	Mrs R. Gale	Owner	12–7–62
Ashdown Sidesaddle	B	Ashdown Exponent	Ashdown Barleysugar	Mr R. Pilkington	Owner	15–6–59
Aysdorn Amanda of Brackenside	B	Ch. Aysdorn Black Zenith	Marla of Brackenside	Mr & Mrs Crowley	Miss K. E. Webb	6–6–59
Droftaw Gay Lady	B	Ashdown Leading Rein	Ingo Fairy of Droftaw	Mr & Mrs G. W. Brown	Owners	22–5–61
Silvae Withywhisper	B	Ch. Silvae Fieldside Freelance	Ch. Withband of Streamside	Mrs Grosvenor Workman	Owner	22–6–61
Aysdorn Black Zinbad	D	Turlshill Pirate	Aysdorn Black Zoreen	Mr & Mrs E. G. Crowley	Owners	20–8–62
Hawkstone Fusilier	D	Heracles vom Liebestraum	Ch. Hawkstone Echo	Mrs J. Lawley	Miss N. Hill	14–10–60
Limberin Timaru Thunderbolt	D	Limberin Dachscroft Bangarde	Macushla of Deugh	Mr A. W. Hague	Mrs P. Dalgetty	3–12–62
Silvae Virgo	D	Ch. Silvae Fieldside Freelance	Silvae Venus	Mrs Grosvenor Workman	Owner	17–4–61
Silvae Vanda	B	Ch. Silvae Fieldside Freelance	Silvae Venus	Mrs Grosvenor Workman	Owner	17–4–61

Name	*Sex*	*Sire*	*Dam*	*Owner*	*Breeder*	*Born*
Silvae Vida	B	Ch. Silvae Fieldside Freelance	Silvae Venus	Mrs Grosvenor Workman	Owner	17–4–61
Womack Imber Starlet	B	Ch. Womack Wainwright	Imber Megora	Mrs R. Gale	Miss K. M. Raine	18–2–62
Womack Wintermorn	B	Ch. Womack Wainwright	Womack Winterstar	Mrs R. Gale	Owner	12–7–62
Aysdorn Black Zaab	D	Aysdorn Zian	Aysdorn Zelda	Mr & Mrs E. G. Crowley	Owners	16–6–63
Dallaberg Dinah	B	Ch. Hawkstone Fusilier	Limberin Latest Lovely	Mrs J. Tryon-Wilson	Owner	20–10–63
Mariners Belinda Belle	B	Ch. Turlshill Lancelot	Ch. Dachscroft Polly Peachum	Mrs M. Harrison	Owner	6–1–63
Silvae Defender	D	Ch. Silvae Virgo	Marlewrai Outset	Mrs Grosvenor Workman	Mrs M. Railton	18–1–64
Selwood Shocking Pink	B	Ch. Hawkstone Fusilier	Selwood Seraphine	Mrs P. Hood-Wright	Mrs I. Eaton	15–6–63
Silvae Frank	D	Ch. Silvae Fieldside Freelance	Silvae Rosette	Mrs Grosvenor Workman	Owner	28–6–64
Silvae Kennet	D	Ch. Silvae For Keeps	Marlewrai Outshine	Mrs Grosvenor Workman	Mrs M. Railton	12–3–62
Thundergay Double-O-Seven	D	Cedavoch Storm	Macushla of Deugh	Mrs P. Dalgetty	Owner	15–12–65
Webelong Legacy	D	Ch. Silvae Blueprint	Webelong Liberty	Mr & Mrs T. H. Thacker	Owners	1–8–64

Silvae Kerris	B	Ch. Silvae Kennet	Silvae Free Will	Mrs Grosvenor Workman	Owner	15-7-64
Cedavoch Seventhveil	B	Ashdown Sinnington	Eilean Mor of Deugh	Mrs J. McNaughton	Owner	22-4-62
Imber Auriga	B	Ch. Womack Wainwright	Imber Megora	Miss K. M. Raine	Owner	18-2-61
Selwood Sigismund	D	Ch. Heidefeld Lohengrin	Selwood Soraya	Mrs P. Hood-Wright	Mrs I. Eaton	17-6-64
Droftaw Tamerslip	D	Turlshill Pirate	Ch. Droftaw Gay Lady	Mr & Mrs G. W. Brown	Owners	30-4-64
Edburton Susan	B	Eastmead Doglann of Dachswald	Joydak Mistress Gretel	Miss G. M. Morgen	Mrs A. J. Dover	23-2-63
Jeremy of Brackenside	D	Ch. Aysdorn Black Zinbad	Carlotta of Brackenside	Miss K. Webb	Owner	2-5-65
Loni of Dunlewey	D	Ch. Heidefeld Lohengrin	Ulrica of Dunlewey	Miss M. H. Hannay	Owner	11-2-63
Polly Flinders of Adyar	B	Launcelot of Adyar	Pollyanna of Adyar	Mrs M. J. Birley	Owner	28-8-63
Aysdorn Black Zebastian	D	Ch. Aysdorn Black Zinbad	Aysdorn Zophia	Mr & Mrs E. G. Crowley	Owners	27-9-65
Ardrahan Petula	B	Ch. Womack Wainwright	Ardrahan Verulamia	Mrs G. Parker	Owner	14-2-65
Silvae Frere	D	Ch. Silvae for Keeps	Marlewrai Outshine	Mrs Grosvenor Workman	Mrs M. Railton	30-3-65
Daksmor Desdemona	B	Ch. Hawkstone Fusilier	Daksmor Tosca	Mrs M. M. Shields	Owner	3-10-64
Rhinefields Cinderella	B	Ch. Rhinefields Corsair	Rhinefields Catalina	Mr & Mrs. J. Gallop	Owners	5-10-64

Name	*Sex*	*Sire*	*Dam*	*Owner*	*Breeder*	*Born*
Greygates Trinket	B	Greygates Rosso	Greygates Telestar	Mrs S. Huet	Owner	20–5–64
Limberin Lorelei	B	Ch. Limberin Timaru Thunder Bolt	Limberin Duskie Beauty	Mr A. W. Hague	Owner	21–2–64
Limberin Leading Light	D	Ch. Hawkstone Fusilier	Limberin Landing Light	Mr A. W. Hague	Owner	22–5–65
Selwood Suleiman	D	Ch. Selwood Sigismund	Selwood Shocking Pink	Mrs P. Hood-Wright	Owner	16–5–66
Selwood Sunfall	D	Ch. Womack Wainwright	Ch. Selwood Sunsprite	Mrs P. Hood-Wright	Owner	17–1–63
Womack Wroyal Parade	D	Ch. Womack Wainwright	Womack Winterstar	Mrs R. Gale	Owner	12–10–65
Womack Winterstarlight	B	Ch. Womack Wrightstarturn	Womack Imber Starlet	Mrs R. Gale	Owner	16–10–64
Rhinefields Diplomat	D	Ch. Silvae Virgo	Rhinefields Catalina	Mr & Mrs J. Gallop	Owners	22–10–65
Rhinefields Dolabella	B	Ch. Silvae Virgo	Rhinefields Catalina	Mr & Mrs J. Gallop	Owners	22–10–65
Womack Droftaw Moselle	B	Ch. Aysdorn Black Zinbad	Ch. Droftaw Tamerslip	Mrs R. Gale	Mr & Mrs Brown	6–1–67
Carinthos Tangletoes Jezabelle	B	Ch. Hawkstone Fusilier	Amber of Carinthos	Mr F. Cobby	Mrs Lawson	21–1–63
Kelvindale Merryman	D	Cedavoch Storm	Ch. Dargarvel Mirth of Deugh	Mrs V. Collins	Miss M. K. Stewart	28–6–65
Dargarvel Merrymaker	B	Cedavoch Storm	Ch. Dargarvel Mirth of Deugh	Miss M. K. Stewart	Owner	28–6–65

Longanlow Louida of Roslaye	B	Longanlow Lawman	Longanlow Howicks Happy Star	Mrs R. Marshall	Mrs B. Beaumont	16–12–65
Cheswold Baystoke Artful Dodger	D	Ch. Hawkstone Fusilier	Cheswold Charmaine	Mrs M. Ree	Mrs Oxton	18–12–63
Mithril Ponselle	B	Mithril Renaud	Mithril Leonora Di Vargas	Mr & Mrs M. E. Triefus	Owners	4–7–65
Dargavel Most Happy Fella of Deugh	D	Cedavoch Storm	Ch. & Ir. Ch. Dargavel Mirth of Deugh	Miss J. Cook	Miss K. M. Stewart	25–4–66
Helice of Hanstown	B	Ch. Heidefeld Lohengrin	Honeysuckle of Hanstown	Mrs B. L. Jacot de Boinod	Owner	1–1–68
Bart of Deugh	D	Ashdown Duke	Ch. Dargavel Bright Spirit of Deugh	Miss J. Cook	Owner	7–7–69
Careless Rapture of Deugh	B	Ch. Dargarvel Most Happy Fella of Deugh	Folly of Deugh	Miss J. Cook	Owner	25–6–68
D'Arisca Satin Sensation	B	Ch. Womack Wrightstarturn	Urdac Electra	Mrs L. Coxon	Owner	24–6–68
D'Arisca Satin Sophisticate	B	Ch. Silvae Kennet	D'Arisca Satin Splendour	Mrs L. Coxon	Owner	17–9–70
Weiden Silvanwood Startime	B	Ch. Silvae Virgo	Silvanwood Samantha	Miss D. P. Dodson	Mesdames Wood and Bargate	21–12–69
Eatina Sunbonnet	B	Ch. Eatina Sundowner	Selwood Shellac	Mrs J. Eaton	Owner	19–6–67
Eatina Sundowner	D	Jarthley Bombardier	Selwood Sunhat	Mrs J. Eaton	Owner	8–4–66

Name	*Sex*	*Sire*	*Dam*	*Owner*	*Breeder*	*Born*
Womack Wrazzamatazz	B	Ch. Rhinefields Diplomat	Ch. Womack Winterstarlight	Mrs R. Gale	Owner	14–2–68
Womack Wrine Maiden	B	Ch. Womack Wrightstarturn	Ch. Womack Draftaw Moselle	Mrs R. Gale	Owner	23–11–68
Womack Wrum Bacardi	B	Ch. Eatina Sundowner	Ch. Womack Wintermorn	Mrs R. Gale	Owner	13–8–69
Kenmardith Black Zeus	D	Ch. Rhinefields Corsair	Dolores of Jarthley	Mr & Mrs K. Fisher	Owners	10–11–67
Rhinefields Marksman	D	Ch. Silvae Virgo	Rhinefields Catalina	Mr & Mrs J. Gallop	Owners	11–11–68
Silvae Jambo	B	Matzell Forrester	Silvae Chamois	Mrs Grosvenor-Workman	Owner	15–11–69
Silvae Rozelle	B	Ch. Silvae Frere	Silvae Rosette	Mrs Grosvenor-Workman	Owner	26–7–67
Dallaberg Dennis	D	Cordun Commander	Tourmaline Tippet	Miss M. Hutchinson	Mrs Tryon-Wilson	6–7–66
Jarthley Wilhelmina	B	Jarthley Bombardier	Selwood Sunhat	Mrs Lawley	Mrs J. Eaton	17–2–67
Zara Poppins of Zyl	B	Ch. Loni of Dunlewey	Zantessa of Zyl	Mrs S. Marston	Owner	25–5–67
Cedavoch Sea Mist	B	Ch. Silvae Blue Print	Ch. Cedavoch Seventh Veil	Mrs J. McNaughton	Owner	10–6–67
Tarkotta Red Bianca	B	Ch. Silvae Kennet	Tarkotta Red Lucia	Mrs B. M. Pugh	Owner	4–4–66
Ch. Dargarvel Merry Andrew	D	Cedavoch Storm	Ch. Dargarvel Mirth of Deugh	Miss K. M. Stewart	Owner	23–4–66
Silvae Thea	B	Ch. Silvae Thackeray	Marlewrai Freya	Mrs Grosvenor-Workman	Mrs M. E. Railton	7–3–69

Silvae Thackeray	D	Silvae Pasteur	Webelong Horizon	Mrs Grosvenor-Workman	Mr & Mrs T. Thacker	1–6–67
Silvae Zeben	B	Ch. Dallaberg Dennis	Silvae Chamois	Mrs Grosvenor-Workman	Owner	26–5–68
Limberin Lamp Lighter	D	Ch. Limberin Leading Light	Ch. Limberin Lore-Lei	Mr A. W. Hague	Owner	1–1–68
Limberin Leading Lady	B	Ch. Limberin Leading Light	Limbering Lisa Lea	Mr A. W. Hague	Mr J. Macauley	8–9–66
Mithril Flagstad	B	Ch. Limberin Leading Light	Mithril Fremstad	Mr R. J. Powley & Mr M. E. Triefus	Mr & Mrs Triefus	9–8–69
Mithril de Reszke	D	Ch. Limberin Leading Light	Mithril Fremstad	Mr & Mrs M. F. Triefus	Owners	9–8–69
Mithril Fleischer-Edel	B	Ch. Limberin Leading Lady	Mithril Fremstad	Mr & Mrs M. F. Triefus	Owners	9–8–69
Silvae Rosin	D	Tourmaline Tripper	Ch. Silvae Rozelle	Mrs E. Grosvenor-Workman	Owner	1–8–70
Mariners Brandy Bubble	B	Ch. Womack Wrightstarturn	Ch. Mariners Belinda Belle	Mrs M. Harrison	Owner	18–6–68
Cedavoch Vanity Fair	B	Ch. Silvae Thackeray	Cedavoch Seabird	Mrs J. McNaughton	Mrs Auld	4–6–69
Berndack Definite	D	Ch. Rhinefields Diplomat	Berndack Rhapsody	Mr & Mrs J. F. Hague	Owners	7–7–70
Roslaye Saffron	B	Roslaye Talisman	Womack Wroyal Ruby	Mrs J. Marshall	Owner	1–7–70
Daksmor Mirabelle	B	Daksmor Don Giovanni	Daksmor Desdemona	Mrs M. M. Shields	Owner	3–5–69
Antway Harvest Moon	**B**	**Aysdorn Zigor**	**Antway Fairy Tale**	**Mrs H. M. Parker**	**Owner**	**16–8–70**

Name	Sex	Sire	Dam	Owner	Breeder	Born
Lindos of Dunlewey	D	Lo[illegible]i of Dunlewey	Vanessa of Dunlewey	Mr. T. Peak	Miss M. Hannay	4–5–71
Mithril Theodorini	B	Ch. Mithril de Reszke	Ch. Silvae Thea	Mr. & Mrs. M. F. Triefus	Mrs Grosvenor Workman	14–8–71
Peredur Salad Days	B	Ch. Rhinefields Dipolmat	Peredur Souvenir	Mrs. R. D. Spong	Owner	25–10–69
Rhinefields Discoverer	D	Ch. Rhinefields Diplomat	Sheumac Satin Slipper	Mr. & Mrs. J. Gallop	Mr & Mrs Degg	23–7–71
Dunlewey Samson	D	Ch. Weiden Silvanwood Startime	Wilma of Dunlewey	Miss M. H. Hannay	Owner	30–12–70
Silvae Mandarin	D	Mithril de Reszke Ch.	Ch. Silva Thea	Mrs. Grosvenor Workman	Owner	14–8–71
Peachcroft Christmas Rose	B	Ch. Womack Wrightstarturn	Peachcroft Bettina	Mrs. J. Peach Lewis	Owner	23–12–71
Oxcliffe Redwood of Belldale	B	Ch. Silvae Rosin	Silvae Verity	Mrs. P. Kelsall	Mrs M. Thornburrow	1–12–71
Rosenket Lady Cornelia	B	Ch. Rhinefields Diplomat	Wallbutt Wanderlust	Mrs. R. A. Rawson	Owner	7–9–72
Limberin Loud Laughter	D	Ch. Limberin Leading Light	Timaru Trendy	Mr. A. W. Hague	Owner	22–4–73
Teilwood Velvet Queen	B	Womack Wrunning Flush	Teilwood Rhodecot Autumn Leaves	Sqn. Ldr. & Mrs. L. Henson	Owners	27–4–72
Aravorny Early Daylight	B	Ch. Limberin Leading Light	Aravorny Daytrip	Mr. T. Peak	Owner	23–7–73

Limberin Light Laughter	D	Ch. Limberin Leading Light	Timaru Trendy	Mr. A. W. Hague	Owner	22–4–73
Auldrigg Elan of Cedavoch	B	Ch. Weiden Silvanwood Startime	Cedavoch Seabird	Mrs. J. McNaughton	Mrs. F. Auld	8–5–72
Limberin Low Laughter	B	Ch. Limberin Leading Light	Timaru Trendy	Mr. A. W. Hague	Owner	22–4–73
Silvae Rodney	D	Ch. Silvae Rosin	Ch. Silvae Thea	Mrs. E. Grosvenor Workman	Owner	21–2–73
Dramatist of Rhinefields	D	Ch. Rhinefields Diplomat	Paxford Straits Black Beauty	Mr. & Mrs. J. Gallop	Mr. H. Roberts	5–4–74
Mariners Christmas Card	D	Mariners Billy Budd	Jarthley Marina	Mrs. M. Harrison	Owner	28–10–72
Imber Veruschka	B	Porthenys Gustav	Imber Antares	Miss K. M. Raine	Owner	1–11–71
D'Arisca Satin Statesman	D	Ch. Dargarvel Most Happy Fella of Deugh	Ch. D'Arisca Satin Sophisticate	Mrs. L. Coxon	Owner	30–6–73
Murantia Janine Marictur	B	Ch. Weiden Silvanwood Startime	Weiden Heidija	Mrs. M. F. Turner	Mrs. Knowles	16–12–71
D'Arisca Satin Selebration	B	Ch. Silvae Thackeray	Ch. D'Arisca Satin Sensation	Mrs. L. Coxon	Owner	16–12–72
Gentleman Jim of Jarthley	D	Jarthley Aristocrat	Harlow Superb	Mrs. J. Lawley	Mr. E. Scothern	7–4–74
Landmark Melchior	D	Longanlow Liberal	Ortrud of Landmark	Mrs. E. Heesom	Owner	17–11–71
Lyzander Jette	D	Khan of Scawdale	Lyzander Lady	Mrs. M. Knowles	Mrs. Read	5–10–70
Womack Wrum Double	D	Ch. Womack Wrightstarturn	Ch. Womack Wrum Bacardi	Mrs. R. Gale	Owner	23–6–74

Name	*Sex*	*Sire*	*Dam*	*Owner*	*Breeder*	*Born*
Swiss Miss of Rosenket	B	Aravorny Montecristo	Astrella of Longwaite	Mrs. R. A. Rawson	Mrs. G. Thynne	19–6–73
Sanday of Deugh	D	Ch. Bart of Deugh	Ch. Careless Rapture of Deugh	Miss J. Cook	Owner	6–9–71
Keidon Konsuella	B	Keidon Katellas	Keidon Kreme of Society	Mrs. R. Miller	Owner	7–5–74
D'Arisca Satin Speculation	B	Mormonstag Wallace	Ch. D'Arisca Satin Sensation	Mrs. L. Coxon	Owner	19–4–74
Benjamin of Ralines	D	William of Dunlewey	Antoinette Parasio	Mr. & Mrs. P. Lockett	Mr. L. Price	9–7–74
Cedavoch Sweet Cyn	B	Cynosure of Cedavoch	Cedavoch Sukina	Mrs. J. McNaughton	Owner	16–10–75
Matzell Mischa	B	Matzell Mixar	Matzell Moondust	Mrs. E. M. E. & Miss M. Norton	Mrs. E. M. E. Norton	2–9–75
Womack Wrum 'n' Coke	B	Ch. Womack Wrightstarturn	Ch. Womack Wrum Bacardi	Mrs. R. Gale	Owner	23–6–74
Descendant of Rhinefields	D	Ch. Dramatist of Rhinefields	Gailey Girl	Mr. & Mrs. J. Gallop	Mr. A. Brooks	16–4–76
Landmark Magician	D	Ch. Landmark Melchior	Silvae Truffle	Mrs. E. Heesom	Owner	15–11–73
Ralines Hildergarde	B	Turlshill Templar	Ralines Limbo Dancer	Mr. & Mr. P. Lockett	Owners	22–7–74
Limberin Lilting Laughter	D	Ch. Limberin Loud Laughter	Limberin Linden Lea	Mr. A. W. Hague	Owner	7–11–74
Roots of Silvae	D	Ch. Silvae Rosin	Erminstrude Fantasque	Mrs. E. Grosvenor Workman	Mrs. P. A. Strong	14–11–73

Name	*Sex*	*Sire*	*Dam*	*Owner*	*Breeder*	*Born*
Scawdale Kristmas Karol	B	Ch. Mariners Christmas Card	Kween of Scawdale	Mrs. M. Knowles	Owner	23–11–75
Teilwood Red Delicious	B	Ch. Landmark Melchior	Teilwood Sadie	Sq. Ldr. & Mrs. L. Henson	Owners	24–2–76
Rhinefields Amapola	B	Ch. Rhinefields Diplomat	Rhinefields Trilby	Mr. & Mrs. J. Gallop	Owners	25–10–75
Teilwood Hot Toddy	B	Ch. Womack Wrum Double	Teilwood Twilight	Sq. Ldr. & Mrs. L. Henson	Owners	29–6–75
Womack Wrum Truffle	B	Ch. Womack Wrum Double	Womack Wrag Quilt	Mr. A. I. & Mrs. H. Rofe	Mrs. R. Gale	9–7–76
Kyreburn Accurist	D	Classridge Caractacus of Athelwood	Tourmaline Tricot	Mrs. R. Jenkins	Owner	17–4–75
Landmark Sebastian	D	Deepfurrows Romeo	Teilwood Rosie Lee	Mrs. E. Heesom	Owner	10–11–77

APPENDIX C (cont.)

STANDARDS

2. LONG HAIRED CHAMPIONS FROM 1955 TO 1978

Name	*Sex*	*Sire*	*Dam*	*Owner*	*Breeder*	*Born*
Danjor Boy Warrior	D	Ch. Rheanda Rheingold of Marlenwood	Danjor Antella	Mr & Mrs H. A. Jordan	Owners	12–10–54
Imber Café Au Lait	D	Ch. Imber Coffee Bean	Liza von Holzner	Mr W. R. Handley	Miss K. M. Raine	13–3–55
Imber Café Noir	D	Ch. Imber Coffee Bean	Wheyenna Pegotty	Miss K. M. Raine & Mr W. R. Handley	Mr F. C. Simmons	22–6–55
Mervyn of Whadaur	D	Zip of Bolivar	Daughter-in-Law of Seton	Miss E. M. Gibson	Owner	15–6–52
Mooncoin Mastrodrasa	D	Ch. Rheanda Rheingold of Marlenwood	Mooncoin Madonna	Mrs R. Chatterton	Owner	7–9–55
Clonyard Cola	B	Ch. Mervyn of Whadaur	Clonyard Cognac	Miss M. S. Tilney	Owner	26–6–54
Danjor Miss Salome	B	Ch. Rheanda Rheingold of Marlenwood	Danjor Antella	Mr & Mrs H. A. Jordan	Owners	12–10–54
Digga of Windgather	B	Rosteague Rinty of Windgather	Polyanna of Windgather	Miss M. R. Mothersill	Owner	29–4–54
Griselda of Bolivar	B	Zip of Bolivar	Veronica of Bolivar	Mrs L. Roberts	Owner	3–11–54
Karla of Hilltrees	B	Bracken of Hilltrees	Rachel of Fenlands	Mr R. Jackson	Lt.-Col. G. Hodge	19–7–51
Reedscottage Rhythm	B	Ch. Jeremy of Buckmead	Ch. Reedscottage Rogueish	Mrs M. E. Buck	Lady Kathleen Hare	16–10–55

Titus of Haverburg	D	**Ch. Jasper of Hilltrees**	**Tessa of Haverburg**	Mrs D. J. Bennett	Mrs E. M. Briggs	30–6–55
Clonyard Coca	B	Ch. Mervyn of Whadaur	Clonyard Cognac	Miss M. S. Tilney	Owner	26–6–54
Jean of Kitenora	B	Ch. Rosteague Rollo	Susan of Kitenora	Mrs A. M. A. Kidner	Owner	16–1–54
Micheline of Pipersbath	B	Ch. Jasper of Hilltrees	Greta of Frejendor	Mr B. A. Smith	Owner	28–2–55
Charlotte of Kitenora	B	Ch. Rheanda Rheingold of Marlenwood	Susan of Kitenora	Dr B. Raven	Mrs A. M. A. Kidner	11–12–55
Clarissa of Kitenora	B	Ch. Rheanda Rheingold of Marlenwood	Susan of Kitenora	Mrs A. M. A. Kidner	Owner	11–12–55
Clonyard Christmas Cracker	B	Ch. Roguish Raconteur	Ch. Clonyard Cola	Miss M. S. Tilney	Owner	25–12–56
Marina von Holzner	B	Ch. Highlight von Holzner	Kyral Chianti	Mrs J. C. Connell	Misses M. & W. Todd	12–2–53
Red Rose	B	Trubru Texan	Elza of Bolivar	Mr R. O. Pickup	Mr & Mrs T. Buckley	21–8–56
Zoe Celeste of Albaney	B	Imber Lancer	Katherine of Albaney	Mrs K. Jensen	Owner	29–5–57
Buckmead Palomino	D	Buckmead Master Miniver	Janetta Kayernel	Mrs M. E. Buck	Mr & Mrs E. Hirst	5–4–56
Buckmead Daemon	D	Ch. Buckmead Palomino	Ch. Reedscottage Rhythm	Mrs M. E. Buck	Owner	10–3–58
Buckmead Dominic	D	Ch. Buckmead Palomino	Ch. Reedscottage Rhythm	Dr B. Raven	Mrs M. E. Buck	10–3–58
Danjor Boy Taza	D	**Ch. Mervyn of Whadaur**	**Ch. Danjor Miss Salome**	**Mr & Mrs H. A. Jordan**	Owners	5–12–57

Name	*Sex*	*Sire*	*Dam*	*Owner*	*Breeder*	*Born*
Imber Café Tinto	D	Ch. Imber Café Noir	Imber Orange Pip	Miss K. M. Raine	Mrs P. Bultitude	20–10–57
Charlotte of Sarfra	B	Ch. Imber Coffee Bean	Rebecca of Spedding	Miss J. Silcock	Owner	21–9–56
Closegarth Cluny	B	Ch. Imber Coffee Bean	Mooncoin Malissa	Mrs M. E. White	Owner	18–7–57
Jane of Bolivar	B	Ch. Imber Coffee Bean	Ch. Griselda of Bolivar	Mrs L. Roberts	Owner	29–4–58
Mooncoin Marsha	B	Buckmead Sherry	Mooncoin Macushla	Mrs R. Chatterton	Owner	23–5–58
Gem of Fairway	D	Ch. Imber Coffee Bean	Sandra of Kitenora	Mr F. J. Green	Owner	19–7–56
Wild Thyme of Antrobus	D	Ch. Imber Café Tinto	Aigubelle of Antrobus	Mrs B. Owen	Owner	12–11–58
Griselda of Maplecott	B	Ch. Imber Coffee Bean	Gelda of Maplecott	Miss E. Murphy	Owner	12–5–58
Katrina of Revilo	B	Don Carlo of Revilo	Madeira von der Howitt	Mr R. O. Pickup	Owner	2–7–59
Rebecca Celeste of Albaney	B	Ch. Imber Café Au Lait	Anita Celeste of Albaney	Mrs K. Jensen	Owner	8–11–60
Courtney of Carloway	D	Ch. Imber Coffee Bean	Prudence of Carloway	Mrs S. Devitt	Owner	27–6–57
Jinglebells Jocular of Mountchlown	D	Amer. Ch. Crespi's Happy New Year	Amer. Ch. Joybell's Jinglebells	Mr B. Emanuel	Mrs M. K. Reed	19–12–58
Robin of Sarfra	D	Ch. Buckmead Daemon	Charlotte of Sarfra	Miss S. J. Silcock	Owner	21–10–59
Closegarth Kiowa	B	Ch. Buckmead Daemon	Ch. Closegarth Cluny	Mrs M. White	Owner	3–6–60
Hermia of Wainsford	B	Ch. Buckmead Daemon	Cherie of Wainsford	Mr J. R. Hickson	Owner	14–7–59
Myfanwy of Sarfra	B	Ch. Buckmead Daemon	Ch. Charlotte of Sarfra	Miss J. Silcock	Owner	21–10–59

Buckmead Hermes	D	Ch. Buckmead Palomino	Ch. Reedscottage Rhythm	Mrs M. E. Buck	Owner	3–4–62
Coobeg Long Jonathan	D	Amer. Ch. Jager of Barcedor	Reedscottage Roguish Wink	Mr B. Emanuel	Mrs M. F. Rhodes	28–4–61
Kennhaven Mark of Bolivar	D	Ch. Buckmead Dominic	Ch. Jane of Bolivar	Dr B. Raven	Mrs H. E. Roberts	15–2–61
Mooncoin Markgraaf	D	Ch. Buckmead Daemon	Mooncoin Marianne	Mrs R. Chatterton	Owner	24–9–60
Red Rebel of Albaney	D	Imber Cafecito	Gay Celeste of Albaney	Mrs K. Jensen	Mr M. J. Moore	24–4–61
Magda of Bolivar	B	Ch. Buckmead Dominic	Ch. Jane of Bolivar	Mrs Roberts & Mrs Boydell	Mrs H. E. Roberts	15–2–61
Shula Celeste of Albaney	B	Ch. Imber Café Au Lait	Anita Celeste of Albaney	Mrs E. Lloyd-Williams	Mrs K. Jensen	3–12–61
Buckmead Hippy	D	Ch. Buckmead Palomino	Ch. Reedscottage Rhythm	Miss S. Brier	Mrs M. E. Buck	3–4–62
Martini von Holzner	D	Ch. Imber Coffee Bean	Ch. Marina von Holzner	Mrs J. C. Connell	Owner	24–5–59
Minte Golden Chance	D	Earlwyn of Pipersbath	Minte Coral of Kumalo	Mrs R. Simmonds	Owner	3–12–61
Red Rock of Albaney	D	Ch. Imber Café Au Lait	Anita Celeste of Albaney	Miss K. M. Raine	Mrs K. Jensen	5–9–62
Sorrel of Windgather	B	Ch. Symphony of Emartag	Sinful of Windgather	Miss M. R. Mothersill	Owner	3–8–62
Clonyard Casserole	B	Clonyard Carlos	Ch. Clonyard Coca	Mrs. L. S. Gatheral	Miss M. Tilney	5–8–61
Lerida of Sarfra	B	Ch. Imber Coffee Bean	Ch. Myfanwy of Sarfra	Miss S. J. Silcock	Owner	23–4–63

Name	*Sex*	*Sire*	*Dam*	*Breeder*	*Owner*	*Born*
Merula of Sarfra	B	Ch. Imber Coffee Bean	Ch. Myfanwy of Sarfra	Mr & Mrs B. G. Spiers	Miss S. J. Silcock	23–4–63
Oranje Celeste of Albaney	B	Ch. Imber Coffee Bean	Anita Celeste of Albaney	Mrs K. Jensen	Owner	31–5–64
Red Simba of Albaney	D	Ch. Red Rebel of Albaney	Deborah Celeste of Albaney	Mrs E. Lloyd-Williams	Mrs K. Jensen	4–7–63
Red Renegade of Albaney	D	Ch. Imber Coffee Bean	Anita Celeste of Albaney	Mrs K. Jensen	Owner	31–5–64
Mooncoin Marigold	B	Ch. Buckmead Daemon	Mooncoin Marianne	Mrs S. M. Brier	Mrs R. Chatterton	24–9–60
Mr Snodgrass of Heckford	D	Bracken of Antrobus	Karen of Heckford	Mr D. J. Brown & Miss E. M. King	Owners	23–2–62
Kennhaven Caesar	D	Ch. Imber Coffee Bean	Kennhaven Wendy	Dr & Mrs B. Raven	Owners	15–2–64
Buckmead Iona	B	Ch. Buckmead Hermes	Buckmead Ferelith	Miss P. Beardsell	Mrs. M. E. Buck	6–9–63
Kennhaven Danielli	B	Ch. Red Simba of Albaney	Kennhaven Sunshine of Vienda	Dr & Mrs B. Raven	Owners	22–12–64
Kennhaven Diarmid	D	Ch. Red Simba of Albaney	Kennhaven Sunshine of Vienda	Dr & Mrs B. Raven	Owners	22–12–64
Murrumbidgee Black Titan of Albaney	D	Ch. Imber Coffee Bean	Ch. Rebecca Celeste of Albaney	Mrs A. Spiers	Mrs K. Jensen	15–3–65
Jacqueline von Holzner	B	Am. Ch. Jinglebells Jocular of Mountchlown	Marina von Holzner	Mrs J. C. Connell	Owner	29–1–62
Closegarth Crinoline	B	Closegarth Cary	Ch. Closegarth Kiowa	Mrs M. White	Owner	12–6–64

Luxon Louise	B	Ch. Red Rock Albaney	Imber Café Lungo	Mrs J. Baker	Miss K. M. Raine	2–10–64
Kennhaven Emma of Emartag	B	Ch. Kennhaven Diarmid	Kennhaven Cleopatra	Mrs M. Griffiths	Dr & Mrs B. Raven	1–1–66
Red Rheingold of Albaney	D	Imber Red Regent of Albaney	Yolande Celeste of Albaney	Mrs K. Jensen	Owner	12–1–67
Lynocree Sabre	D	Ch. Kennhaven Mark of Bolivar	Ch. Shula Celeste of Albaney	Mrs E. Lloyd-Williams	Owner	17–8–64
Lynocree Solero	D	Ch. Kennhaven Mark of Bolivar	Ch. Shula Celeste of Albaney	Mrs E. Lloyd-Williams	Owner	17–8–64
Pandora of Murrumbidgee	B	Ch. Kennhaven Diarmid	Banzen Ravil of Murrumbidgee	Mr & Mrs B. G. Spiers	Owners	16–2–66
Kennhaven Francesca	B	Ch. Kennhaven Caesar	Kennhaven Sunshine of Vienda	Mr & Mrs E. Cunningham	Dr & Mrs B. Raven	1–9–66
Denberg Donella	B	Denberg Luxonfield Laird	Denberg Delilah	Mrs E. Harrison	Owner	28–3–69
Camilla Celeste of Albaney	B	Ch. Red Rheingold of Albaney	Ch. Oranje Celeste of Albaney	Mrs. K. Jensen	Owner	30–3–69
Claudette Celeste of Albaney	B	Imber Café Kaunus	Yolanda Celeste of Albaney	Mrs K. Jensen	Owner	27–2–68
Metadale Minuet	B	Ch. Kennhaven Caesar	Metadale Music Maker	Mrs P. R. Marlow	Mr R. Metcalfe	7–3–67
Julius of Penerley	D	Ch. Kennhaven Caesar	Cristobel of Mountchlown	Mrs J. C. Martin	Owner	9–9–66
Mormonstag Replica	B	Ch. Kennhaven Caesar	Roberta Celeste of Albaney	Mrs J. I. Martin	Owner	14–3–67

Name	*Sex*	*Sire*	*Dam*	*Owner*	*Breeder*	*Born*
Mormonstag Rhoderick	D	Ch. Kennhaven Caesar	Roberta Celeste of Albaney	Mrs J. I. Martin	Owner	14–3–67
Coobeg Barbarossa	D	Ch. Murrumbidgee Black Titan of Albaney	Coobeg Cleopatra	Mrs M. Rhodes	Mrs P. A. Cooper	8–6–68
Coobeg Christmas Rose	B	Ch. Coobeg Coquina	Am. Ch. Jessell's Sea Witch of Mountchlown	Mr M. Rhodes	Owner	10–12–67
Marie Celeste of Albaney	B	Ch. Red Renegade of Albaney	Deborah Celeste of Albaney	Mrs D. M. Sandland	Mrs K. Jensen	20–1–67
Endora of Murrumbidgee	B	Pimpernel of Murrumbidgee	Ch. Merula of Sarfra	Mr & Mrs A. D. Swann	Mr & Mrs B. G. Spiers	28–5–68
Swansford Brigg of Truanbru	D	Ch. Murrumbidgee Black Titan of Albaney	Ch. Kennhaven Francesca	Mr & Mrs A. D. Swann	Mr & Mrs E. Cunningham	7–10–69
Mormonstag Canny Lad	D	Ch. Kennhaven Caesar	Roberta Celeste of Albaney	Mrs Raven	Mrs J. I. Martin	15–12–68
Exeview Shanagea	B	Ch. Red Renegade of Albaney	Exeview Minte Mona Liza	Mrs I. Tozer	Owner	5–1–68
Nadine Celeste of Albaney	B	Ch. Red Rheingold of Albaney	Ch. Oranje Celeste of Albaney	Mrs K. Jensen	Owner	24–4–70
Haygars Kerry	D	Dondine of Sarfra	Adrian of Revidge	Mrs E. Hayes	Owner	3–7–68
Lowenbournes Lydia	B	Ch. Red Rheingold of Albaney	Ch. Marie Celeste of Albaney	Mrs D. M. Sandland	Owner	20–11–68
Swansford Murrumbidgee Isadora	B	Dante of Murrumbidgee	Ch. Pandora of Murrumbidgee	Mrs M. Swann	Mr & Mrs B. G. Spiers	4–9–70
Swansford Adora	B	Ch. Kennhaven Caesar	Ch. Endora of Murrumbidgee	Mr & Mrs A. D. Swann	Owners	9–5–71

Albaney's Red Rheinhart	**D**	**Imber Café Paulista**	**Camilla Celeste of Albaney Ch.**	**Mrs. K. Jensen**	**Owner**	**5–11–71**
Imber Café Russe of Voryn	B	**Imber Red Regent of Albaney**	**Imber Samantha Celeste of Albaney**	Mr. J. V. Crawford	Miss K. Raine & Mrs J. Baker	23–9–70
Murrumbridgee Paganini	D	Imber Café Paulista	**Ch. Pandora of Murrumbridgee**	Mr.T. L. Johnson	Mr. & Mrs. B. G. Spiers	8–2–70
Swanford Estee	B	Ch. Swansford Brigg of Truanbru	Ch. Endora of **Murrumbridgee**	**Mr. & Mrs. A. D. Swann**	Owners	27–4–72
Dunbrook Cuddl-e-Dudley	D	Bemaric Adonis	Belazieth's Tina	**Mrs. J. M. Duncombe**	**Owner**	17–2–73
Imber Hot Coffee	D	Ch. Albaney's Red **Rheinhart**	**Imber Kaffa Moka**	Miss K. M. Raine & Mr. J. V. Crawford	Miss K. M. Raine	16–1–73
Pamaron Beanochen Conrad	D	**Rudolf of Langton Paddock**	**Littlehound Juliana**	**Mr. & Mrs. P. L. Johnson**	Mrs. S. Kirby	9–9–70
Arnfield Amanda	B	Ch. Mormonstag Canny Lad	Yasmin Celeste of Albaney	Mrs. E. Lloyd Williams	Mrs. D. Quayle	12–7–72
Mooncoin Maccabean	D	Mooncoin Marshabronze	Closegarth Charm	Mrs. R. Chatterton	Owner	2–11–72
Voryn's Volga Olga	B	Rudolf of Langton Paddock	Ch. Imber Cafe Russe of Voryn	Mr. & Mrs. W. E. Robinson	Mr. J. V. Crawford	4–3–72
Swansford Ambassador	D	Ch. Kennhaven Caesar	Ch. Endora of Murrumbidgee	Mr. A. D. Swann	Mr. A. D. & Mrs. M. Swann	9–5–71
Nicola Celeste of Albaney	B	Ch. Red Rheingold of Albaney	Ch. Oranje Celeste of Albaney	Mrs. K. Jensen	Owner	24–4–70
Swansford Toreador	D	Ch. Swansford Brigg of Truanbru	Ch. Endora of Murrumbidgee	Mrs. M. Swann	Mr. A. D. & Mrs. M. Swann	10–2–74

Name	*Sex*	*Sire*	*Dam*	*Owner*	*Breeder*	*Born*
Arnfield Annabel	B	Ch. Mormonstag Canny Lad	Yasmin Celeste of Albaney	Mrs. G. Burrough	Mrs. D. Quayle	12–7–72
Albaney's Claire Celeste	B	Imber Cafe Paulista	Ch. Camilla Celeste of Albaney	Mrs. K. Jensen	Owner	5–11–71
Jamanean Maria	B	Imber Cafe Paulista	Imber Cafe Rosa	Mr. & Mrs. W. E. Robinson	Owners	3–7–73
Pamaron Abracadabra	D	Ch. Pamaron Beanochen Conrad	Amerfair Fritha	Mrs. H. M. Johnson	Owner	10–6–74
Murrumbidgee Isabella	B	Dante of Murrumbidgee	Ch. Pandora of Murrumbidgee	Mr. T. L. Johnson	Mrs. A. Spiers	4–9–70
Swansford Emminence	D	Ch. Swansford Brigg of Truanbru	Ch. Endora of Murrumbidgee	Mr. W. Horrocks	Mr. A. D. & Mrs. M. Swann	27–4–72
Swansford Liesl	B	Ch. Imber Hot Coffee	Ch. Swansford Murrumbidgee Isadora	Mrs. M. Swann	Owner	17–9–74
Swansford Betadora of Bronia	B	Africandawns Night Banner	Ch. Swansford Estée	Mrs. M. Swann	Mr. A. D. Swann	1–2–75
Lynjoy Shaswinning Way	B	Lynjoy Sinbenali	Lynjoy Tuftytail Angel	Mrs. K. J. Shaw	Owner	16–2–71
Phaeland Phreeranger	D	Ch. Albaney's Red Rheinhart	Silksworth Gold Braid	Miss S. D. A. Gatheral	Owner	24–6–74
Albaney's Miranda Celeste	B	Imber Cafe Paulista	Ch. Camilla Celeste of Albaney	Mrs. K. Jensen	Owner	29–1–75
Bronia Zodiac	D	Ch. Swansford Brigg of Truanbru	Phaeland Juniper	Mrs. M. Hall	Mrs. D. Hanney	26–9–72

Pamaron Abacus	D	Ch. Pamaron Beanochen Conrad	Amerfair Fritha	Mrs. H. M. Johnson	Owner	10–6–74
Truanbru Bunbury Blossom	B	Ch. Mormonstag Canny Lad	Truanbru Bambi	Mr. & Mrs. E. Cunningham	Owners	20–9–74
Rosenket Royal Flame	B	Ch. Imber Hot Coffee	Ritterburg Rhine Romantica	Mrs. R. A. Rawson	Owner	23–8–74
Frankanwen Gold Spinner of Swansford	B	Swansford Shenondor	Frankanwen Golden Girl	Mrs. M. Swann & Mrs. W. Dixon	Mrs. W. Dixon	30–6–76
Swansford Odora from Brianolf	B	Africandawns Night Banner	Ch. Swansford Estée	Mr. & Mrs. J. B. Winchurch	Mrs. M. Swann	19–3–76
Truanbru Beau Brummel of Africandawns	D	Ch. Mormonstag Canny Lad	Truanbru Bambi	Mr. T. L. Johnson	Mr. & Mrs. E. Cunningham	20–9–74
Swansford Waldeman	D	Ch. Swansford Toreador	Swansford Misadora	Mrs. M. Swann & Mr. & Mrs. J. B. Winchurch	Mrs. M. Swann	3–6–76

APPENDIX C (cont.)

STANDARDS

3. WIRE HAIRED CHAMPIONS FROM 1955 TO 1978

Name	*Sex*	*Sire*	*Dam*	*Owner*	*Breeder*	*Born*
Osbert of Seale	D	Ch. Oklahoma of Shennis	Primavera of Seale	Mrs M. Howard	Owner	26–3–52
Simonswood Stiletto	D	Ch. Altair of Clouds	Ch. Simonswood Sabina	Dr T. H. Rigg	Owner	8–6–54
Cliftonhill Jinks	D	Ch. Simonswood Stiletto	Cliftonhill Vogue	Mrs Glover	Owner	18–8–55
Coq d'Or of Seton	D	Ch. Grunwald Graduate	Dansomaine of Seton	Mrs D. Besson & Mrs B. Farrand	Owners	26–10–56
Ch. Orkneyinga Raven	D	Grunwald Grampion	Orkneyinga Sylvan Songthrush	Gp. Capt. & Mrs W. A. J. Satchell	Owners	19–2–55
Coral of Seton	B	Ch. Grunwald Graduate	Dansomaine of Seton	Mrs K. Besson & Mrs B. Farrand	Owners	26–10–56
Simonswood Sheba	B	Ch. Altair of Clouds	Ch. Simonswood Sabina	Dr T. H. Rigg	Owner	8–6–54
Simonswood Solange	B	Ch. Altair of Clouds	Ch. Simonswood Sabina	Dr T. H. Rigg	Owner	8–6–54
Oklahoma of Seale	D	Ch. Osbert of Seale	Katinka of Seale	Mrs M. Howard	Owner	8–8–55
Tumlow Black Magic	D	Shvan Quentin	Tumlow Lollipop	Miss E. Hoxey	Owner	6–7–57
Victor of Seale	D	Ch. Gerry of Seale	Viola of Seale	Mrs M. Howard	Owner	19–3–55
Paula of Arodsel	B	Nilbor Nisam	Wylde Palaver	Mr & Mrs L. J. Dring & Mr B. A. Smith	Mrs M. Roblin	18–12–55

Rytona Jolly Roger	D	Clouds Elinda Terceiro	Tanya of the Moat	Mrs N. L. Levis	Mrs M. Bates	30–7–58
Seale Weavers Rudolph	D	Ch. Osbert of Seale	Weavers Trudi	Mrs V. MacNaughton	Owner	6–4–56
Kelvindale Bottine	B	Kelvindale Dusty Boots of Dargavel	Kelvindale Maria	Mrs V. Collins & Miss M. K. Stewart	Mrs V. Collins	21–12–54
Orkneyinga Tommy Brock	D	Ch. Orkneyinga Raven	Orkneyinga Venus	Gp.-Capt. & Mrs W. A. J. Satchell	Mr D. C. Fortun	28–10–58
Rambler of Seale	D	Ch. Seale Weavers Rudolph	Marygold of Seale	Mrs M. Howard	Owner	25–1–60
Greygates Slippers	B	Irish Ch. Cobbler	Greygates the Bean	Mrs S. Huet	Owner	18–3–60
Rytona Twinkle	B	Clouds Elinda Terceiro	Tanya of the Moat	Miss J. Hughes	Mrs M. E. Bates	30–7–58
Fichtenwald Keiler	D	Wupty of Jagendorf	Dinwelsbuhl Eicne	Mr R. Mathews	Owner	8–8–60
Gisbourne Inca	D	Gisbourne Indigo	Gisbourne Camilla	Mrs B. Farrand	Mrs E. Quick	6–10–61
Hot Cross Bun of Seale	D	Ch. Seale Weavers Rudolph	Honey Bun of Seale	Mrs M. Howard	Owner	14–3–60
Rambler of Seale	D	Ch. Seale Weavers Rudolph	Marygold of Seale	Mrs M. Howard	Owner	25–1–60
Tumlow Magicote of Seale	D	Ch. Tumlow Black Magic	Honey Bun of Seale	Miss E. Hoxey	Mrs M. Howard	24–7–61
Holly Berry of Seton	B	Ch. Greygates Jive Dancer	Dansomaine of Seton	Mrs D. Besson & Mrs B. Farrand	Owners	1–10–61
Mordax Merry Music	B	Ch. Grunwald Graduate	Hardanger Mitzi	Mrs N. Shields	Mrs M. M. Senior & Mrs D. Kennedy	14–11–58
Pandora of Seton	B	Grunwald Grampion	Creation of Seton	Mrs D. Besson & Mrs B. Farrand	Owners	15–6–60

Name	*Sex*	*Sire*	*Dam*	*Owner*	*Breeder*	*Born*
Culdees Katinka	B	Titania's Crispin Boy	Rytona Tinsel	Mrs M. Flynn	Mrs M. Flynn & Mrs A. Wilson	31–7–61
Mordax Miss Mint	B	Grunwald Grampion	Mordax Mamselle Maupin	Mrs V. V. Gower	Mrs B. Farrand	25–6–62
Rytona Tip Toe	B	Clouds Elinda Tercerio	Tanya of the Moat	Mrs A. Wilson	Mrs M. E. Bates	30–7–58
Magic Moon of Seale	B	Ch. Tumlow Black Magic	Honey Bun of Seale	Mrs M. Howard	Owner	29–12–62
Malisa of Arodsel	B	Democrat of Arodsel	Mercedes of Brockbane	Mr & Mrs J. L. Dring	Mrs D. Greenwood	11–1–63
Moon Girl of Andyc	B	Ch. Gisbourne Inca	Tumlow Chocolate Sundae	Miss S. M. Raphael	Owner	10–1–64
Silenus Scarlett	B	Ch. Gisbourne Inca	Ch. Mordax Merry Music	Mrs N. Shields	Owner	26–7–63
Tumlow Fruitcake	D	Ch. Gisbourne Inca	Tumlow Coconut Kisses	Miss E. Hoxey	Owner	29–8–63
Tosca of Meeching	B	Ch. Gisbourne Inca	Ch. Rytona Twinkle	Miss J. Hughes	Owner	12–5–64
Mordax Model Maid	B	Mordax Master Michael	Gisbourne Camilla	Mrs B. Farrand	Mrs E. Quick	3–6–64
Bernadette of Modillion	B	Ch. Altair of Clouds	Selwood Sweet Marjoram	Mrs H. Clegg	Owner	29–7–57
Greygates Jive Dancer	D	Greygates Jive	Greygates Irish Dancer	Mrs S. Huet	Owner	17–2–57
Tentsmuir Keith Marshal	D	Ch. Gisbourne Inca	Tentsmuir Cara Dulce	Dr G. Blair	Owner	19–6–63
Trumpeter of Meeching	D	Ch. Gisbourne Inca	Ch. Rytona Twinkle	Miss J. Hughes	Owner	12–5–64

Mordax Modern Masterpiece	D	Mordax Master Michael	Gisbourne Camilla	Mrs B. Farrand	Mrs E. Quick	3–6–64
Lydia of Haverburg	B	Culdees Konz	Liverdale Laura	Mrs E. M. Briggs	Mrs A. Wilson	15–7–64
Tumlow Sugar and Spice	B	Ch. Tumlow Fruit Cake	Tumlow Gigi Kyon	Mrs E. Hoxey-Harris	Mrs Hoxey-Harris and Mrs N. Shields	16–11–65
Imber the Baker's Man	D	Ch. Tumlow Fruit Cake	Imber the Comeback	Miss K. M. Raine	Owner	5–5–65
Wanderer of Seale	D	Stroller of Seale	Red Pepper of Seale	Mrs McNaughton	Mrs M. Howard	16–10–66
Brambleglen Barbarossa	D	Timon of Meeching	Tanglewood Tabitha	Mrs F. J. Bird	Owner	30–4–66
Tentsmuir Vanity Girl	B	Ch. Tumlow Fruit Cake	Tentsmuir Kate Dalrymple	Dr G. Blair	Owner	2–9–66
Kelvingarvel Japonica	B	Ch. Gisbourne Inca	Kelvingarvel Pansy	Mrs Collins & Miss Stewart	Owners	25–9–68
Gisbourne Milton	D	Gisbourne Memorandum	Gisbourne Imogen	Mrs B. Farrand	Mrs Quick	19–9–68
Mordax Music Master	D	Ch. Gisbourne Inca	Brockbane Red Rachel	Mrs B. Farrand	Mrs Henniker-Heaton	29–4–70
Amphletts Imperial Star	B	Moat Imperial	Amphletts Apricot Sauce	Mrs V. V. Gower	Mrs Lloyd	28–8–67
Lowinlim Heidi	B	Ch. Gisbourne Inca	Longanlow Golden Slippers	Mr & Mrs K. J. Harris	Owners	9–7–68
Tentsmuir Vanity Fair	B	Ch. Tumlow Fruit Cake	Tentsmuir Kate Dalrymple	Dr Mary Jolly	Dr G Blair.	2–9–66
Mistress Jane of Paxford	B	**Ch. Gisbourne Inca**	**Denholm la Boheme of Paxford**	Mrs. H. Naylor	**Miss M. Gray**	10–5–68

Gisbourne Mirabelle	B	Gisbourne Ilex	Gisbourne Camilla	Mrs. P. Lawless	Mrs. E. Quick	20–12–66
Munstrike of Andyc	D	Ch. Gisbourne Inca	Ch. Moongirl of Andyc	Miss. S. M. Raphael	Owner	30–11–66
Silvanwood Stiletto	B	Ch. Gisbourne Inca	Brockbane Red Rachel	Mesdames Bargate & Wood	Mrs. L. Henniker-Heaton	29–4–70
Andyc Moonlight Rhapsody	B	Ch. Mordax Music Master	Moonmist of Andyc	Miss. S. M. Raphael	Owner	17–7–71
Gisbourne Greensleeves	B	Gisbourne Ilex	Gisbourne Camilla	Mrs. E. Quick	Owner	25–10–69
Pickhill Golden Minstrel	D	Ch. Mordax Music Master	Pickhill Dusty	Mrs. B. Farrand	Owner	21–2–72
Brockbane Red Rondo	D	Ch. Mordax Music Master	Brockbane Dark Design	Mrs. I. V. Beynon & Mr. E. E. Gross	Owners	3–2–72
Tan Trudi of Thornton	B	Ch. Mordax Music Master	Rheinhessia of Appletrees	Mr. & Mrs. Pearson	Mrs. Campbell	15–12–72
Mocking Bird of Mordax	B	Ch. Pickhill Golden Minstrel	Paxford Greygates Willow	Mrs. B. Farrand	Mr. H. C. Smith	3–9–73
Daxglade Dancing Major of Swansford	D	Ch. Brockbane Red Rondo	Tumlow Crumpet	Mrs. M. Swann	Mr. & Mrs. Griffiths & Mrs. E. Hoxey-Harris	4–3–74
Monteagle Sharpshooter	D	Ch. Pickhill Golden Minstrel	Greygates Bobo	Mrs. S. Owen	Mr. H. C. Smith	12–4–73
Tentsmuir Maid Maria	B	Ch. Mordax Music Master	Tentsmuir Seans Maid	Dr. G. Blair	Owner	3–1–74
Meeching Tina	B	Ch. Mordax Music Master	Ch. Tosca of Meeching	Mr. J. P. Green	Miss J. Hughes	22–7–72
Brockbane Rough Music	B	Ch. Mordax Music Master	Brockbane Dark Design	Mrs. I. V. Beynon & Mr. E. E. Gross	Owners	3–2–72

Tentsmuir Maid Margo	B	Ch. Mordax Music Master	Tentsmuir Seans Maid	Mmes. J. Naylor & B. Farrand	Dr. G. Blair	3–1–74
Fraserwood Neon Star	D	Ch. Pickhill Golden Minstrel	D'Arisca Tweed 'N' Tawny	Mrs. B. Farrand	Mrs. Fraser	28–12–74
Silvanwood High Society	B	Ch. Mordax Music Master	Friendly Shaycroft	Mmes. Bargate & Wood	Owners	15–3–75
Mydax Roamer	B	Holmesdale Gambler	Mydax Breakers Eager	Mrs. J. Menin	Owner	17–5–74
Joydonia French Mustard	D	Ch. Brockbane Red Rondo	Billnmare Pepperpot	Mrs. J. M. Mildon	Owner	15–6–74
Silvae Cotillion	B	Ch. Daxglade Dancing Major of Swansford	Silvae Joyful	Mrs. E. Grosvenor Workman	Owner	8–8–75
Andyc Midnight Rhapsody	B	Aus. & N.Z. Ch. Andyc Grand Master	Ch. Andyc Moonlight Rhapsody	Miss S. M. Raphael	Owner	11–8–76
Quitrutec Friendly Persuasion	B	Quitrutec Lohengrin	Daxglade Dancing Maid	Mr. & Mrs. G. W. Owen	Owners	23–3–77
Daxene Yukonly	D	Ch. Daxglade Dancing Major of Swansford	Monteagle Camilla	Mr. J. P. Green	Owner	18–10–75

APPENDIX D

MINIATURES

1. MINIATURE SMOOTH CHAMPIONS FROM 1955 TO 1978

Name	*Sex*	*Sire*	*Dam*	*Owner*	*Breeder*	*Born*
Challenge of Wendlitt	D	Ch. Otter of Wendlitt	Sara Ann of Wendlitt	Mrs J. E. Littmoden	Owner	30–7–55
Merryweather Magic	D	Ch. Minivale Melvin	Merryweather Matilda	Mrs E. Bassett	Owner	28–8–53
Merryweather Marvellous	D	Ch. Merryweather Marvel	Sidegate Tiny Tot	Mrs E. Bassett	Mrs D. Groom	19–1–55
Shepherdsdene Spring Song of Kersheen	B	Ch. Shepherdsdene Sensation	Easter of Shepherdsdene	Miss S. Ferris	Mr & Mrs E. Fox	18–10–53
Trudie of Bettmark	B	Ch. Merryweather Magic	Limpsfield Garnet	Mrs B. V. Samuel	Mrs M. N. Molesworth	23–3–55
Courtney of Montreux	D	Ch. Otter of Wendlitt	Cressida of Montreux	Mr A. Negal	Owner	26–7–56
Merryweather Mathew	D	Ch. Merryweather Marvel	Davaars Isabel	Mrs E. Bassett	Mrs A. Hay	17–3–56
Shepherdsdene Sans Egal	D	Ch. Shepherdsdene Sovereign	Glitter of Shepherdsdene	Mr & Mrs E. Fox	Owners	24–9–54
Chocoletta of Montreux	B	Ch. Romulus of Montreux	Berengaria of Montreux	Mr A. Negal	Owner	10–9–56
Dalegarth Teilwood Sally	B	Ch. Otter of Wendlitt	Wee Greta of Teil	Mr & Mrs F. T. Newbury	Mrs A. Forsyth	19–10–55
Embassy Firedancer	B	Ch. Merryweather Marvel	Embassy Firefly	Mr & Mrs W. E. Hickling	Owners	21–3–55

Flower of Wendlitt	B	Goldenstar of Wendlitt	Golden Girl of Wendlitt	Mrs J. E. Littmoden	Owner	4–8–55
Minivale Perry	D	Ch. Minivale Melvin	Minivale Petronella	Mrs E. A. Winder	Owner	22–1–57
Minivale Pure Gold	D	Ch. Minivale Melvin	Minivale Petronella	Mrs E. A. Winder	Owner	22–1–57
Romulus of Montreux	D	Cassandra of Montreux	Titania of Montreux	Mr A. Negal	Owner	3–10–55
St Neots Tiny Tim	D	Minivale Page Boy	St Neots Bebe	Mrs Wrycroft	Owner	18–7–56
Carminetta of Montreux	B	Ch. Romulus of Montreux	Helene of Montreux	Mr A. Negal	Owner	12–4–57
Dalegarth Limelight	B	Goldenstar of Wendlitt	Krishna of Kinghurst	Mr & Mrs G. A. Lloyd	Mr & Mrs F. T. Newbury	19–7–56
Minivale Primula	B	Ch. Minivale Miraculous	Minivale Perle	Mrs E. A. Winder	Owner	14–4–56
Sauminda Sally	B	Ch. Merryweather Magic	Sauminda Wendy	Mr & Mrs J. Sauvage	Owner	22–8–56
Shadmor Fantasia of Wendlitt	B	Ch. Otter of Wendlitt	Shadmor Stephanie	Mrs J. E. Littmoden	Mrs E. R. Moore	22–6–55
Shulamede of Montreux	B	Ch. Romulus of Montreux	Cressida of Montreux	Mr A. Negal	Owner	11–4–57
Bartolo of Montreux	D	Ch. Romulus of Montreux	Helene of Montreux	Mr A. Negal	Owner	21–6–58
Dalegarth Dabster	D	Jack-a-Dandy of Wendlitt	Ch. Dalegarth Teil-wood Sally	Mr & Mrs F. T. Newbury	Owners	1–10–57
Merryweather Murgatroyd	D	Ch. Merryweather Mathew	Limpsfield Topaz	Mrs E. Bassett	Mrs E. M. Clarke	31–7–58

Name	*Sex*	*Sire*	*Dam*	*Owner*	*Breeder*	*Born*
Gloriana of Davenbrook	B	Limpsfield Earlybird	Cherie of Mallards	Mrs A. Finlayson	Owner	4–7–57
Magdaliene of Montreux	B	Ch. Romulus of Montreux	Cressida of Montreux	Mr A Negal	Owner	11–4–57
Monken Manuela	B	Ch. Merryweather Magic	Monken Morgedal	Mrs J. Nunn	Owner	12–5–57
Sheumac Scorer of Booth	B	Marikamos Zingo	Thanatos Jacobea	Mrs J. M. Foden	Mrs M. I. Kirkham	10–2–58
Truelove of Bettmark	B	Limpsfield Earlybird	Trudie of Bettmark	Mrs B. V. Samuel	Owner	15–1–57
Cedric of Montreux	D	Ch. Romulus of Montreux	Helene of Montreux	Mr A. Negal	Owner	21–6–58
Dalegarth Delicate Air	B	Ch. Merryweather Magic	Ch. Dalegarth Teilwood Sally	Mr & Mrs F. T. Newbury	Owners	10–2–59
Merryweather Marcella	B	Ch. Merryweather Magic	Arabella	Mrs B. V. Samuel	Mr R. Kyall	10–3–58
Berndack Mini-Minor	D	Ch. Minivale Pure Gold	Berndack Bruna	Mrs D. Hague	Owner	1–8–59
Dalegarth Charlie Brown	D	Ch. Dalegarth Dabster	Dalegarth Lynette	Mr & Mrs F. T. Newbury	Mr & Mrs A. R. Barker	16–6–59
Flaunden Senator	D	Ch. Romulus of Montreux	Flaunden Silk	Mrs K. Gordon	Owner	16–2–59
Merryweather Mills	D	Ch. Merryweather Magic	Ch. Truelove of Bettmark	Mrs E. Bassett	Mrs B. V. Samuel	3–6–60
Minivale Nugget	D	Ch. Minivale President	Dinglebank Golden Guinea	Mrs E. A. Winder	Mrs B. Gardner	15–2–60
Minivale President	D	Ch. Minivale Miraculous	Minivale Petronella	Mrs E. A. Winder	Owner	11–7–58

Berndack Martina	B	Ch. Minivale Pure Gold	Minivale Bruna	Mr & Mrs J. F. Hague	Mrs Hague	1–8–59
Elaine of Montreux	B	Ch. Courtney of Montreux	Ch. Chocoletta of Montreux	Mr A. Negal	Owner	3–1–59
Embassy Cream Caramel	B	Ch. Shepherdsdene Sans Egal	Ch. Embassy Firedancer	Mr & Mrs W. E. Hickling	Owners	14–6–58
Embassy Old Coin	B	Grunwald Geoffrey	Embassy Firefairy	Mrs P. Donaldson	Mr & Mrs W. E. Hickling	10–5–59
Kay Ann of Wendlitt	B	Ch. Otter of Wendlitt	Pamela Ann of Wendlitt	Mrs J. E. Littmoden	Owner	23–8–59
Sheumac Skeeter	B	Marikamas Zingo	Sheumac Squib	Mrs J. Foden	Mrs E. A. Sandiland	14–3–59
Kelvingarvel Dominic	D	Ch. Merryweather Magic	Kelvingarvel Annabelle	Mrs V. Collins & Miss M. K. Stewart	Owners	11–7–60
Septimus of Wendlitt	D	Ch. Otter of Wendlitt	Daffodil of Wendlitt	Mrs J. E. Littmoden & Mrs B. Munt	Mrs J. E. Littmoden	10–9–61
Shepherdsdene Satellite	D	Ch. Shepherdsdene Sans Egal	Shepherdsdene Scandal	Mr & Mrs E. Fox	Owners	5–5–58
Wirraldene Scampie Kellermeister	D	Embassy Gilt Edged	Karol Kellermeister	Mrs M. J. Jackson	Mrs E. Butler	18–9–60
Constance of Montreux	B	Ramiro of Montreux	Ch. Shulamede of Montreux	Mr A. Negal	Owner	27–8–61
Lansing Lovely Janet	B	Sauminda Austin	Sauminda Garforths Jane	Mrs M. F. Commeline	Mr J. L. Richardson	13–1–61
Michaela of Montreux	B	Ramiro of Montreux	Magnolia of Montreux	Mr A. Negal	Owner	17–1–61
Potsdown Woolly Pots	B	Paddy of Wendlitt	Pamela Ann of Wendlitt	Miss G. H. Barker & Mr H. M. Woollam	Mrs A. W. Neal	21–10–60

Name	*Sex*	*Sire*	*Dam*	*Owner*	*Breeder*	*Born*
Starlet of Bettmark	B	Ch. Merryweather Magic	Sapphire of Bettmark	Mrs B. V. Samuel	Owner	26–7–59
Cavalier of Montreux	D	Ramiro of Montreux	Magnolia of Montreux	Mr A Negal	Owner	17–7–61
Dalegarth Charleston	D	Ch. Dalegarth Charlie Brown	Dalegarth Lucky Star	Mr & Mrs F. T. Newbury	Owners	12–10–61
Limberin Americano	D	Ch. Minivale President	Limberin Firefly	Mr A. W. Hague	Owner	4–7–62
Limberin Pimpernel	D	Ch. Merryweather Magic	Limberin Firefly	Mr A. W. Hague	Owner	12–6–60
Merryweather Marcello	D	Ch. Merryweather Mathew	Ch. Merryweather Marcella	Mrs E. Bassett	Mrs B. V. Samuel	8–5–61
Timson of Wendlitt	D	Tiny Tim of Wendlitt	Forestford Cleopatra	Mrs J. E. Littmoden	Mrs J. Mills	12–10–61
Booth Minnehaha	B	Sheumac Starlighter	Booth Between	Mrs J. M. Foden	Owner	23–9–51
Hippolyta of Ballygunge	B	Ch. Flaunden Senator	Colynbawn Kumari of Ballygunge	Mr & Mrs J. Varley	Mrs Varley	18–3–62
Limberin Penny Black	B	Ch. Merryweather Magic	Limberin Firefly	Mr A. W. Hague	Owner	12–6–60
Limberin Marienina	B	Ch. Merryweather Marvel	Limberin Lilting Lullaby	Mr A. W. Hague	Owner	2–1–60
Pamela Jane of Wendlitt	B	Paddy of Wendlitt	Pamela Ann of Wendlitt	Mrs J. E. Littmoden & Mrs B. Munt	Mr A. W. Neal	21–10–60
Phyllis of Montreux	B	Ramiro of Montreux	Magnolia of Montreux	Mr A. Negal	Owner	16–3–62

Potsdown Pride	B	Ch. Merryweather Marvel	Ch. Potsdown Woollypots	Miss G. H. Barker & Mr H. M. Woollam	Owners	27–12–61
Sara of Montreux	B	Geoffrey of Montreux	Sarita of Montreux	Mr A. Negal	Owner	4–11–62
Adrian of Montreux	D	Ch. Cavalier of Montreux	Shulamede of Montreux	Mr A. Negal	Owner	23–10–63
Bellini of Montreux	D	Ch. Cavalier of Montreux	Rosemary of Montreux	Mr A. Negal	Owner	14–9–62
Dalegarth Designer	D	Ch. Dalegarth Dabster	Ch. Dalegarth Teilwood Sally	Mr & Mrs F. T. Newbury	Owners	23–9–62
Geoffrey of Montreux	D	Ramiro of Montreux	Shulamede of Montreux	Mr A. Negal	Owner	27–8–61
Shepherdsdene Pippin	D	Ch. Shepherdsdene Satellite	Shepherdsdene Apple Sauce	Mr & Mrs E. Fox	Owners	14– –62
Chiquita of Montreux	B	Ramiro of Montreux	Magnolia of Montreux	Mr A. Negal	Owner	24–5–63
Banastre Birthday Girl	B	Ch. Shepherdsdene Sans Egal	Banastre Blue Moon	Mrs J. Cusworth	Owner	12–6–62
Fenella of Montreux	B	Ch. Cavalier of Montreux	Ch. Magdaleine of Montreux	Mr A. Negal	Owner	20–3–63
Flaunden Sea Urchin	B	Ch. Flaunden Senator	Wirraldene Wild Rose	Mrs K. Gordon	Mrs J. Marshall	24–7–62
Hannah of Hobbithill	B	Ch. Merryweather Magic	Chloe of Hobbithill	Dr S. Kershaw	Owner	20–6–60
Bowbank Red Riley	D	Bowbank Ferrari	Bowbank Red Rosette	Mrs D. Solomon	Owner	28–2–64
Flaunden Sir Lionel	D	Ch. Flaunden Senator	Wirraldene Wild Rose	Mrs G. Chivers	Mrs K. Gordon	5–6–63

Name	*Sex*	*Sire*	*Dam*	*Owner*	*Breeder*	*Born*
Merryweather Moreover	D	Ch. Merryweather Mills	Foxcote Flirt	Mrs E. Bassett	Owner	11–8–63
Monken Manilla	B	Sauminda Austin	Ch. Monken Manuela	Mrs J. Nunn	Owner	10–2–64
Petronella of Montreux	B	Ch. Geoffrey of Montreux	Sarita of Montreux	Mr A. Negal	Owner	30–6–64
Slovanna of Montreux	B	Ramiro of Montreux	Ch. Elaine of Montreux	Mr A. Negal	Owner	27–6–63
Telstar of Hobbithill	D	Ch. Limberin Americano	Ch. Hannah of Hobbithill	Mr A. W. Hague	Dr. Kershaw	30–3–64
Twiland Fidelity	B	Sheumac Starshot	Twiland Crevette	Mrs E. Williams	Owner	11–8–63
Wendlitt Tessa of Hobbithill	B	Ch. Limberin Americano	Ch. Hannah of Hobbithill	Mrs J. Littmoden	Dr S. Kershaw	30–3–64
Bowbank Red Riordan	D	Ch. Bowbank Red Riley	Bowbank Frolic	Mrs D. Solomon	Owner	17–5–65
Tarkotta Red Titania	B	Wimoway Wilberforce	Sunsprite of Wimoway	Flt.-Lt. J. Pugh	Owner	25–11–61
Patricia of Montreux	B	Ch. Cavalier of Montreux	Dubarry of Montreux	Mr A. Negal	Owner	19–7–64
Evelyn of Montreux	B	Ch. Courtney of Montreux	Ch. Chocoletta of Montreux	Mr A. Negal	Owner	19–6–58
Potsdown Morgan	D	Tarkotta Potsdown Preceptor	Potsdown Philippa	Mr & Mrs H. Woollam	Owners	14–7–64
Wimoway Washington Rose	B	Ch. Flaunden Senator	Wimoway Coleen	Mrs E. P. Smith	Owner	8–10–64

Dandy Dan of Wendlitt	**D**	**Jack-a-Dandy of Wendlitt**	**Petronella of Wendlitt**	**Mrs J. E. Littmoden**	**Owner**	**19–1–65**
Heldomur Golden Girl	B	Bowbank Fledermaus	Heldomur Wahead	Mr D. J. Mold	Owner	16–4–63
Hatchmead Sophia	B	Hatchmead Black Magic	Hatchmead Helena	Mrs J. D. M. Thomas	Owner	6–12–62
Booth Mayfly	B	Zebo of Bettmark	Ch. Sheumac Skeeter	Mrs J. M. Foden	Owner	3–5–64
Melba of Duningham	B	Merryman of Duningham	Duskie Flower of Duningham	Mr & Mrs T. Dunn	Owners	2–9–61
Pipersvale Chocoletta	B	Ch. Septimus of Wendlitt	Berndack Katie	Mrs B. Munt	Owner	23–4–65
Vienda Kitty Fisher	B	Mr Acker Bilk	Kennhaven Minty	Miss H. Harriman	Owner	12–3–64
Winston of Hobbithill	D	Ch. Limberin Americano	Ch. Hannah of Hobbithill	Mr A. W. Hague	Dr S. Kershaw	29–7–65
Shepherdsdene Jonathan	D	Shepherdsdene St. Julian	Shepherdsdene Ciderette	Mr & Mrs E. Fox	Owners	24–8–65
Booth Christina	B	Ch. Merryweather Moreover	Selwood Sybil	Mrs J. Foden	Owner	29–5–66
Flaunden Student Prince	D	Ch. Flaunden Senator	Wirraldene Wild Rose	Mrs J. Blandford	Mrs K. Gordon	5–6–63
Playboy of Duningham	D	Ch. Dalegarth Designer	Melba of Duningham	Miss H. Harriman	Mr & Mrs T. Dunn	10–11–64
Potsdown Limelight	B	Ch. Potsdown Morgan	Griselda of Ktima	Miss G. Barker and Mr H. Woollam	Mrs J. Leach	27–5–66
Runnel Petticoat	B	Ch. Merryweather Moreover	Runnel Poppy	Mrs M. Gracey	Owner	1–6–65

Name	*Sex*	*Sire*	*Dam*	*Owner*	*Breeder*	*Born*
Limberin El Dorado	D	Ch. Limberin Americano	Limberin Delilah	Mr A. W. Hague	Owner	25–6–66
Limberin Tarantella	B	Ch. Telstar of Hobbithill	Baxby Belinda	Mr A. W. Hague	Mrs S. Buffey	26–4–66
Prince Albert of Wendlitt	D	Ch. Dandy Dan of Wendlitt	Ch. Wendlitt Tessa of Hobbithill	Mrs J. E. Littmoden	Owner	14–10–66
Dalegarth Lichen	B	Dalegarth Day Boy	Dalegarth Amelia Brown	Mr & Mrs F. T. Newbury	Owner	10–4–67
Regenfurt Regan	B	Ch. Shepherdsdene Pippin	Regentfurt Dimini	Mrs D. S. Rainford	Owner	20–8–66
Wimoway Water Lily	B	Ch. Bowbank Red Riordan	Ch. Wimoway Washington Rose	Mr & Mrs P. Smith	Mrs E. Smith	1–1–67
Merryweather Miss Miranda	B	Ch. Merryweather Moreover	Merryweather Miss Rhapsody	Mrs E. Bassett	Mrs E. H. Jones	1–6–66
Merryweather Masquerade	D	Ch. Merryweather Moreover	Merryweather Miss Rhapsody	Mrs E. Bassett	Mrs M. Jones	26–10–67
Merryweather Maddalo Sweet Honey	B	Ch. Merryweather Masquerade	Maddalo Sweet Thoughts	Mrs E. Bassett	Mrs & Miss Glover	1–9–69
Wingcrest Principal Girl	B	Greenmynd Jasper	Wingcrest Leritia	Mrs M. Batteson	Owner	24–6–68
Lollypop of Dermatt	D	Ch. Prince Albert of Wendlitt	Lydia of Dermatt	Mrs M. L. Brook-man	Owner	23–10–69
Amberleigh Red Rufus of Gilston	D	Ch. Merryweather Masquerade	Amberleigh Aconite of Gilston	Mesdames Evans & Angus	Mrs Marshall	27–1–70

Booth Sienna	B	Justin of Shalamar	Booth Beverley	Mrs J. Foden	Owner	9–12–69
Shepherdsdene Rhine Wine	D	Shepherdsdene Hock	Shepherdsdene Ciderette	Mr & Mrs E. Fox	Owners	15–4–68
Bowbank Delight	B	Bowbank Fledermaus	Bowbank Duskie Delight	Mrs A. G. Gladwyn	Mr & Mrs. H. Solomons	30–7–66
Runnel Apron Strings	B	Ch. Merryweather Marcello	Ch. Runnell Petticoat	Mrs M. Gracey	Owner	5–5–68
Fleur of Hobbithill	B	Ch. Prince Albert of Wendlitt	Araminta of Hobbithill	Dr Sylvia Kershaw	Owner	6–3–69
Silvae Tarkotta Red Tiki Roa	D	Wimoway Wilberforce	Tarkotta Wee Willie Winkie	Mrs E. Grosvenor Workman	Mrs B. Pugh	11–4–67
Silvae Tickey	B	Silvae Tarkotta Red Tiki Roa	Silvae Wisket	Mrs E. Grosvenor Workman	Owner	28–7–68
Fabian of Hobbithill	D	Ch. Prince Albert of Wendlitt	Araminta of Hobbithill	Mr A. W. Hague	Dr S. Kershaw	6–3–69
Limberin Honor Bright	B	Ch. Winston of Hobbithill	Limberin Fancy	Mr A. W. Hague	Owner	26–10–68
Limberin Mini Skirt	B	Ch. Limberin Topper	Ch. Booth Minnehaha	Mr A. W. Hague	Mrs J. Foden	4–9–69
Limberin Pan American	D	Ch. Limberin Americano	Booth Firefly	Mr A. W. Hague	Mrs J. Foden	24–7–68
Limberin Topper	D	Ch. Merryweather Moreover	Topsy of Hobbithill	Mr A. W. Hague	Dr S. Kershaw	15–12–66
Dormy Frederick of Wendlitt	D	Ch. Dandy Dan of Wendlitt	Arabella of Hobbithill	Mrs J. E. Littmoden	Mrs D. Goff	1–7–69

Name	*Sex*	*Sire*	*Dam*	*Owner*	*Breeder*	*Born*
Arcturus of Montreux	D	Ch. Geoffrey of Montreux	Beverley of Montreux	Mr A. Negal	Owner	22–1–67
Irving of Montreux	D	Hobart of Montreux	Fionnula of Montreux	Mr A. Negal	Owner	22–5–68
Soraya of Montreux	B	Hobart of Montreux	Ch. Slovanna of Montreux	Mr A. Negal	Owner	5–10–67
Hatchmead Selena	B	Ch. Dandy Dan of Wendlitt	Ch. Hatchmead Sophia	Mrs J. D. M. Thomas	Owner	1–9–67
Pipersvale Octavius	D	Ch. Septimus of Wendlitt	Amanda Jane of Wendlitt	Mrs. B. Munt	Owner	15–7–67
Bowbank Colombine	B	Bowbank Black Jester	Bowbank Caramello	Mrs D. Solomon	Mrs G. Dennison	24–1–69
Tarkotta Tzarbrina	B	Ch. Prince Albert of Wendlitt	Ch. Tarkotta Red Titania	Ft/Lt A. J. Pugh	Owner	27–8–68
Festoon of Bettmark	B	Merryweather Marciano	Floret of Bettmark	Mrs B. Samuel	Owner	29–6–67
Trinket of Bettmark	B	Ch. Timson of Wendlitt	Titania of Bettmark	Mrs B. Samuel	Owner	21–4–70
Wimoway Abbots Habit	D	Justin of Shalamar	Meadow Mist of Dunningham	Mr & Mrs P. Smith	Owners	16–6–70
Wimoway Chocolate Soldier	D	Hobart of Montreux	Meadow Mist of Dunningham	Mr & Mrs P. Smith	Owners	19–7–67
Flaunden Stage Struck	D	Ch. Merryweather Masquerade	Flaunden Sonic Boom	Mrs Blandford	Owner	29–11–69

Potsdown Sunshine	B	Ch. Potsdown Morgan	Potsdown Pilla Plack	Miss G. Barker & Mr H. Woollam	Owners	20–4–70
Limberin Ladybird	B	Limberin Carbon Copy	Limberin Endora	Mr A. W. Hague	Owner	23–6–71
Potsdown Miss Morgan	B	Ch. Potsdown Morgan	Potsdown Pilla Plack	Miss G. Barker & Mr H. Woollam	Owners	20–4–70
Roslaye Rigby	D	Ch. Prince Albert of Wendlitt	Roslaye Bubbles	Mrs J. Marshall	Owner	7–2–71
Limberin Golden Glory	B	Ch. Winston of Hobbithill	Baxby Belinda	Mr A. W. Hague	Mrs S. Buffey	14–9–71
Bowbank Drambuie	D	Ch. Bowbank Red Riley	Bowbank Darling Daughter	Mrs B. Munt	Mrs D. Solomon	4–10–70
Braishvale Jumping Jack	D	Ch. Dormy Frederick of Wendlitt	Braishvale Lively Lady	Mrs. H. Fidler	Owner	11–3–71
Flaunden the Sailor Man	D	Ch. Flaunden Stage Struck	Flaunden Sandrey	Mrs. Blandford & Miss Clarke	Owners	12–12–70
Wendlitt Frederica	B	Ch. Frederick of Wendlitt	Betsy Jayne of Wendlitt	Mrs. J. E. Littmoden	Owner	18–9–70
Harmony of Booth	B	Ch. Merryweather Masquerade	Booth Vitesse	Mrs. J. M. Foden	Owner	22–11–71
Montreux Siegfried	D	Ch. Irving of Montreux	Theodosia of Montreux	Mr. A. Negal	Owner	1–4–72
Chocolate Maid of Cardax	B	Ch. Wimoway Abbots Habit	Wimoway Chocolate Box	Messrs. C. V. & P. A. Millard	Owners	7–7–71
Wendlitt Remy	D	Braishvale Jumping Jack	Charming Louise of Wendlitt	Mrs. J. E. Littmoden	Owner	15–9–72

Name	*Sex*	*Sire*	*Dam*	*Owner*	*Breeder*	*Born*
Hobbithill Odette	B	Ch. Flaunden Stage Struck	Ch. Fleur of Hobbithill	Dr. S. Kershaw	Owner	20–8–71
Wimoway Waikiki	B	Ch. Wimoway Abbots Habit	Wimoway Wallflower	Mr. & Mrs. E. P. Smith	Owners	16–7–71
Pipersvale Tia Maria	B	Ch. Bowbank Drambuie	Pipersvale Penelope Ann	Mrs. B. Munt	Owner	5–8–72
Berrycourt Robin	D	Ch. Bowbank Red Riordan	Betsy Jayne of Wendlitt	Mr. & Mrs. R. L. Voaden	Owners	17–5–72
Braishvale Star of Redcliffe	D	Ch. Dormy Frederick of Wendlitt	Braishvale Lively Lady	Mrs. S. Barlow	Mrs. H. Fidler	27–11–71
Luxonfield Black Magic of Wimoway	B	Ch. Wimoway Chocolate Soldier	Luxonfield Nutty	Mr. & Mrs. E. P. Smith	Mrs. J. M. Baker	1–5–72
Lindy of Dermatt	B	Ch. Prince Albert of Wendlitt	Lydia of Dermatt	Mrs. M. L. Brookman	Owner	23–10–69
Bowbank Celandine	B	Bowbank Red Rory	Ch. Bowbank Colombine	Mrs. D. Solomon	Owner	15–7–71
Cannobio Silken Tassle	B	Ch. Dalegarth Designer	Cannobio Bowbank Red Rondolette	Mrs. B. Castle	Owner	7–8–72
Tourmaline Jet	B	Ch. Fabian of Hobbithill	Tourmaline Tapestry	Mrs. D. Hilton	Owner	8–3–72
Wimoway William Tell	D	Justin of Shalamar	Wimoway Wallflower	Mr. & Mrs. E. P. Smith	Owners	6–6–73
Amberleigh Atlanta	B	Ch. Lollipop of Dermatt	Ch. Amberleigh Allouette	Mrs K. M. Evans & Mrs Angus	Owners	12–2–72
Cannobio Schoolmarm	B	Dalegarth Dominick	Cannobio Lucky Lucy Jane	Mrs. B. Castle	Owner	26–7–73

Silvae in the Red	D	Kimarden Little Mark	Silvae Pound Foolish	Mrs. E. Grosvenor Workman	Owner	16–3–74
Amberleigh Allouette	B	Ch. Amberleigh Red Rufus of Gilston	Amberleigh Airsangraces	Mmes. K. Evans & I. Angus	Owners	19–5–71
Stargang Wurlitzer	D	Red Mask of Davenbrook	Stargang Carousel	Mrs. E. P. Blackburn	Owner	8–4–74
Runnel Ruff of Wendlitt	B	Ch. Prince Albert of Wendlitt	Ch. Runnel Apron Strings	Mrs. J. E. Littmoden	Mrs. M. Gracey	4–8–73
Honey Brandy of Pipersvale	B	Ch. Bowbank Drambuie	Vienda Betsy Trotwood	Mrs. B. Munt	Mrs. L. Penswick	5–7–74
Monken Mocking Bird	B	Justin of Shalamar	Monken Moondust	Mrs. J. Nunn	Owner	14–7–74
Hobbithill Zebedee of Tarkotta	D	Ch. Braishvale Jumping Jack	Hobbithill Polly	Flt.-Lt. A. J. & Mrs. B. M. Pugh	Dr. S. Kershaw	3–8–74
Cannobio Such a Smoothie	D	Ch. Cannobio So Smart	Cannobio Sauce Box	Mrs. B. Castle	Owner	17–10–74
Red Rover of Limberin	D	Ch. Winston of Hobbithill	Ripecorn of Merryriver	Mr. A. W. Hague	Messrs. J. R. & M. H. Jones	11–11–74
Royal Brandy of Pipersvale	D	Ch. Bowbank Drambuie	Vienda Betsy Trotwood	Mrs. B. Munt	Mrs. L. Penswick	14–4–75
Hobbithill Zephania	B	Ch. Braishvale Jumping Jack	Hobbithill Polly	Dr. S. Kershaw	Owner	3–8–74
Vienda Extravagancia	B	Ch. Bowbank Drambuie	Regentfurt Santa Rosalia	Mrs. L. Penswick	Owner	17–6–74
Lornapete Red Revie	D	Bowbank Red Ramsey	Lornapete Red Queen	Mr. P. H. Tinkler	Owner	9–3–72
Regenfurt Charlotte	B	Ch. Wendlitt Remy	Regenfurt Carolina	Mrs. D. Fainford	Owner	30–9–73

Name	*Sex*	*Sire*	*Dam*	*Owner*	*Breeder*	*Born*
Booth Buccaneer	D	Muttley of Merryweather	Booth Rosira	Mrs. J. Foden	Owner	24–12–72
Cannobio So Smart	D	Dalegarth Dominick	Cannobio Lucky Lucy Jane	Mrs. B. Castle	Owner	26–7–73
Roslaye Calypso Girl	B	Ch. Roslaye Rigby	Roslaye Charlotte	Mrs. J. Marshall	Owner	4–10–74
Bowbank Tamarisk	B	Ch. Bowbank Drambuie	Ch. Bowbank Celendine	Mrs. B. Munt	Mrs. D. Solomon	12–8–75
Wimoway Whispering Grass	B	Ch. Roslaye Rigby	Ch. Luxonfield Black Magic of Wimoway	Mr. & Mrs. E. P.	Owners	8–5–75
Kimarden Josephina	B	Ch. Berrycourt Robin	Kimarden Elfreda	Mrs. E. R. Leaver	Owner	2–10–75
Willowfield Sweet William	B	Ch. Wimoway William Tell	Amberleigh Amaryllis	Mrs. E. Bassett	Lady Dick-Lauder	9–7–75
Cardax Matchmaker	D	Dermatt Latimer	Ch. Chocolate Maid of Cardax	Mr. & Mrs. C. Millard	Owners	24–11–75
Willowfield Windflower	B	Ch. Gilston Antar of Amberleigh	Amberligh Amaryllis	Lady Dick-Lauder	Mmes. K. Evans & I. Angus	14–1–74
Hobbithill Erica	B	Ch. Braishvale Jumping Jack	Ch. Fleur of Hobbithill	Dr. S. Kershaw	Owner	15–9–75
Amberleigh Aquamarine	B	Ch. Gilston Antar of Amberleigh	Ch. Amberleigh Atlanta	Mrs. C. Craig	Mmes. K. Evans I. Angus	14–10–75
Limberin Vermilion	B	Ch. Red Rover of Limberin	Royal Tansie	Mr. A. W. Hague	Mrs. S. Storey	14–1–76
Braishvale Danny Boy	D	Ch. Cannobio Such a Smoothie	Braishvale Mary-Loo	Mrs. H. Fidler	Owner	31–5–76

Name	Sex	Sire	Dam	Owner	Breeder	Born
Bowbank Nijinsky	D	S.A. Ch. Bowbank Bernard	Bowbank Dancing Daughter	Mrs. D. Solomon	Owner	20–7–74
Cannobio Hanky Panky of Wingcrest	D	Ch. Braishvale Jumping Jack	Cannobio Something Else	Mrs. M. Batteson-Webster & Miss L. Prudence	Mrs. B. Castle	6–4–76
Monksmile Dandelion	D	Manikin of Monksmile	Sweetmount Samantha	Mrs. B. Munt	Mrs. S. McNeilly	29–6–76
Braishvale Crackerjack	D	Ch. Prince Albert of Wendlitt	Braishvale Sallie	Mrs. H. Fidler	Owner	31–5–76
Wimoway Bertie Wooster	D	Ch. Braishvale Jumping Jack	Ch. Luxonfield Black Magic of Wimoway	Mr. & Mrs. E. P. Smith	Owners	22–8–76
Hobbithill Fescue of Wingcrest	D	Ch. Cannobio Such a Smoothie	Ch. Hobbithill Odette	Mrs. M. Batteson-Webster & Miss L. Prudence	Dr. S. Kershaw	20–5–76
Pipersvale Beaujolais	B	Ch. Royal Brandy of Pipersvale	Ch. Pipersvale Tia Maria	Mrs. B. Munt	Owner	15–5–77
Maundowne Mardianna	B	Hobbithill Toby	Maundowne Mardi Gras	Mrs. N. Winterbourne	Owner	30–11–76
Stargang Mother Goose	B	Eng. & Aus. Ch. Stargang Wurlitzer	Stargang Pantomime	Mrs. E. P. Blackburn	Owner	4–12–75

APPENDIX D (*cont.*)

2. MINIATURE LONG HAIRED CHAMPIONS FROM 1955 TO 1978

Name	*Sex*	*Sire*	*Dam*	*Owner*	*Breeder*	*Born*
Dragon Fly von Walder	D	Meltis von Walder	Ballyteckel Gertie Gad	Mrs L. S. Bellamy	Owner	16–5–54
Armorel Black Magic	D	Gunther of Lenches	Priorsgate Armorel	Mrs I. Stevenson	Owner	3–7–54
Crackers of Farick	B	Marlenwood Marten of Fairmaine	Pep of Farick	Miss J. Fardell	Owner	28–5–55
Josephine of Hoylin	B	Ch. John of Morny-varna	Hopeborough Jasmine	Miss M. Fletcher	Owner	1–4–53
Neeky Nook of Farick	B	Marlenwood Micke	Morceau of Farick	Miss J. Fardell	Owner	11–1–54
Armorel Craghill Dandy	D	Ch. Springmount Madrigal	Priorsgate Armorel	Mrs I. Stevenson	Owner	14–11–55
Badgerswood Martin von Walder	D	Meltis von Walder	Jenny Wren von Walder	Mrs L. S. Bellamy	Mrs L. Smith	19–8–54
Priorsgate Tom Thumb	D	Ch. Priorsgate Marlen-wood Royce	Priorsgate Miss Muffet	Miss M. C. Sherer	Owner	11–8–54
Joy Sagittary	B	Paris Kellermeister	Juno Sagittary	Mrs Y. J. Oswell	Mrs J. Hall-Fletcher	30–10–55
Solon Sagittary	D	Paris Kellermeister	Juno Sagittary	Mrs H. E. Fielding	Mrs J. Hall-Fletcher	30–10–55
Didgemere Caesar	D	Spendthrift Sambo	Primrosepatch Frederica	Mrs J. Mills & Mrs J. Littmoden	Mrs B. Abbey	8–11–56
Javan of Jaldon	D	Ch. Priorsgate Marlenwood Royce	Sari of Waldberg	Messrs C. Crabtree & H. Jordan	Mrs J. Durant	23–6–56

Nicholas of Petersfield	D	Ch. Springmount Madrigal	Marlenwood Merrily	Mr F. C. Gee	Owner	25–12–56
Springmount Esquire	D	Ch. Priorsgate Marlenwood Royce	Priorsgate Honey	Mrs B. Morris	Mrs I. M. C. Marsh	16–3–56
Primrosepatch Lady Brown	B	Primrosepatch Tiny Man	Primrosepatch Fairy Fay	Mrs A. Sidgwick	Mrs O. Smith Rewse	5–12–55
Priorsgate Yvonne	B	Ch. Priorsgate Marlenwood Royce	Priorsgate Miss Muffet	Miss M. C. Sherer	Owner	9–4–53
Taschen Tappet	B	Ch. Jeremy Fisher of Hoylin	Taschen Tippet	Dr M. Blakiston & Miss A. M. New	Owners	7–6–55
Zactly Zosia of Bordak	B	Rytona Red Rust	Milady Lisa of Bordak	Mrs E. T. Franczak	Mrs. D. Dove	14–2–54
Dazzle of Dawning	D	Shaun of Helenarth	Sooky of Dawning	Mrs M. A. Kirkham	Owner	2–9–56
Don Basilio of Mallards	D	Ch. Springmount Madrigal	Ch. Fricassee of Mallards	Mrs R. K. B. Cole-Hamilton	Mrs S. M. Gale	12–3–58
Esspeejay Sunglow	D	Marlenwood Micke	Esspeejay Begum	Mr & Mrs S. G. Christmas	Owners	14–4–57
Rapture of Bowerbank	B	Ch. Jamie of Marlenwood	Caprice of Bowerbank	Miss T. J. Millburn	Owner	10–7–55
Ravenhead Anna	B	Surprise of Arundover	Wolfox Teazie Weazie	Miss G. Percival	Miss M. S. Down	23–3–57
Sheilagh of Hoylin	B	Shaun of Helenarth	Jacqueline of Hoylin	Mrs M. A. Kirkham	Miss M. Fletcher	25–11–53
Armorel Morninglow	D	Ch. Springmount Madrigal	Priorsgate Armorel	Mrs I. Stevenson	Owner	20–9–58
Daxene Golden Gigli	D	Ch. Armorel Black Magic	Norbrook Rieke	Mr J. P. Green	Owner	15–5–58

Name	*Sex*	*Sire*	*Dam*	*Owner*	*Breeder*	*Born*
Moselle von Walder	D	John of Petersfield	Miss Cherry of Arundover	Mrs L. S. Bellamy	Miss M. S. Down	17–9–58
Priorsgate Alexander	D	Priorsgate Fireking	Ermintrude of Pyrford	Miss M. C. Sherer	Mrs M. Payne	29–6–58
Bijou of Mallards	B	Merryweather Mahogany	Madrilene of Mallards	Mrs S. M. Gale	Owner	24–2–59
J'árrive of Farick	B	Marlenwood Duke Anton	Neeky Nook of Farick	Miss J. Fardell	Owner	25–4–58
Priorsgate Philippa	B	Cary of the Yeld	Fifinella von Walder	Miss M. C. Sherer	Owner	30–6–55
Rejoyce of Mertynabbot	B	Primrose Patch Periwinkle	Ch. Joy Sagittary	Mrs Y. J. Oswell	Owner	12–6–59
Mertynabbot Byworth Comet	D	Marlenwood Duke Anton	Byworth Carousel of Mertynabbot	Mrs Y. J. Oswell	Mrs M. King	29–4–60
Mighty Fine von Walder	D	Buttons of Arundover	Miss Cherry of Arundover	Mrs L. S. Bellamy	Miss M. S. Down	26–9–60
Springmount Saxon of Bowerbank	D	Priorsgate Joseph	Springmount Tansy	Miss T. J. Millburn	Mrs B. Harcourt Wood	16–1–59
Armorel Lady Sylvia	B	Ch. Springmount Madrigal	Priorsgate Armorel	Mrs I. Stevenson	Owner	14–6–59
Jiroska of Jaldon	B	Ch. Priorsgate Marlenwood Royce	Sari of Waldberg	Mrs N. Leadbeater	Mrs J. Durant	12–7–57
Primrosepatch Jasmine	B	Ch. Springmount Madrigal	Japonica of Daisyclose	Mrs A. Sidgwick	Mrs J. F. Nunn	14–5–58
Armorel Golden Monarch	D	Ch. Armorel Morninglow	Armorel Glenfarg Mitzi	Mrs I. Stevenson	Owner	7–6–60

Jon of Marlenwood	D	Marlenwood Red Willow	Marlenwood Clover	Mrs F. Gwyer	Mrs M. F. Rhodes	18–10–60
Priorsgate Rob Roy	D	Longanlow Black Bramble	Priorsgate Christmas Day	Miss M. C. Sherer	Owner	21–6–60
Raleigh of Bowerbank	D	Goldsmith of Langaller	Springmount Fiona	Miss T. J. Millburn	Owner	19–4–60
Tammy of Bardival	D	Ch. Springmount Madrigal	Elizabeth of Walberg	Mr & Mrs W. Fletcher	Owner	11–8–58
Armorel Morning Glory	B	Ch. Springmount Madrigal	Priorsgate Armorel	Mrs I. Stevenson	Owner	20–9–58
Cedavoch Cherry Sweet	B	Ch. Don Basilio of Mallards	Miss Rebecca of Marpheld	Miss M. K. Stewart & Mrs. V. Collins	Mrs J. McNaughton	27–11–60
Kinghurst Janita of Jaldon	B	Ch. Priorsgate Marlenwood Royce	Sari of Waldberg	Mrs H. Wolstenholme	Mrs J. Durant	12–7–57
Mertynabbot Little Model	B	Ch. Mertynabbot Byworth Comet	Ch. Joy Sagittary	Mrs Y. J. Oswell	Owner	28–3–61
Delphik Derry	D	Reedscottage Rattan	Delphik Lisba Yvonne	Mrs H. Fielding	Owner	5–3–62
Dunlossit Bright Boy	D	Ch. Armorel Morninglow	Armorel April Magic	Mrs Donaldson & Mrs Raven	Mr M. Duckworth	30–7–61
Wenbarn Peregrine	D	Ch. Armorel Morninglow	Wenbarn Mimosa of Primrosepatch	Mrs Barnes & Mrs Faulkner	Owners	5–7–62
Armorel Madame Dieudonne	B	Phaeland Honey Bee	Armorel Rose Queen	Mr & Mrs W. E. Hickling	Mrs I. Stevenson	16–4–62
Armorel Pearly Queen	B	Ch. Armorel Golden Monarch	Armorel May Blossom	Mrs I. Stevenson	Mr K. Waterworth	1–10–61
Miranda von Walder	B	Ch. Moselle von Walder	Millicent von Walder	Mrs L. S. Bellamy	Owner	22–5–62

Name	*Sex*	*Sire*	*Dam*	*Owner*	*Breeder*	*Born*
Ridgebar Esspeejay Teresa	B	Esspeejay Black Emperor	Esspeejay Britannia	Mrs B. C. Jolly	Mr & Mrs Christmas	5–7–58
Dominantly Dirk of Bordak	D	Mostly May of Bordak	Talento Tatiana	Mrs D. Dove	Mrs R. McGregor Cheers	11–4–63
Brigmerston Loop de Loop	B	Ch. Raleigh of Bowerbank	Marlenwood Milady Jill	Mrs A. Green	Owner	19–12–62
Fireflash of Farick	B	Ch. Didgemere Caesar	Ch. Crackers of Farick	Miss J. Fardell	Owner	18–7–59
Minutist Storm	B	Minutist Moonlight	Minutist Amara Gretel	Mrs N. E. Parsons	Owner	8–6–62
Ridgebar Festina Lente	B	Marlenwood Red Willow	Ridgebar Robsvarl Tabitha Titmouse	Mrs N. Moon	Mrs B. G. Jolly	4–7–60
Trumond Tamara	B	Zwarthax Tom Tit	Trumond Trudy	Mr & Mrs F. F. Thomas	Owners	18–4–61
Wenbo Peta	B	Ch. Esspeejay Sunglow	Wenbo Cinderella	Mr & Mrs W. L. B. Bowen	Owners	7–4–61
Trumond Truella	B	Zwarthax Tom Tit	Trumond Troufle	Mr & Mrs F. F. Thomas	Owners	28–4–63
Delphik Dhobi	B	Reedscottage Rattan	Lisba Yvonne	Mrs H. E. Fielding	Owner	5–3–62
Esspeejay Skyrider	D	Esspeejay Lochinvar	Wenbo Odette	Mr & Mrs S. G. Christmas	Owners	16–6–62
Mertynabbott Birthday Present	D	Ch. Mertynabbot Byworth Comet	Charlotte of Mertynabbot	Mrs F. J. O'Meara	Mrs Y. J. Oswell	8–12–61
Ravenhead Edwina	B	Ch. Delphik Derry	Ch. Ravenhead Anna	Miss G. B. Percival	Owner	27–12–63

Ridgebar Patsyanna Polly	B	Ridgebar Christopher Robin	Wayvick Quinka	Mrs B. G. Jolly	Owner	31–7–62
Sunara Mertynabbot Pollyanna	B	Ch. Delphik Derry	Mertynabbot Rigalong Tangerine	Mrs M. Fraser-Gibson	Mrs Y. J. Oswell	27–4–63
Mertynabbot Lancelot	D	Ch. Wenbarn Peregrine	Mertynabbot Baby Doll	Mrs J. Blandford	Mrs Y. J. Oswell	30–6–63
Minutist Hooligan	D	Minutist Diabolo	Minutist Berryland Lucky Charm	Mrs N. E. Parsons	Owner	19–11–64
Judith of Jaldon	B	Ch. Priorsgate Marlenwood Royce	Sari of Waldberg	Mrs J. Durrant	Owner	23–6–56
Puckridge Sonatina	B	Ch. Springmount Madrigal	Puckridge Red Pincushion	Mrs J. Waddington	Owner	25–6–62
Coobeg Martini of Bowerbank	D	Ch. Raleigh of Bowerbank	Coobeg Daxene Golden Meadow	Mr H. Oliver	Mrs M. F. Rhodes	2–10–62
Delphik Dodonna	B	Ch. Delphik Derry	Rigalong Galaxy	Mrs H. Fielding & Mrs Dawson	Mrs H. Fielding	1–6–64
Delphik Dario	D	Ch. Delphik Derry	Delphik Delta	Mrs H. Fielding	Owner	1–4–65
Marpheld Maybelle	B	Ch. Tammy of Bardival	Morag of Marpheld	Mrs M. B. Hunt	Owner	6–5–63
Minutist Mikado	D	Minutist Diabolo	Minutist Tosca	Mrs N. E. Parsons	Owner	19–7–64
Prospecthill Penny From Rokeby	B	Wee Geordie of Beltrim	Prospecthill Tuppence	Mrs B. Eglin	Mrs A. Taylor	23–1–63
Tingrith Tango	D	Martyn of Mertynabbot	Vanity of Mertynabbot	Mrs Commeline	Mrs F. J. O'Meara	18–7–58

Name	*Sex*	*Sire*	*Dam*	*Owner*	*Breeder*	*Born*
Urdax Sibylla	**B**	**Baylegate Kingfisher**	**Fishermaid Firefly**	**Mrs B. I. Urwin**	**Owner**	**20–8–62**
Armorel André	D	Armorel Minutest Gerry	Armorel Sundance	Mrs I. Stevenson	Owner	6–4–66
Delphik Donamos	D	Ch. Delphik Derry	Delphik Della	Mrs H. Fielding	Owner	24–4–65
Titian Sagittary	D	Ch. Dunlossit Bright Boy	Scarlett Sagittary	Mrs Hall-Fletcher	Owner	20–12–63
Delphik Dekosi	B	Ch. Delphik Derry	Delphik Della	Mrs H. Fielding	Owner	24–4–65
Sunara Sweet Thoughts	B	Sunara Mertynabbot Goblin	Sunara Mertynabbot Delightful	Mrs Fraser-Gibson	Owner	28–5–66
Mertynabbot Nicola	B	Sunara Wayward Wind	Byworth Cobnut	Mrs Y. J. Oswell	Owner	2–3–65
Brigmerston Sir Percival	D	Brigmerston Ravenhead Eamon	Brigmerston Angelique	Mrs A. Green	Owner	30–10–65
Sunara Gloire of Dijon	B	Minutist Diabolo	Imber Demi-Tasse	Mrs Fraser-Gibson	Owner	22–1–66
Martin von Holzner	D	Brigmerston Ravenhead Eamon	Honeysuckle von Holzner	Mrs J. C. Connell	Owner	24–9–66
Sunara Sorrento	D	Sunara Mertynabbot Goblin	Imber Demi Tasse	Mrs F. Fraser-Gibson	Owner	28–12–64
Brigmerston Sir Francis	D	Brigmerston Ravenhead Eamon	Ch. Brigmerston Loup de Loup	Mrs A. Green	Owner	14–5–67
Embassy Bridesmaid	B	Embassy Jason Sagittary	Lorelei Lumpenhund	Mrs V. Hickling	Mrs B. Whipp	26–3–66
Embassy Master Sagittary	D	Ch. Dunlossit Bright Boy	Scarlett Sagittary	Mrs V. Hickling	Mrs J. Hall-Fletcher	3–6–65
Champ of Wildcroft	D	Jasper of Bardival	Lady of Bardival	Mr H. Oliver	Mr & Mrs W. Fletcher	9–1–65

Mertynabbot Kind Sir	D	Ch. Mertunabbot Lancelot	Mertynabbot Eclair	Mrs. Y. J. Oswell	Owner	6–8–66
Danjor Little Oriole	B	Ch. Coobeg Martini of Bowerbank	Danjor Little Jay	Mrs B. V. Samuel	Mr. H. Jordan	9–1–65
Minutist Praline	B	Ch. Minutist Mikado	Ch. Minutist Fatima	Mrs N. E. Parsons	Owner	9–4–66
Trumond Trimble of Primrosepatch	D	Trumond Tarquin	Trumond Tricia	Mrs A. Sidgwick	Mr & Mrs F. Thomas	
Minutist Ottoman	D	Am. Ch. Minutist Goliath	Minutist Wavelet	Mrs J. Blandford	Mrs N. Parsons	10–10–69
Rossglen Merrymaid	B	Rossglen Wizard	Auberjean Picklescott Judy	Mrs P. J. Dutson	Owner	11–11–67
Rossglen Red Tammy	D	Ch. Delphik Derry	Rossglen Rowena	Mrs P. J. Dutson	Owner	24–10–66
Modern Millie von Holzner	B	Ch. Martin von Holzner	Brigmerston Angelique	Mrs J. C. Connell	Mrs A. Green	11–8–67
Meonfalk Caracas	D	Ch. Wenbarn Peregrin	Puckridge Darlin Bud	Mrs A. Gildersleeve	Owner	12–3–69
Delphik Diplomat	D	Ch. Delphik Derry	Ch. Delphik Dekosi	Mrs H. Fielding	Owner	20–1–70
Delphik Debbret	B	Ch. Delphik Donamos	Ch. Delphik Dhobi	Mrs H. Fielding	Owner	1–9–67
Delphik Deanna	B	Ch. Delphik Derry	Delphik Della	Mrs H. Fielding	Owner	18–1–67
Bardival Black Princess	B	Ch. Sunara Sorrento	Bardival Sweet Caress	Mr & Mrs W. Fletcher	Owners	12–9–69
Sunara Fiery Miss	B	Ch. Delphik Derry	Ch. Sunara Gloire of Dijon	Mrs M. Fraser-Gibson	Owner	7–7–68

Name	*Sex*	*Sire*	*Dam*	*Owner*	*Breeder*	*Born*
Ravenhead Edward	D	Ch. Delphik Derry	Ch. Ravenhead Anna	Miss C. L. M. Gatheral	Miss G. Percival	27–12–63
Flaunden Busy Lizzie of Glenmoris	B	Ch. Mertynabbot Lancelot	Mertynabbot Nymph	Mr A. L. Hammond	Mrs J. Blandford	9–6–69
Woodreed Little Footman	D	Woodreed Sunara Gold Star	Woodreed Fleur-de-Lys	Mrs N. Moon	Owner	30–9–67
Minutist Sophistication	B	Ch. Minutist Mikado	Minutist Favourite	Mrs N. E. Parsons	Owner	14–4–67
Brigmerston Lord Charles of Primrose Patch	D	Ch. Brigmerston Sir Francis	Brigmerston Angelique	Mrs A. Sidgwick	Mrs A. Green	6–8–68
Mayville Bitter Sweet	B	Mayville Sultan	Minutist Ninon	Mr & Mrs Sourbuts	Owners	14–6–69
Puckridge Melba	B	Ch. Mertynabbot Byworth Comet	Puckridge Partita	Mrs J. Waddington	Owner	10–7–66
Urdac Hadrian	D	Urdac Sweet Sultan	Urdac Margarita	Mrs B. I. Urwin	Owner	20–7–67
Minutist Ascot	D	Ch. Wenbarn Peregrine	Minutist Favourite	Mrs N. Winterbourne	Mrs N. Parsons	11–5–65
Littlehound Halleluya	D	Mertynabbot Namoos	Especially Emma of Bordak	Mrs F. Klin	Owner	24–12–67
Bardival Drummer Boi	D	Ch. Delphik Derry	Bramble of Bardival	Mr & Mrs W. Fletcher	Owners	10–8–69
Tingrith Blue Jacket	D	Ch. Mertynabbot Birthday Present	Mertynabbot Love Affair	Mrs R. Steele	Mrs J. O'Meara	20–5–67
Delphik Mannequin	B	Ch. Delphik Dario	Delphik Dekker	Mrs H. Fielding	Mrs S. Lambert	1–71
Embassy Wat a Boy	D	Ch. Dunlossit Bright Boy	Ch. Armorel Madame Dieudonne	Mrs. K. V. Hickling	Owner and Mr Hickling	30–11–66

Trumond The Toff	D	Ch. Martin von Holzner	Trumond Tamoshanta	Mr & Mrs F. F. Thomas	Owners	9–7–70
Sunara Midnight Star	B	Sunara Debonair	Sunara Miss Fabulous	Miss Williams	Mrs Fraser-Gibson	30–5–70
Minutist Biltong	B	Minutist Hiawatha	Minutist Fatima	Mrs N. Moon	Mrs N. Parsons	16–4–70
Rossglen Elegant	B	Ch. Rossglen Red Tammy	Rosslgen Reisa	Mrs P. J. Dutson	Owner	22–7–69
Delphik Distinguished	D	Ch. Delphik Diplomatic	Ch. Delphic Debbret	Mrs. H. Fielding	Owner	1–6–71
Bushcot Hazel	B	Minutist Hutchinson	Berryland Desirable	Mrs. Fishwick	Owner	5–9–71
Minutist Casino	D	Minutist Hiawatha	Minutist Juniper	Mrs. R. K. Cole-Hamilton	Mrs. N. Parsons	12–1–70
Forestford Darling Lili	B	Ch. Brigmerston Sir Francis	Forestford Deborah	Mesdames Fielding & Mills	Mr. J. Smith	18–2–70
Jackanordie Jolyon	D	Jackanordie Solo	Jackanordie Seemly Samantha of Boroak	Mrs. N. Wakefield	Owner	9–5–70
Conyers Coffeemate	D	Ch. Ravenhead Edward	Conyers Cinderella	Mrs. C. A. Blaxall	Miss S. D. A. Gatheral	13–7–69
Mareth Sofia	B	Ch. Delphik Derry	Woodheath Decibelle	Mrs. J. Mather	Owner	26–5–71
Candover Black Cherry	B	Ch. Brigmerston Sir Francis	Wild Honeysuckle	Mrs. I. M. L. Pain	Owner	5–6–69
Pantry Boy von Holzner	D	Ch. Martin von Holzner	Maria von Holzner	Mrs. J. C. Connell	Owner	18–3–71
Sunara Regal Artist	B	Ch. Sunara Sorrento	Sunara Miss Fabulous	Mrs. M. Fraser-Gibson	Owner	18–6–72

Name	*Sex*	*Sire*	*Dam*	*Owner*	*Breeder*	*Born*
Glenmoris Sovereign Maid	B	Delrene Golden Sovereign	Ch. Flaunden Busy Lizzie of Glenmoris	A. L. Hammond	Owner	1–6–72
Ridgeview Romeo	D	Minutist Costa	Radiant Rachel of Ridgeview	Mrs. C. J. Wilson	Owner	18–11–71
Southcliff Salvatore	D	Ch. Martin von Holzner	Ch. Southcliff Salome	Mr. A. Sharman & Mrs. R. Heighton	Mr. A. Sharman	22–1–72
Beltrim Carlo	D	Minutist Casino	Tricia of Beltrim	Mrs. R. A. Cole-Hamilton	Owner	13–5–72
Delphik Double Diamond	B	Ch. Delphik Diplomatic	Ch. Delphic Debbret	Mrs. I. M. L. Pain	Mrs. H. Fielding	1–6–71
Jackanordie Digby	D	Ch. Jackanordie Jolyon	Jackanordie Delysia	Mrs. N. Wakefield	Owner	17–2–72
Southcliff Salome	B	Ch. Mertynabbot Lancelot	Southcliff Sieglinde	Mr. A. Sharman	Owner	18–10–70
Littlenodes Silver Smoke	D	Littlenodes Quick Silver	Littlenodes Changeling	Mrs. B. Owen	Mrs. P. Wharton	4–8–72
Woodreed Lord David	D	S.A. Ch. Flaunden Libretto	Woodreed Little Chatelaine	Mrs. B. J. Bayne	Mrs. N. Moon	4–10–71
Mareth Moonraker	D	Aus. Ch. Woodheath Simply Simon	Mareth Frances	Mrs. M. Fraser-Gibson	Mrs. J. Mather	23–1–72
Southcliff Satin Sash	B	Ch. Sunara Sorrento	Sunara Golden Melody of Southcliff	Mrs. A. Sharman	Owner	28–4–73
Southcliff Selika	B	Ch. Sunara Sorrento	Sunara Golden Melody of Southcliff	Mr. A. Sharman	Owner	31–7–71
Alicia of Ringlingisle	B	Piper Pan of Bowerbank	Helmend Miss Mouse Mole	Mr. & Mrs. R. Gow	Mrs. R. Cole-Hamilton	24–1–71

Rhinestar Dedication	D	Ch. Sunara Sorrento	Woodreed Little Blessing	Mr. & Mrs. Corn	Owners	30–9–73
Delrene Dignified Kingpin	D	Ch. Delphik Distinguished	Delrene Dignified Dame	Mrs. E. M. Rabone	Owner	24–4–73
Rossglen Raison D'Être	B	Ch. Rossglen Red Tammy	Auberjean Picklescott Judy	Mrs. P. J. Dutson	Owner	25–5–72
Trumond Toffynose	D	Ch. Trumond The Toff	Trumond Trevita	Mr. & Mrs. F. F. Thomas	Owners	30–7–72
Tupee Tweedledee of Ridgeview	D	Ch. & S.A. Ch. Minutist Ottoman	Littlenodes Black Tulip	Mrs. C. J. Wilson	Mrs. Attfield	26–6–74
Minard Mini Maestro	D	Ch. Trumond Trimble of Primrosepatch	Garmston Shady Lady	Mr. & Mrs. T. Goddard	Owners	4–7–73
Delphik Derryson	D	Ch. Delphik Derry	Delphik Duplicate	Mr. & Mrs. W. McKay	Mrs. H. Fielding	24–3–73
Antrobus Silver Sparkle of Delphik	B	Ch. Littlenodes Silver Smoke	Hilgreg Holly Queen	Mrs. H. Fielding	Mrs. H. Gregory	4–7–74
Grasteve Solitaire	B	Lemonbank Landowner of Grasteve	Grasteve Sequin	Mrs. A. G. Gladwin	Owner	31–10–73
Antrobus Adulation	B	Ch. Littlenodes Silver Smoke	Hilgreg Harella	Mrs. T. Palmer	Mrs. B. Owen	29–11–74
Southcliff Seretse	D	Ch. Southcliff Salvatore	Ch. Southcliff Selika	Mr. A. Sharman	Owner	10–11–73
Western Star of Sunara	D	Ch. Sunara Sorrento	Ch. Sunara Midnight Star	Mrs. D. Varney	Owner	25–5–73
Delrene Elegant Queen	B	Ch. Delrene Dignified Kingpin	Delrene Prim and Proper	Mrs. E. M. Rabone	Owner	3–5–74
Jackanordie Val'n'tine	D	Ch. Jackanordie Digby	Jackanordie Selina	Mrs. N. Wakefield	Owner	3–1–73

Name	*Sex*	*Sire*	*Dam*	*Owner*	*Breeder*	*Born*
Mertynabbot Yara Nicola	B	N.Z. Ch. Burntbarn Crackerjack	Mertynabbot Angela	Mrs. P. Hampton	Mrs. Y. Oswell	27–6–73
Bushcot Dandelion of Rhinestar	D	Ch. Rhinestar Dedication	Ch. Bushcot Hazel	Mr. & Mrs. Corn	Mrs. S. Fishwick	19–7–75
Delphik Doretta	B	Ch. Delphik Diplomatic	Delphik Daniella	Mrs. I. M. L. Pain	Mrs. H. Fielding	6–4–72
Verdigo Elete Eliza	B	Sunara Sunwillow	Wilkent Ottilie	Mrs. L. Pike	Owner	25–7–73
Castlenovary's Fellow	D	Ch. Sunara Sorrento	Firefly Mischief of Castlenovary	Mr. & Mrs. Spier & Miss B. Francis	Owners	16–8–74
Southcliff Sweet Music	B	Ch. Southcliff Salvatore	Sunara Golden Melody of Southcliff	Mr. A. Sharman	Owner	19–9–75
Woodheath Lunar Eclipse	B	N.Z. Ch. Burntbarn Crackerjack	Woodheath Lunar Lady	Mrs. B. O'Neill & Mrs. S. J. Storkey	Mrs. B. O'Neill	29–4–73
Delphik Brigg	D	Ch. Brigmerston Sir Francis	Delphik Directrice	Mrs. H. Fielding	Owner	16–10–75
Southcliff Schubert	D	Ch. Sunara Sorrento	Sunara Golden Melody of Southcliff	Mrs. B. G. Jolly	Mr. A. Sharman	28–9–74
Antrobus Antique Silver	D	Ch. Littlenodes Silver Smoke	Mertynabbot Simone	Mrs. J. Middleton	Mrs. B. Hyde	7–1–74
Voryn's Joseph	D	Ch. Jackanordie Jolyon	Primrosepatch Dawn Sky	Mrs. N. Wakefield & Mr. J. V. Crawford	Mr. J. V. Crawford	30–1–74
Urdac Trump Coup	B	Ch. Urdac Hadrian	Minutist Cameora	Mrs. B. I. Urwin	Owner	19–6–75
Delphik Doodlebug	D	Ch. Delphik Brigg	Delphik Diorling	Mrs. H. Fielding	Owner	22–1–77
Cannobio Sukina	B	Ridgeview Ruggles	Cannobio Sweet Dessert	Mrs. B. Castle	Owner	28–6–76

Beltrim Raffles	D	Wauchopes Andy	Antrobus Amanda	Mrs. R. Cole-Hamilton	Owner and Miss Menzies	1–2–77
Lornapete Silver Swag	B	Woodreed Little Swagman	Silver of Lornapete	Mr. P. Tinkler	Owner	1–1–76
Minard Mini Magnum	D	Ch. Minard Mini Maestro	Minard Moonlight Ebony	Mr. & Mrs. T. Goddard	Owners	9–4–76
Calico of Candover	B	Ch. Urdac Hadrian	Beltrim Taspy	Mrs. I. M. L. Pain	Mr. & Mrs. J. Hendrie	12–7–74
Mareth Brut of Meonfalk	D	Cannobio Bowerbank Sacha	Moon Maiden of Mareth	Mrs. A. F. G. Gildersleeve	Mrs. J. Mather	26–10–74
Rhinestar Buttercup	B	Ch. Bushcot Dandelion of Rhinestar	Woodreed Little Blessing	Mr. & Mrs. Corn	Owners	20–2–77
Woodheath Bismark	D	N.Z. Ch. Burntbarn Crackerjack	Woodheath Lunar Lady	Mrs. B. O'Neill	Owner	29–4–73
Southcliff Sonosash	D	Southcliff Sonolarri	Ch. Southcliff Satin Sash	Mr. A. Sharman	Owner	9–10–76
Sunara Sea Symphony	D	Ch. Sunara Sorrento	Ch. Sunara Regal Artist	Mrs. M. Fraser-Gibson	Owner	27–5–75
Ridgeview Dark Brown Tweed	D	Ch. Tupee Tweedledee of Ridgeview	Minutist Hooplara	Mrs. C. J. Wilson	Owner	3–5–76

APPENDIX D (cont.)

3. MINIATURE WIRE HAIRED CHAMPIONS FROM 1955 TO 1978

Name	*Sex*	*Sire*	*Dam*	*Owner*	*Breeder*	*Born*
Jane of Sillwood	B	Liseson of Sillwood	Sillwood Paula of of Dunkerque	Mrs R. Wakefield	Owner	20–8–57
Coobeg Ballyteckel Walt Weevil	D	Huntersbroad Minoru	Ballyteckel Win Wireworm	Mrs M. F. Rhodes	Mrs K. G. Besson	25–9–56
Brownsugar of Sillwood	D	Jason of Sillwood	Lisette of Sillwood	Mrs R. Wakefield	Owner	3–6–59
Coobeg Punch	D	Ch. Coobeg Ballyteckel Walt Weevil	Oxleaze Judy	Mrs M. F. Rhodes	Mrs J. Mann	31–1–60
Gisbourne Polka Dot	D	Ballyteckel Peter Pest	Gisbourne Georgina	Mrs D. Wilson	Mrs E. Quick	9–12–59
Orkneyinga Nutshell	D	Orkneyinga Trojan of Gladsmuir	Orkneyinga Hunters-broad Harriet	Gp. Capt. & Mrs W. A. J. Satchell	Owners	13–6–58
Gisbourne Petite Point	B	Ballyteckel Peter Pest	Gisbourne Georgina	Mrs D. Wilson	Mrs E. Quick	9–12–59
Monteagle Ha'poth	B	Dudleston Huskie	Monteagle Mudlark	Mr R. W. B. Pinches	Mr C. Smith	15–8–60
Orkneyinga Red Gauntlet	D	Orkneyinga Oscar	Orkneyinga Blinkbonny Twig	Gp. Capt. & Mrs W. A. J. Satchell	Owners	23–7–60
Rigol Willy Dhu	D	Redenhall Silver Wings	Rigol Susie's Liquorice	Mrs S. de Bernes	Owner	20–1–61
Teak of Granta	D	Redenhall Gold Braid	Paulette of Sillwood	Mrs K. Gordon	S.-Ldr. & Mrs E. R. Whitehouse	15–5–61
Bluefelt Honeysuckle of Darlaston	B	Bluefelt Buzzbee	Lapwing of Fellisfeld	Mrs C. Taylor	Mrs G. Tanasiewicz	15–12–59

Gold Bracken of Granta	B	Redenhall Gold Braid	Paulette of Sillwood	S.-Ldr. & Mrs E. R. Whitehouse	Owners	13–9–60
Orkneyinga Nerina	B	Orkneyinga Oscar	Simonswood Sylphine	Gp. Capt. & Mrs W. A. J. Satchell	Owners	13–7–60
Omah of Seale	D	Orkneyinga Oscar	Victoria of Seale	Mrs M. Howard	Owner	22–7–62
Peredur Pimento	D	Merryweather Moustachio	Orkneyinga Nereid	Mrs R. Spong	Owner	8–6–62
Erica of Yewden	B	Bronze Knight of Yewden	Huntersbroad Serena	Mrs E. Mitchell	Mrs M. Commeline	18–3–59
Gold Ilex of Granta	B	Redenhall Gold Braid	Paulette of Sillwood	S.-Ldr. & Mrs E. R. Whitehouse	Owners	15–5–61
Petite Poupee of Kavmar	B	Ballyteckel Peter Pest	Minuet of Kavmar	Mrs M. J. Hone	Owner	29–7–60
Rigol Phantom Phoebe	B	Rigol Phantom Philip	Milkichoc of Marpheld	Mrs S. de Bernes	Mr F. Borrowdale	3–9–62
Flaunden Wentworth	D	Ch. Teak of Granta	Moatenden Debutante	S.-Ldr. & Mrs E. R. Whitehouse	Mrs J. A. Marshall	2–8–62
Wandleston Lulu	B	Wandleston Lupus	Wandleston Dalucia	Mrs K. P. Butcher	Owner	28–1–63
Okay of Seale	B	Orkneyinga Oscar	Victoria of Seale	Mrs M. Howard	Owner	1–7–63
Hansel of Tornquist	D	Redenhall Black Beret	Merryweather Musquash	Mrs M. E. Reade	Owner	3–6–62
Peredur Sinful Skinful	B	Ch. Peredur Pimento	Orkneyinga Nereid	Mrs R. Spong	Owner	8–8–64
Peredur Wee Taffy of Paxford	D	Ch. Peredur Pimento	Orkneyinga Nereid	Miss M. E. Gray	Mrs R. Spong	8–8–64

Name	*Sex*	*Sire*	*Dam*	*Owner*	*Breeder*	*Born*
Orkneyinga Vottr	D	Ch. Orkneyinga Redgauntlet	Ch. Orkneyinga Nerrina	Gp. Capt & Mrs W. A. J. Satchell	Owners	28–10–64
Kelvindeugh Lauder Likely	D	Rigol Phantom Philip	Kelvindeugh Susan	Mrs V. Collins & Miss J. Cook	Owners	3–3–65
Selwood Marguerite	B	Ch. Peredur Pimento	Selwood Marigold	Mrs P. Hood-Wright	Owner	22–8–65
Culdees Ulric	D	Rigol Rough Shod	Rigol Pearl Buttons	Mrs M. Flynn	Owner	16–10–65
Grunwald Guyler	D	Grunwald Geoffrey	Rigol Rough Spun	Mr & Mrs J. Lloyd	Owners	26–10–66
Redenhall Silver Mint	B	Redenhall Silver Quill	Redenhall Moth	Mrs S. de Bernes	Mrs R. J. Colbourne	19–1–65
Redenhall Yewberry	D	Kummel of Granta	Redenhall Blossom	Mrs J. Hone	Mrs R. J. Colbourne	30–9–63
Flaunden the Whitehouse	D	Ch. Flaunden Wentworth	Flaunden Whimsy	Mrs J. Blandford	Owner	20–3–66
Bryn of Paxford	D	Ch. Redenhall Yewberry	Ch. Peredur Wee Taffy of Paxford	Miss M. E. Gray	Owner	18–12–66
Silvae The Mouse	B	Ch. Redenhall Yewberry	Monteagle War Paint	Mrs Grosvenor-Workman	Mr H. C. Smith	16–9–66
Selwood Marguerite	B	Ch. Peredur Pimento	Selwood Marigold	Mrs P. Hood-Wright	Owner	22–8–65
Daxene Black Unity	B	Ch. Redendall Yewberry	Daxene Silver Medallist	Mrs J. Lawley	Mr. J. P. Green	26–10–66
Field Hill Martie	D	Owlsnest Popcorn	Field Hill Muffin	Mrs B. Wilson	Owner	20–11–65
Brenkhill Honey Boy	D	Vienda Strikealight	Micholwood Busy Bee	Mr. & Mrs. D. Penswick	Owners	7–3–72

Flaunden What-not	D	Ch. Flaunden The Whitehouse	Tanglewood Twiddlemina	Mrs J. Blandford & Mrs Moate	Mrs Parsell	4–2–69
Flaunden Mr Whippy	D	Flaunden Winter Waistcoat	Flaunden Whipsy	Mrs J. Blandford	Miss A. M. Stewart	12–7–70
Flaunden Wimpole Street	D	Ch. Redenhall Yewberry	Flaunden Whimsy	Mrs J. Blandford	Owner	4–7–69
Silvae Enormouse	D	Ch. Bryn of Paxford	Ch. Silvae The Mouse	Mrs E. Grosvenor-Workman	Owner	2–7–69
Redenhall Black Clasp	B	Kummel of Granta	Redenhall Silver Skein	Miss H. Harriman	Mr Colbourne	28–6–67
Vienda Live Wire	B	Ch. Bryn of Paxford	Ch. Redenhall Black Clasp	Miss H. Harriman & Mrs Haresnape	Miss H. Harriman	22–11–68
Selwood Poinsettia	B	Bluefelt Buckle	Selwood Small Fry	Mrs P. Hood-Wright	Owner	11–4–66
Daxene Yewenda	B	Ch. Redenhall Yewberry	Daxene Silver Medallist	Mrs J. Lawley	Mr J. P. Green	6–6–68
Andyc Dolly Rocker	D	Ch. Andyc Topper	Gisbourne Paper Doll	Miss S. M. Raphael	Owner	26–6–69
Andyc Tansy	B	Ch. Bryn of Paxford	Threepenny Opera of Cumtru	Miss S. M. Raphael	Owner	18–2–68
Andyc Topper	D	Ch. Bryn of Paxford	Threepenny Opera of Cumtru	Miss S. M. Raphael	Owner	18–2–68
Peredur Wicked Wangler	B	Ch. Stormerbanks Vandal	Peredur Sinful Skinful	Mrs R. D. Spong	Owner	4–5–70
Porthurst Billee-Jean	B	Little Drummer Boy of Cumtru	Peredur Flora Dora	Mrs R. E. Ticehurst	Owner	14–9–69
Yankee Doodle of Cumtru	D	Porthurst Timmy Tiptoes of Cumtru	Mistletoe of Cumtru	Mrs R. E. Ticehurst	Mrs S. Willoughby	4–7–69

Name	*Sex*	*Sire*	*Dam*	*Owner*	*Breeder*	*Born*
Witch Doctor of Cumtru	D	Chipmunk of Cumtru	Witch of Seale	Mrs. S Willoughby	Owner	30–6–68
Andyc Miss Topper	B	Ch. Andyc Topper	Gisbourne Rachel	Miss S. M. Raphael	Mrs B. Fitzmaurice	4–9–69
Gwyn of Paxford	B	Ch. Bryn of Paxford	Selwood Primula	Miss M. E. Gray	Mrs P. Hood-Wright	2–4–69
Selwood Dittany	D	Peredur Oddjob	Selwood Buttercup	Miss S. M. Raphael	Mrs B. Hammett	16–10–70
Doctrinair of Cumtru	B	Ch. Witchdoctor of Cumtru	D'Abernon Debonair	Mrs T. Dixon	Mrs S. Willoughby	2–1–70
Daxene Silver Dawn	B	Ch. Redenhall Yewberry	Daxene Silver Medallist	Mr. J. P. Green	Owner	17–5–71
Drakesleat Hussy	B	Selwood Penstemon	Drakesleat Silvae Mandymouse	Mrs. Z. Andrews	Owner	19–10–71
Menwinnion Golden Rod	D	Ch. Bryn of Paxford	Menwinnion Golden Glow	Miss M. E. H. Marshall	Owner	25–2–71
Silvae Tuftymouse	B	Swatchway Superb	Silvae Winkymouse	Mrs. Grosvenor Workman	Owner	8–2–71
Stargang Moonshine	B	Stargang Pink Pill of Cumtru	Vienda Coffee Liqueur	Mrs. E. P. Blackburn	Owner	23–1–71
Brenkhill Honey Boy	D	Vienda Strikealight	Nicholwood Busy Bee	Mr. & Mrs. D. Penswick	Owners	7–3–72
Vienda Shining Star	B	Redenhall Singing Star	Ch. Redenhall Black Clasp	Mr. & Mrs D. Penswick	Owners	12–10–70
Dianamo Paddina	B	Dianamo Thats Life	Majorette of Cumtru	Mrs. D. W. Moate	Owner	6–12–72
Deerdax Bumble Bee	B	Ch. Brenkhill Honeyboy	Vienda Cor Blimy	Mrs. L. Penswick	Mrs. H. D. Roberts	27–3–73

Stargang Badger	D	Ch. Bryn of Paxford	Stargang Twilight	Mrs. E. P. Blackburn	Owner	23–1–73
Peredur Sam Gamgee	D	Ch. Peredur Pimento	Peredur Howrytuar	Mrs. R. D. Spong	Owner	22–11–72
Silvae Handymouse	D	Ch. Selwood Dittany	Silvae Itsamouse	Mrs. E. Grosvenor Workman	Owner	14–7–73
Drakesleat Klunk Klick of Andyc	D	Ch. Selwood Dittany	Ch. Drakesleat Hussy	Miss S. M. Raphael	Mrs. Z. Andrews	29–10–73
Vienda Queen Bee	B	Ch. Brenkhill Honeyboy	Ch. Vienda Live Wire	Mrs. L. Penswick	Owner	10–4–74
Drakesleat Kalamity Kate	B	Ch. Selwood Dittany	Ch. Drakesleat Hussy	Mrs. Z. Andrews	Owner	29–10–73
Bankonit From Andyc	B	Banker of Benk	Asbach Wasserburg	Miss S. M. Raphael	Mr. & Miss Wilson	22–6–74
Cratloe Double Topping	D	Ch. Andyc Topper	Cratloe Dream Topping	Mrs. E. Fountain	Owner	18–7–73
Silvae Cider	B	Paxford Evan Jones	Kelvindeugh Lauder Laurel	Mrs. E. Grosvenor Workman	Owner	7–8–73
Daxene Red Arkle	D	Jarthley Top Hat	Daxene Anita	Mr. J. P. Green	Owner	4–7–74
Lovells Lancelot of Andyc	D	Ch. Cratloe Double Topping	Mini Model of Andyc	Miss S. M. Raphael	Mrs. Ryves-Hopkins	4–7–74
Drakesleat Scarlet Woman	B	Eng. & N.Z. Ch. Silvae Handymouse	Ch. Drakesleat Hussy	Mrs. Z. Andrews	Owner	22–1–75
Andyc Honeypot	D	Ch. Brenkhill Honeyboy	Selwood Arabis of Lovells	Mrs. L. Penswick	Miss S. M. Raphael	8–6–74
Peredur Springtime	B	Ch. Peredur Sam Gamgee	Peredur Springsong	Mrs. R. D. Spong	Owner	2–11–74

Name	*Sex*	*Sire*	*Dam*	*Owner*	*Breeder*	*Born*
Silvae Rubbermouse	D	Eng. & N.Z. Ch. Silvae Handymouse	Silvae Nuttymouse	Mrs. E. Grosvenor Workman	Owner	19–9–75
Stargang Vixen of Sutina	B	Ch. Stargang Badger	Stargang Moonbeam	Mr. & Mrs. J. Elkington	Mrs. E. P. Blackburn	2–4–74
Cannobio Winnie Womble	B	Ch. Stargang Badger	Dalegarth Thankful	Mrs. B. Castle	Owner	19–10–74
Stargang Madam Butterfly	B	Ch. Flaunden Mr. Whippy	Stargang Otter	Mrs. E. P. Blackburn	Owner	21–4–75
Ludworth Easter Snow	B	Ch. Cratloe Double Topping	Peredur Flora Dora	Mrs. V. Stott	Owner	30–3–75
Drakesleat Miss Alliance of Brackenacre	B	Drakesleat Range Rover	Ch. Drakesleat Hussy	Mr. & Mrs. J. Nixon	Mrs. Z. Andrews	29–3–76
Gisbourne Little Lotus	B	Little Black Sambo of Ouston	Gisbourne Babycham	Mrs. E. Quick	Owner	2–7–74
Silvae Crackermouse	B	Eng. & N.Z. Ch. Silvae Handymouse	Kelvindeugh Lauder Laurel	Mrs. E. Grosvenor Workman	Owner	1–9–75
Dalegarth Jus' William	D	Dalegarth Key Man	Dalegarth Streaker	Mr. & Mrs. F. T. Newbury	Owners	9–10–76
Lovells Larkabout at Andyc	B	Ch. Cratloe Double Topping	Mini Model of Andyc	Miss S. M. Raphael	Mrs. Ryves-Hopkins	1–11–75
Drakesleat Ai Jail	B	Drakesleat Dick Dastardly	Ch. Drakesleat Kalamity Kate	Mrs. Z. Andrews	Owner	10–10–76
Ludworth Easter Topping	B	Ch. Cratloe Double Topping	Peredur Flora Dora	Mrs. E. Fountain	Mrs. V. Stott	30–3–75
Silvae Crazymouse	D	Eng. & N.Z. Ch. Silvae Handymouse	Silvae Nuttymouse	Mrs. E. Grosvenor Workman	Owner	19–9–75

Drakesleat Riff Raff	B	Drakesleat Dick Dastardly	Ch. Drakesleat Kalamity Kate	Mrs. Z. Andrews	Owner	10–4–75
Dalegarth Ragamuffin	D	Dalegarth Key Man	Beannchor Dormouse	Mr. & Mrs. F. T. Newbury	Owners	7–8–76
Silvae Scrumpy	B	Ch. Silvae Rubbermouse	Ch. Silvae Cider	Mrs. E. Grosvenor Workman	Owner	19–10–76
Fighting Chance of Bothlyn	D	Ch. Brenkhill Honey Boy	Maid Marrion of Bothlyn	Miss E. Egan	Mrs. I. Young	19–12–76
Cannobio Teddy Bear	D	Dalegarth Key Man	Cannobio Wishful Thinking	Mrs. B. Castle	Owner	10–9–77

INDEX